Venice

WHAT'S NEW | **WHAT'S ON** | **WHAT'S BEST**

www.timeout.com/venice

D1395803

Contents

Venice by Area

Essentials

Time Out Digital Ltd
4th Floor
125 Shaftesbury Avenue
London WC2H 8AD
Tel: + 44 (0)20 7813 3000
Email: guides@timeout.com
www.timeout.com

Published by Time Out Digital Ltd, a wholly owned subsidiary of Time Out Group Ltd.
Time Out and the Time Out logo are trademarks of Time Out Group Ltd.

© **Time Out Group Ltd 2015**
Previous edition 2007.

Editorial Director Sarah Guy
Group Finance Controller Margaret Wright

© **Time Out Group Ltd**
Chairman & Founder Tony Elliott
Chief Executive Officer Tim Arthur
Chief Financial Officer Matt White
Publisher Alex Batho

10 9 8 7 6 5 4 3 2 1

This edition first published in Great Britain in 2015 by Ebury Publishing
20 Vauxhall Bridge Road, London SW1V 2SA

Ebury Publishing is part of the Penguin Random House group of companies whose addresses
can be found at global.penguinrandomhouse.com

Distributed in the US and Latin America by Publishers Group West (1-510-809-3700)

For further distribution details, see www.timeout.com

ISBN: 978-1-90504-295-1

A CIP catalogue record for this book is available from the British Library.

Printed and bound in China by Leo Paper Products Ltd.

Venice Shortlist

The **Time Out Venice Shortlist** is one of a series of guides that draws on Time Out's background as a magazine publisher to keep you current with everything that's going on in town. As well as Venice's classic sights and the best of its eating, drinking and leisure options, the guide picks out the most exciting venues and gives a full calendar of annual events. It also includes features on the important news, trends and developments, all compiled by locally based editors and writers. Whether you're visiting for the first time in your life or you're a frequent visitor, you'll find the *Time Out Venice Shortlist* contains all you need to know, in a portable and easy-to-use format.

The guide divides central Venice into seven areas, each containing listings for Sights & Museums, Eating & Drinking, Shopping, Nightlife and Arts & Leisure, along with maps pinpointing their locations. At the front of the book are chapters rounding up these scenes city-wide, and giving a shortlist of our overall picks in a variety of categories. We also include itineraries for days out, plus essentials such as transport information and hotels.

Our listings give phone numbers as dialled from within Italy. From abroad, use your country's exit code followed by 39 (the country code for Italy) and the number given, including the initial '0'.

We have noted price categories by using one to four euro signs (**€-€€€€**), representing budget, moderate, expensive and luxury. Major credit cards are accepted unless otherwise stated.

All our listings are double-checked, but places do sometimes close or change their hours or prices, so it's a good idea to call a venue before visiting if you're making a special trip. While every effort has been made to ensure accuracy, the publishers cannot accept responsibility for any errors that this guide may contain.

Venues are marked on the maps using symbols numbered according to their order within the chapter and colour-coded as follows:

❶ Sights & Museums
❶ Eating & Drinking
❶ Shopping
❶ Nightlife
❶ Arts & Leisure

Time Out **Venice** Shortlist

EDITORIAL
Editor Anne Hanley
Proofreader John Shandy Watson

DESIGN & PICTURE DESK
Senior Designer Kei Ishimaru
Group Commercial Senior Designer
 Jason Tansley
Picture Editor Jael Marschner
Deputy Picture Editor Ben Rowe
Picture Researcher Lizzy Owen

ADVERTISING
Managing Director St John Betteridge

MARKETING
Senior Publishing Brand Manager
 Luthfa Begum
Head of Circulation Dan Collins

PRODUCTION
Production Controller
 Katie Mulhern-Bhudia

CONTRIBUTORS
This guide was researched and written by Anne Hanley, with the exception of Tintoretto's Last Suppers (Gregory Dowling) and additional work by Clara Marshall.

PHOTOGRAPHY
Pages 2 (bottom left), 29 Vogalonga; 2 (top right), 41 Philip Bird LRPS CPAGB/Shutterstock.com; 2 (bottom right), 37, 68, 94 (top left and top right), 121 (top), 124, 141 (top right and bottom) Renata Sedmakova/Shutterstock.com; 3 (top left and bottom left), 9, 55 (middle and bottom), 141 (top left), 157 (bottom), 160 (top and middle) Oleg Znamenskiy/Shutterstock.com; 3 (top right and bottom right), 16, 22, 101 (top left), 157 (top left and middle right), 169, 172, 176 Olivia Rutherford; 5 Banet/Shutterstock.com; 7 Lisa S./Shutterstock.com; 8 Mongolo1984/Wikimedia Commons; 11 lapas71/Shutterstock.com; 13 ©Francesco Galifi; 15, 24, 77, 80, 90, 97, 110 (top), 136 Alessandra Santarelli; 17 Rostislav Glinsky/Shutterstock.com; 20/21 Michele Gamberinini; 23 Greta Gabaglio/Shutterstock.com; 26, 35 MagSpace/Shutterstock.com; 28 taniavolobueva/Shutterstock.com; 30 Rolf_52/Shutterstock.com; 31, 40 Andrea Avezzù; 32/33 Laborant/Shutterstock.com; 34 Circumnavigation/Shutterstock.com; 36 s74/Shutterstock.com; 38 De Agostini/Getty Images; 43 irisphoto1/Shutterstock.com; 44 g215/Shutterstock.com; 45 Janis Smits/Shutterstock.com; 48 (top) Andrei Nekrassov/Shutterstock.com; 48 (bottom) Evgeny Shmulev/Shutterstock.com; 55 (top) saaton/Shutterstock.com; 60 (top left and top right) Marc De Tollenaere; 60 (bottom) Nick_Nick/Shutterstock.com; 72, 101 (bottom) gab90/Shutterstock.com; 79 Adriano Castelli/Shutterstock.com; 82 Alessandro Colle/Shutterstock.com; 95 Mariusz Niedzwiedzki/Shutterstock.com; 101 (middle left) hipproductions/Shutterstock.com; 101 (top right) Annalisa Bombarda/Shutterstock.com; 102 ChinellatoPhoto/Shutterstock.com; 104 Robert Crum/Shutterstock.com; 107 Catarina Belova/Shutterstock.com; 112 ChiccoDodiFC/Shutterstock.com; 121 (bottom) maigi/Shutterstock.com; 128 zebra0209/Shutterstock.com; 144 © ORCH orsenigo_chemollo); 147 Valeri Potapova/Shutterstock.com; 148 contact Vision; 153 (top) keko64/Shutterstock.com; 153 (middle) Vito Poma; 154 BasPhoto/Shutterstock.com; 155 Angelo Giampiccolo/Shutterstock.com; 157 (top right) Ralf Siemieniec/Shutterstock.com; 160 (bottom) catalunyastock/Shutterstock.com; 179 Nikolas Koenig

The following images were supplied by the featured establishments: 2 (top left), 14, 18, 19, 25, 27, 67, 88, 110 (bottom left and bottom right), 117, 153 (bottom), 165, 166, 170

Cover photography: Visions Of Our Land/Getty Images

MAPS
LS International Cartography, via Decemviri 8, 20138 Milan, Italy (www.mapmovie.it)

About **Time Out**

Founded in 1968, Time Out has expanded from humble London beginnings into the leading resource for those wanting to know what's happening in the world's greatest cities. As well as our influential what's-on weeklies in London and New York, we publish nearly 30 other listings magazines in cities as varied as Beijing and Mumbai. The magazines established Time Out's trademark style: sharp writing, informed reviewing and bang up-to-date inside knowledge of every scene.

Time Out made the natural leap into travel guides in the 1980s with the City Guide series, which now extends to over 50 destinations around the world. Written and researched by expert local writers and generously illustrated with original photography, the full-size guides cover a larger area than our Shortlist guides and include many more venue reviews, along with additional background features and a full set of maps.

Throughout this rapid growth, the company has remained proudly independent, still owned by Tony Elliott four decades after he started Time Out London as a single fold-out sheet of A5 paper. This independence extends to the editorial content of all our publications, this Shortlist included. No establishment has been featured because it has advertised, and no payment has influenced any of our reviews. And, for our critics, there's definitely no such thing as a free lunch: all restaurants and bars are visited and reviewed anonymously, and Time Out always picks up the bill.

For more about the company, see www.timeout.com.

Don't Miss

Gallerie dell'Accademia

Sights & Museums

There's a strange dichotomy about the way Venice displays its immense cultural wealth. For the most part, it's not cutting edge – or even remotely modern. In fact were they to return today, the visitors who have flocked to this watery city since the 15th century – for commerce, edification or just plain fun – would have no difficulty recognising the city they saw then: the same exquisite masterpieces hanging in corners of dim churches, the same rippling reflections of Titianesque colours in quiet canals and the same architectural mish-mash of stunning and endlessly absorbing originality.

Certainly, Napoleon concentrated a lot of church art in the Gallerie dell'Accademia (p140), but the overall impression of art and beauty being an intrinsic part of the city's fabric has never changed – to the point, at times, where little effort has been made to exalt those very features that make the city unique.

Yet there have been upgrades and novelties of late: the Accademia's interminable extension and restoration programme is gradually bearing fruit, and the Palazzo Grassi (p63) and Punta della Dogana (p143) galleries rival the world's greatest exhibition spaces. The Biennale, too, excites international admiration. Don't expect all the city's museums to be state-of-the-art with all mod cons; instead they offer beauty beyond your wildest expectations.

Nobody comes to Venice without some idea of what to expect; the big surprise is that it's true. The streets are full of water, and there's an otherworldly quality to the place.

Grand Canal

There are, of course, highlights: St Mark's basilica (p45), the Gallerie dell'Accademia (p140) and the Rialto bridge (p107) to name but a few. But in these tourist hotspots you'll never get an impression of Venice's full diversity; for that, you'll have to take your courage (and your map) in your hands and leave the main routes.

Venice is divided into six *sestieri* (districts). They're worth getting to grips with, firstly because all addresses include the *sestiere* name, and secondly because each has a different flavour. Cradled by the great lower bend of the Grand Canal is the *sestiere* of San Marco, the heart of the city; east of here is Castello; stretching to the west and north is Cannaregio. To the west of the Rialto bridge is San Polo; north of that is Santa Croce; while further to the south is Dorsoduro, with its wide Zattere promenade looking across to the long residential island of the Giudecca – the honorary seventh *sestiere*.

St Mark's square p9

Churches

Venice began life as a host of separate island communities, each clustered around its own parish church. There are still well over 100 religious buildings. They contain inestimable artistic treasures. Most of the major churches have reliable opening times; hours in minor churches depend on the whim of the priest or sacristan. It's well worth exploring these too, since there is not a single one that does not contain some item of interest.

No Sunday opening times are given in listings for churches that open only for Mass. Remember that churches are places of worship: shorts and bare shoulders are frowned upon, as are visits while services are going on.

Museums, galleries & scuole

On the whole, Venice's museums and galleries are rather old-fashioned containers for beautiful and/or instructive things, rather than innovative exhibition experience spaces. Slowly, the city is catching up with new exhibiting techniques, but it still has a way to go.

In the meantime, the city's beautiful things are peerlessly lovely, and traditional Venetian instruction can be fun. The Museo Storico Navale (p84) provides a colourful introduction to Venice's maritime past, while a grasp of the elaborate mechanisms of Venetian government will turn the slog around the Palazzo Ducale (Doge's Palace, p53) into a voyage of discovery.

Then there are the curiosities – Palazzo Mocenigo (p119) where Venetian costume and Venetian perfumes are beautifully presented; Ca' Rezzonico (p134), where 18th-century Venice is recreated in all its finery and foppery; and the smaller but eclectic Museo della Fondazione Querini Stampalia (p73), with a fascinating collection of scenes of 18th-century Venetian life and a glorious Bellini.

As well as museums in the strict sense of the word, Venice also boasts *scuole*, establishments that were a blend of art-treasure house and social institution. Essentially, they were devotional lay brotherhoods, subject to the state rather than the church. The earliest were founded in the 13th century; by the 15th century, there were six *scuole grandi* and as many as 400 minor ones. The *scuole grandi* had annually elected officers drawn from the 'citizen' class (those sandwiched between the governing *patriciate* and the unenfranchised *popolani*). While the *scuole grandi* – such as Scuola di San Rocco (p126) and Scuola di San Giovanni Evangelista (p126)– drew their members mainly from the wealthier professional classes, the humbler *scuole piccole* were either exclusively devotional groups, trade guilds or confraternities of foreign communities, as with Scuola di San Giorgio degli Schiavoni (p86).

The wealthier confraternities devoted a great deal of time and expense to beautifying their meeting houses (the *scuole* themselves), sometimes hiring one major painter to decorate the whole building; this was the case of Tintoretto in the Scuola di San Rocco and Carpaccio in the Scuola di San Giorgio degli Schiavoni.

Admission & tickets

In high season, expect to queue to enter St Mark's, the Accademia and the Palazzo Ducale (Doge's Palace). Other sights rarely present any overcrowding problems except during special exhibitions. April and May are traditional months for Italian school trips: this can mean sharing your Titians and Tintorettos with gangs of bored teenagers. Entry to all state-owned museums is, theoretically, free for under-18s and reduced for under-26s. Charges and concessions at city-run and privately owned museums vary; it pays to carry whatever ID cards you can muster (student card, press card, motoring association card and so on).

Multi-entrance tickets

Many of Venice's landmarks offer multi-entrance tickets, cutting costs if you are planning to visit all the sights covered by a given ticket. See also p187 for information on pre-purchasing passes through Venezia Unica.

Museum passes

The Musei Civici Veneziani, Venice's city-owned museums, offer two multi-entrance options, both of which can be bought at participating establishments. The major museums (Musei di Piazza San Marco, Ca' Rezzonico and Ca' Pesaro) accept credit cards. Note that the Musei di Piazza San Marco can **only** be entered on a cumulative ticket.

For the others (Ca' Rezzonico, Carlo Goldoni's House, Museo di Palazzo Mocenigo, Ca' Pesaro, Museo Fortuny, the Glass Museum and Lace Museum), individual tickets are also available. See also www.visitmuve.it.

• **Musei di Piazza San Marco** (Palazzo Ducale, Biblioteca Marciana, Museo Correr, Museo Archeologico, Torre dell'Orologio; valid three months) €16; €10 reductions.
• **Museum Pass** (all the Musei Civici; valid six months) €24; €18 reductions.

State museums

The state-owned Gallerie dell'Accademia and Palazzo Grimani can be visited on a multi-entrance ticket costing €9 (€6 reductions) available from either. No credit cards except for online advance bookings. Information on www.gallerieaccademia.org.

Chorus

Many of Venice's finest churches belong to the Chorus scheme (www.chorusvenezia.org), which funds upkeep by charging for entry. There's a fee of €3 for each church, or you can get a multi-entrance ticket (€12; €8 reductions; free under-10s). Single and multi-entrance tickets can be bought in participating churches. No credit cards.

Venissa p15

Eating & Drinking

More than any other Italian city, Venice has its own particular customs when it comes to dining and drinking out.

Of course there are *ristoranti* (many of them, in this tourist-oriented place, of execrable quality and exorbitant prices); but there are also *bàcari* – a cross between a drinking den and a traditional fast-food outlet. It is this latter eaterie that sets Venice apart… and that has spearheaded a recent renaissance in Venetian cuisine.

Venetians differ from other Italians, too, in that they are drinkers. Not to excess, mind you: but a shot of fiery grappa in your breakfast coffee takes the damp from the canals out of your marrow, and a stopover – or four, or five – on the way home from work for a quick *spritz* or an *ombra* (a small, often remarkably cheap, glass of red or white wine) with friends is an essential part of socialising *alla veneziana*.

What's on the plate

The lagoon city has a long culinary tradition based on fresh seafood, game and vegetables, backed up by northern Italy's three main carbohydrate fixes: pasta, risotto rice and polenta. (Pizza is a southern import: good pizza in Venice is a rarity.) Outside of a handful of top-notch restaurants, you will invariably eat better if you go with the flow of *la cucina veneta*.

This requires a certain spirit of experimentation. If you've never eaten *garusoli* (sea snails) or *canoce* (mantis shrimps), Venice is the place to try these marine curios.

All'Amarone

The once-strong local tradition of creative ways with meat is kept alive in a handful of restaurants – Ai Gondolieri (p145), for example – and one marvellous trattoria, Dalla Marisa (p103); it can also be found in *bàcaro*-counter *cicheti* such as *nervetti* (veal cartilage) and *cotechino* (spicy pig's intestine parcels filled with pork).

Vegetarians may be horrified to learn that there's not a single vegetarian restaurant in the city. But Venetian cuisine relies heavily on seasonal veggies, so eating a meat-free meal is not difficult. Alla Zucca (p122) is always a safe bet, and Algiubagiò (p105) offers a range of vegetarian dishes.

There is something of the Spanish tapas mentality about the Venetian approach to eating: *antipasti* (hors d'oeuvres) often engulf the whole meal. If you nodded vigorously when the waiter suggested bringing 'one or two' seafood *antipasti*, you may start to regret it when the fifth plate arrives – but it is perfectly OK just to eat some pasta afterwards, or to skip to the *secondo*, or even dessert.

What's in the glass

Except in the more upmarket restaurants and one or two born-again *bàcari*, wines will mostly be local. Luckily, the wine-growing area that stretches from the Veneto north-east to Friuli is one of Italy's strongest, with good white wines such as Soave backed up by solid red wines such as Valpolicella. This means that, even in humbler establishments, the house wine is usually drinkable and often surprisingly refined. For more on the wines of north east Italy, see p112.

Eating

Restaurants

Steer well clear of those restaurants – mainly around St Mark's and the Rialto – that employ sharply dressed waiters to stand outside and persuade passing tourists to come in for a meal: an immediate recipe for mediocre fare at rip-off prices. Following our recommendations will spare you unpleasant surprises.

Bàcari

With their blackened beams and rickety wooden tables, *bàcari* (accent on the first syllable) are often hidden down backstreets or in quiet *campi*. Most look age-old; many, however, are recent arrivals or makeovers… which doesn't detract from the bounty of what's on offer.

Locals crowd the bar, swiftly downing a glass or two of wine (*un'ombra*), and taking the edge off their appetites with one of the *cicheti* (snacks) that line the counter. Eat enough of these, and you've had a good-value meal.

If you sit down at a table and order from the menu – which will include more abundant portions of those *cicheti*, plus a few hot dishes – you can expect prices to be a bit higher.

Pizzerie

Venice has its fair share of pizza joints, though the standard here is not particularly high. Still, prices in *pizzerie* are low-ish, which makes them a good standby between more

Alla Ciurma

DON'T MISS

expensive meals. Note that beer, rather than wine, is the traditional accompaniment for pizza.

Drinking

Cafés & bars

Italian bars and cafés (the terms are pretty much interchangeable) are multi-purpose establishments. To the usual Italian breakfast, light snacks, pastries and alcoholic beverages routine, Venice adds its own specialities: the *ombra* and the *spritz* (see p79).

Many of Venice's bars also double up as cake and ice-cream emporia. Locals consume freshly prepared goodies throughout the day, and with early-evening *aperitivi*.

Rules of engagement

There are two timescales for eating in Venice. Smart restaurants serve lunch from around 1pm to 3pm and dinner from 7.30pm until at least 10pm. *Bàcari* and neighbourhood *trattorie* follow Venetian workers' rhythms, with lunch running from noon to 2pm and dinner from 6.30pm to 9pm.

Rosa Salva p15

Menus are often recited out loud; waiters are used to doing off-the-cuff English translations. If you want to know how much dishes cost, ask. Note that the price of fish is often quoted by weight – generally by the *etto* (100 grammes). A double-pricing policy applies in many eateries, with one tariff for locals and another (the one on the menu, if it exists) for tourists. There is not much you can do about this unofficial congestion charge.

Always ask for a written *conto* (bill) at the end of the meal, as it is, in theory, illegal to leave the restaurant without one.

The usual practice in Italian bars is to decide what you want, pay at the till, then order at the counter. Note that anything ordered at the counter must be consumed there. If you want to sit at a café table, you should sit down and order (or at the very least indicate that you are planning to sit down); the privilege of occupying a table will push your bill up – a little in smaller, more hidden-away places; but jaw-droppingly in, say, St Mark's square, especially in the evening, when a surcharge is added for the palm orchestras.

For advice on tipping, see p186.

Reading the listings

In this guide, we have used the € symbol to indicate price ranges. € means a cheaper meal at €25 or less; €€ is anything up to €40; €€€ is up to €60; €€€€ is over €60. These figures cover a three-course meal for one, with house wine. Prices may seem high, but remember that it is perfectly okay just to order a pasta course, a salad and a coffee – which may halve the price.

Where we have given 'meals served' times, this refers to the kitchen's opening hours, when full meals can be ordered; establishments may function well before and/or after these times as wine- and snack-serving *bàcari*.

Shopping

This extraordinary *entrepôt* between East and West was where merchants from Europe and the Levant came together for centuries. An endless array of goods, from exotic spices and raw silks to humble salt, was imported for resale by Venetian traders. During the Renaissance, the two-week La Sensa trade fair drew people from all over the Mediterranean basin and further north in Europe; it was particularly popular for purchasing wedding trousseaux.

Traders of different nations each had their *fondaco* (alternatively spelled *fontaco* or *fondego*), a lodging-cum-warehouse. So successful – and so desirous of making an impression – were the German traders in Venice that their Fondego dei Tedeschi (currently being made over to become – perhaps fittingly – a shopping mall

administered by the Louis Vuitton group) was adorned with frescoes by Titian and Giorgione.

The sumptuous brocades and damasks, Burano lace and Murano glassware still produced and found in the city are all legacies of *La Serenissima*'s thriving commerce. Though the prices of such authentic Venetian-made goods can sometimes be eye-watering, a recent resurgence of local artisans – cobblers, jewellers, carpenters, mask-makers and blacksmiths – at least means that the traditional techniques are being kept alive.

Where & what to buy

The Mercerie – the maze of crowded, narrow alleyways leading from piazza San Marco to the Rialto – and the streets known collectively as the

Venetia Studium

Frezzeria, immediately to the west of St Mark's square, have been the main retail areas in this city for the past 600 years or so. The densest concentration of big name fashion outlets can be found around calle larga XXII Marzo, where top names such as Prada, Fendi, Versace and Gucci all have boutiques.

Devotees of kitsch should not miss the stalls and shops near the train station, where plastic gondolas, illuminated gondolas, flashing gondolas, musical gondolas and even gondola cigarette lighters reign supreme. Stalls around both ends of the Rialto bridge are also a good source of tack, though nylon football strips and fake Nikes dominate here. Throughout the city, that most un-Venetian product – leather handbags – can be purchased cheaply in near-identical shops manned by Chinese staff.

For more tasteful souvenirs, Venice's glass, lace, fabrics and handmade paper are legendary – as are the made-in-Taiwan substitutes that are passed off as the genuine article by unscrupulous traders. Sticking to the outlets listed in our Venice by Area chapters will help you to avoid unpleasant surprises.

The steady drop in population has led to the demise of 'everyday' shops, squeezing out many of the few remaining greengrocers, bakers and butchers. Corner supermarkets (notably the Co-op) have been filling the gap, however, fitting huge amounts of produce into minuscule spaces.

There is one corner of Venice where food shopping has changed little for centuries. For fresh fruit, vegetables and fish, along with a magnificent taste of exuberant Venetian life, head for the open-air market at the north-west foot of the Rialto bridge (Monday to Saturday mornings). Fruit and vegetables can also be purchased from the market-boats that are moored at the eastern end of via Garibaldi in the *sestiere* of Castello, and on the rio San Barnaba in Dorsoduro.

Opening hours

Most smaller food shops are closed on Wednesday afternoons, while some non-food shops stay shut on Monday mornings. During high season, many shops abandon their lunchtime closing and stay open all day, even opening on Sundays.

It pays to be sceptical about the hours posted on the doors of smaller shops. If you want to be sure of not finding the shutters drawn, call before you set out.

Tax rebates

If you are not an EU citizen, remember to keep your official receipt (*scontrino*) as you are entitled to a rebate on IVA (sales tax) paid on purchases of personal goods costing more than €155, as long as they leave the country unused and are bought from a shop that provides this service. In shops displaying the tax-free sign in the window, ask for the form, which you'll need to show at customs upon departure. See the Italian government website www.agenziadogane.gov.it for more information (in English) about customs.

Giovanna Zanella

SHORTLIST

Lace & linen
- Annelie (p138)
- Chiarastella Cattana (p65)
- Martinuzzi (p58)

Gorgeous textiles
- Antichità Marciana (p70)
- Arras (p138)
- Fortuny Tessuti Artistici (p150)
- Gaggio (p65)
- Trois Antichità (p71)
- Venetia Studium (p71)

Glass
- Genninger Studio (p146)
- L'Isola – Carlo Moretti (p65)
- Marina & Susanna Sent (p146 and p159)
- Vittorio Costantini (p106)

Scrumptious sweets
- Dolceamaro (p62)
- Marchini Pasticceria (p62)
- Pasticceria Melita (p89)
- VizioVirtù (p127)

Eye-catching footwear
- Daniela Ghezzo Segalin Venezia (p61)
- Giovanna Zanella (p81)
- Kalimala (p81)
- Piedàterre (p114)

Reading matter
- Filippi Editore Venezia (p81)
- Libreria Marco Polo (p106)
- Libreria Toletta (p138)
- Wellington BooKs (p66)

Masks
- Ca' Macana (p138)
- Papier Mâché (p81)
- Tragicomica (p118)

Beast Club

Nightlife

Venice offers many pleasures, but its nightlife isn't one of them. The city described by Byron as 'revel of the Earth' can no longer lay any claim to the status of Europe's party capital. But despite appearances, the place isn't totally dead: if you know where to go, there's plenty of scope for a pleasant if undemanding evening out.

A typical Venetian night out starts with a post-work, pre-prandial *spritz* in one of the bars around the Rialto market area; this might develop into a *giro de ombre*, a bar-crawl Venetian style, comprising numbers of small glasses of white or red wine, which are best left uncounted. For those still standing when the traditional *bàcari* (wine bars) close, there's a network of late-opening bars hidden away all over town – by the Rialto,

along the northern fondamenta della Misericordia, in ever-lively campo Santa Margherita or around San Pantalon.

Stringent noise regulations combined with a lack of adequate venues have effectively pulled the plug on large music events, except during Carnevale (during the months of January and February) and summer festivals. There's better news for serious jazz-heads: regular high quality jazz and experimental music events are put on by local cultural organisations such as Caligola (www.caligola.it), at the hugely active Teatro Fondamenta Nuove (www.teatrofondamentanuove.it) or at the Venezia Jazz Club (p139).

Thanks to the tenacity of the few bar owners still willing to wrestle with red tape and persist in the

SHORTLIST

Spritz to start
- Al Mercà (p111)
- Al Timon (p103)
- Da Bonifacio (p79)
- El Refolo (p87)
- Muro Rialto (p113)

Dancefloor
- Piccolo Mondo (p146)

Live sounds
- Caffè Centrale – various nights (left)
- El Chioschetto – Wed & Sun (p132)
- El Sbarlefo – Fri (p137)
- F30 – Sat (p98)
- Venice Jazz Club – most nights (p139)

Good wines
- Al Prosecco (p122)
- La Mascareta (p79)
- Naranzaria (p113)

Beer buffs
- Irish Pub (p106)
- La Mascareta (p79)
- Naranzaria (p113)
- Santo Bevitore (98)

Drinking till late
- Café Noir (p135)
- Café Rosso (p135)
- El Refolo (p87)
- La Mascareta (p79)
- Orange (p137)

face of party-pooping petitioning neighbours, it's still possible, however, to hear live music in a handful of *locali* around town. Venetian vibes tend to be laid-back, and these small, free gigs are almost always reggae, jazz or blues, with the odd rock, Latino or world session.

Note that many of the bars listed under Eating & Drinking operate through the day as regular cafés and even lunch spots, then stay open into the evening becoming *aperitivo* and after-hours meeting and drinking spots. A handful of sleeker, more international-style venues – such as Caffè Centrale (San Marco 1659B, piscina Frezzeria, www.caffecentrale venezia.com) complete the city's nightlife scene.

Clubs

If it's clubs you're after, you've come to the wrong city. Old-fashioned Piccolo Mondo (see p146) has a small dancefloor. For serious club culture, make for the mainland to

venues such as Beast Club at via Don Federico Tosatto 9 in Mestre; see www.beastclub.it or the club's Facebook page for events details.

Information & tickets

Listings are carried by the two local dailies, *Il Gazzettino* and *La Nuova Venezia*. For a more complete overview of concerts and festivals, with English translations, the monthly listings magazine *Venezia News* is indispensable. Also keep your eyes peeled around town for posters advertising upcoming gigs and events. Tickets are usually available at venues.

Gay & lesbian

Venice might seem to provide the perfect, gay-embracing, hassle-free and ridiculously romantic backdrop for most fantasies. But gays and lesbians looking for something fast-paced will be disappointed.

In Venice proper, the laid-back gay scene is tucked neatly away in the private sphere, where dinner parties or quiet drinks at the local *bàcaro* or wine bar define the way the city's (by no means small) gay community goes about its business. Il Muro (at the lagoon end of the piazzetta San Marco, turn right towards the Giardinetti Reale and keep walking), one of the city's oldest cruising institutions, is no

longer as popular as it once was, but it still attracts a fair number of post-midnight visitors in the summer months.

Across on the mainland, however, Mestre and Marghera have newer, flashier clubs and bars pulling in a younger crowd from around the province. Check out PDM Porto da Mar (www.portodomar.com) in Marghera or make your way to the Flexo Club (www.flexopadova.it) in Padua for something more lively.

In the summer, everyone converges at Alberoni on the Lido, its rather secluded beach area and surrounding dunes allowing people to indulge in nude sunbathing and cruising.

The national gay rights group ArciGay (www.arcigay.it) sponsors activities, festivals and counselling services. ArciGay membership is needed for entry to certain venues. A one-month ArciGay *tessera* (membership card) costs €15 and can be purchased at the door of the venues that require it.

Caffè Centrale p21

La Fenice

Arts & Leisure

Theatre was a key element of Venice's famously frenetic party scene in the 17th and 18th centuries. With audiences demanding constant novelty, competing playhouses renewed their repertoires frequently. As a result, play production was prolific, as was operatic output, with as many as 1,274 operas being produced in Venice in just over a generation.

There's rather less on offer for today's playgoers than for their 18th-century counterparts, though recent years have seen considerable improvement. The growth and revamping in recent years of small theatres have finally given a little more space for experiments in the avant-garde.

But the performing arts scene remains a victim of Venice's musical tradition, with Vivaldi pouring out of its churches and *scuole*, more often than not performed by bewigged and costumed players of varying standards. Exceptions are the Venice Baroque Orchestra, a global success story, and the orchestra of La Fenice (p71), one of the best in the country. As well as its opera and ballet seasons, La Fenice has at least two concert seasons a year. The Teatro Malibran (p98) shares La Fenice's programmes and also has its own chamber-music season.

Lovers of sacred music should catch two regular Sunday events: the sung Mass at St Mark's (10.30am; p45) and the Gregorian chant on the island of San Giorgio (11am; p151). Visiting foreign choirs often give free one-off performances in Venice's fabulous churches, including St Mark's (phone 041 522 5697 for information). Look out for posters.

Multisala Rossini

The city also has its own gospel choir in the Joy Singers of Venice (www.joysingers.it), which performs at various venues.

What's on when

Venice's theatre and dance season stretches from November to June – though La Fenice keeps on going most of the year, closing only for August. Tourist-oriented classical music concerts are held all year. The dance, music and theatre sections of the Biennale arts umbrella (www.labiennale.org) hold festivals and events from spring to autumn; many dance performances took place among the exhibits of the Biennale's Contemporary Art fest in summer 2014.

Summer also brings a chance to watch or even join in tango performances in campo San Giacomo dell'Orio (www.tangoaction.com).

Information & tickets

Tickets can usually be purchased at theatre box offices immediately prior to shows, at the tourist information office near piazza San Marco and at HelloVenezia/VeneziaUnica offices (p187). For high-profile or first-night productions at prestigious venues such as La Fenice or Teatro Malibran, seats sell out days or even weeks in advance: reserve at the theatres themselves or online. Local newspapers *Il Gazzettino* and *La Nuova Venezia* carry listings of theatrical events, as does the bilingual monthly *Venezia News* (www.venezianews.it).

The silver screen

Once, Venice had a host of cinemas; these days, most of them have been converted into supermarkets. But it's a pretty accurate reflection of local demand, with a diminishing population signifying decreasing numbers of movie goers.

Two institutions inject a little life into the film scene. The annual Film Festival (p28) takes place in September, when the Lido's bikini-clad hordes rub shoulders with photographers, journalists and a

Interpreti Veneziani

SHORTLIST

Classic venues
- La Fenice – opera, concerts and classical dance (p71)
- Teatro Carlo Goldoni – from Goldoni classics to 20th-century plays (p63)
- Teatro Malibran – chamber music, opera and dance (p98)

Sporting fixtures
- Stadio PL Penzo – Venice's football stadium (p83)

Experimental theatre
- Biennale – Teatro (p27)
- Teatro Fondamenta Nuove (p106)

Film
- Biennale – Venice Film Festival (p28)
- Multisala Rossini (p66)

Vivaldi & Co
- Palazzo Bru Zane – French Romantic music (p127)
- La Pietà – Vivaldi in Vivaldi's church (p89)
- San Vidal – Interpreti Veneziani (p66)

constellation of international stars. Screenings at the massive PalaBiennale tent on the Lido are open to the public: tickets can be bought through the Biennale website or at the HQ in Ca' Giustinian. The Circuito Cinema (www.comune.venezia.it/cinema), a city council-backed hive of film-related research and activity, runs and programmes a group of local arthouse cinemas, the newest of which is the three-screen Multisala Rossini (p66).

The dearth of original-language films infuriates expats and cinema buffs alike. Outside the festival, screenings in anything but Italian are few and far between; look out for '*versione originale*' on programmes.

The sporting life

No other Italian city puts its inhabitants through their paces like Venice. In return for tramping miles on foot each day and being forced into compulsory step aerobics every ten paces, Venetians are rewarded with longevity and general good health into ripe old age.

Watery pursuits are what Venetians like best. Over 120 regattas are held a year (see box p29).

As for more usual exercise routines, many of the city's rowing clubs have well-equipped gyms. If you like to run in company, head for the lagoon-side pavement near the Giardini Pubblici or in the park by the Sant'Elena vaporetto stop. Cycling is best done on the Lido or around the island of Sant'Erasmo. If spectating is more appealing, then catch a football match at the PL Penzo stadium, on an island off Castello – a truly unique experience.

Carnevale p30

French and Austrian occupiers put paid to Venice's reputation for non-stop extravagant revels when they moved into town in the early 18th century. By that time Venice's celebrations had become frantic and excessive, the tawdry death throes of a city in terminal decline. In the Republic's heyday, however, Venice's rulers used pageantry both to assert the hierarchical nature of society and to give the lower orders the chance to let off steam. Official celebrations were declared in honour of anything from the end of a plague epidemic to victory in a naval battle. For the working classes, there were the *corse al toro* (bullfights) in campo Santo Stefano, or bloody battles between rival factions of the populace.

It wasn't until the second half of the 20th century, in fact, that the city's best-known festivals – **Carnevale**, for example, and the **Regata Storica** – were reintroduced. Nowadays, you could be forgiven for thinking that

feste such as Carnevale are merely media and tourism events. Yet Venetians continue to take festivals seriously, especially if they take place on the water. There are more than 120 regattas on the lagoon each year (p29).

The following are the pick of the annual events that take place in Venice. Further information and exact dates can be found nearer the time in the city's two dailies, *Il Gazzettino* and *La Nuova Venezia*, and in the monthly *Venezia News*. Posters around the city advertise concerts and other happenings. Dates highlighted in bold are public holidays. See also www.comune. venezia.it.

Spring

Mar/Apr **Pasqua (Easter)**
Basilica di San Marco & various locations
At dusk on Maundy Thursday, the lights are turned off inside St Mark's

basilica, and a fire is lit in the narthex (entrance porch) for the *benedizione del fuoco* (blessing of fire). Pasquetta (Easter Monday) is a public holiday, and museums and galleries may be closed.

Sun in mid Apr **Su e Zo per i Ponti**
www.suezo.it
Literally 'Up and Down Bridges'. Participants in this non-competitive, jolly race are given a map and a list of checkpoints (many of them bars) in the city of Venice to tick off. Proceeds go to charity.

25 Apr **Feast of San Marco**
Mass in the basilica, followed by a gondola regatta between the island of Sant'Elena and the punta della Dogana. Red rosebuds are given to wives and lovers.

1 May **Festa del Lavoro (Labour Day)**

Weekend after Ascension **Festa & Regata della Sensa**
Under the Republic, the doge boarded a glorious state barge and threw a gold ring overboard near the outlet to the Adriatic, to symbolise *lo sposalizio del mare* – marriage with the sea. Today, the mayor throws a wreath at San Nicolò on the Lido; a regatta follows.

Sun in late May/early June **Vogalonga**
www.vogalonga.com
Venetians – together with many out-of-towners – cover a 33km/20.5mile route in non-motorised boats of all descriptions. The event starts in front of the lagoon façade of the Doge's Palace at 8.30am. See also p29.

Summer

June-Nov **Biennale d'Arte (d'Architettura) Contemporanea**
Giardini della Biennale, Arsenale & various other venues
www.labiennale.org
This contemporary art jamboree has been going strong since 1895, and takes place on odd-numbered years. Since 1980, the architecture equivalent has occupied the Biennale venues in even-numbered years.

Biennale d'Arte

Film Festival

Week around 29 June **Feast of San Pietro**
San Pietro in Castello
The most villagey of Venice's local festivals, this one has a week of concerts, food stands and bouncy castles.

3rd weekend in July **Feast of the Redentore**
A pontoon bridge is built from San Marco to the Giudecca, to allow church and civic dignitaries to process to the Redentore church. On Saturday evening, illuminated boats full of picnickers gather off the punta della Dogana to watch a firework display.

Week around 25 July **Feast of San Giacomo dell'Orio**
Concerts, barbecues and a charity raffle in the eponymous campo.

15 Aug **Ferragosto (Feast of the Assumption)**
Venice closes down for this public holiday, and there's usually a free concert on the island of Torcello.

Late Aug-early Sept **Mostra Internazionale d'Arte Cinematografica (Film Festival)**
Various venues on the Lido
www.labiennale.org
The brightest stars of the film firmament descend on Venice for this festival. Tickets for public showings are available online or from Ca' Giustinian (San Marco 1364A, calle Ridotto).

Autumn

Ongoing **Biennale d'Arte (d'Architettura) Contemporanea**

1st Sun in Sept **Regata Storica**
Grand Canal
After an historical procession, rowing races take place along the Grand Canal. See also p29.

3rd Sun in Sept **Sagra del Pesce**
Burano

Messing about in boats

Venetians in their element.

Vogalonga

It doesn't take much to get a Venetian into a boat: give them a blue-skied Sunday or even a dry evening after a frustrating day at work, and they'll take to the water for a leisurely cruise to a deserted sandbank for a picnic, or a punishing, head-clearing row across a lonely backwater.

Two traditional activities dominate on the mosquito-infested lagoon: Venetian rowing (*voga alla veneta*) and Venetian sailing (*vela al terzo*) with a junk-shaped sail.

In *voga alla veneta*, the rower stands up, facing the direction of travel. There are various types of *voga alla veneta*: team rowing is one; the solo, cross-handed, two-oar method called *voga alla valesana* is another; and the most famous is *voga ad un solo remo* (one-oar rowing) as practised by Venetian gondoliers. The gondolier only ever puts his oar in the water on the right side of the boat, where it rests in a *forcola* (rowlock). Pushing on the oar makes the craft turn to the left. The trick consists in using the downstroke

to correct the direction. In theory, a gondolier uses little energy rowing a gondola, though that doesn't quite explain how they get those bodybuilder biceps.

All of these boating methods are employed by participants in the 120-plus regattas that take place on the lagoon each year. The most famous is the **Regata Storica**, held on the first Sunday of September: the pageantry may make it look like a tourist-board creation, but locals take the racing part of it very seriously indeed.

For sheer numbers of craft in the water, the joyously chaotic **Vogalonga** – held one Sunday in May or June – takes the prize. Anything without a motor can, and does, take part, from all the regular variations on the gondola, to dragon boats and things that look suspiciously like bathtubs.

The city's website does have a list (in Italian) of the major rowing events but it's not easy to find: search for 'stagione remiera' and the appropriate year on www.comune.venezia.it.

Fried fish and lots of white wine are consumed amid Burano's brightly painted houses.

1st weekend in Oct **Sagra del Mosto**
Sant'Erasmo

This festival is a great excuse for Venetians to get light-headed on the first pressing of wine.

Last Sun in Oct **Venice Marathon**
www.venicemarathon.it

The marathon starts in the town of Stra, near Padua, and ends on the riva dei Sette Martiri.

1 Nov **Ognissanti (All Saints' Day)**

11 Nov **Feast of San Martino**

Children armed with mamma's pots and spoons raise a ruckus around the city centre. Horse-and-rider-shaped San Martino cakes can be found in cake shops all over Venice.

21 Nov **Feast of the Madonna della Salute**

The patriarch (archbishop) leads a procession across the Grand Canal on a pontoon bridge from campo Santa Maria del Giglio to the Salute church.

Winter

8 Dec **L'Immacolata (Feast of the Immaculate Conception)**

25 Dec **Natale (Christmas Day)**

26 Dec **Santo Stefano (St Stephen's Day/Boxing Day)**

31 Dec **San Silvestro (New Year's Eve)**
Piazza San Marco

A massive outdoor party in the square has light shows, live music and DJ sets.

1 Jan **New Year's Day**

Hardy swimmers take a bracing dip in the waters off the Lido.

6 Jan **La Befana (Epiphany)**

A rowing race along the Grand Canal. Competitors, all aged over 50, are dressed up as an ugly witch, La Befana.

3 weeks leading up to Lent
Carnevale

Venice's 'traditional' pre-Lent Carnevale festivities were resuscitated in the late 1970s, and draw masked revellers from all over the world for celebrations that now last almost three weeks.

Marathon

Itineraries

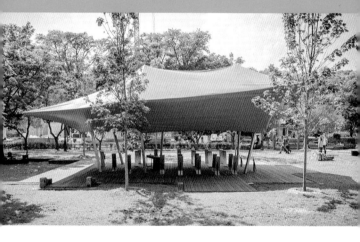

The Grand Canal

Venice's extraordinary high street is like nothing else: three-and-a-half kilometres (2.2 miles) of watery grandeur, lined with magnificent *palazzi*. Nothing will give you the same grasp of what this extraordinary city is all about like a trip down the Grand Canal. In quintessentially Venetian fashion, the magnificent *palazzi* that line the water way were both statement of clout and taste, and solid commercial enterprise: their design is as practical as it is eye-catching.

Most of the buildings date from between the 12th and 18th centuries. When a palazzo was rebuilt, the basic structure was retained, for the good reason that the same foundations could be used. A palazzo typically had a water entrance opening on to a large hall with storage space on either side; a *mezzanino* with offices; a piano nobile with spacious reception halls and residential rooms; and a land entrance at the back.

Setting out from the railway station towards San Marco, the façades of the Scalzi (left bank) and San Simeone (right bank) churches greet the visitor before the vaporetto passes beneath the **Scalzi bridge**, built in 1934.

Beyond, the church of San Geremia (left bank) stands just before the wide Cannaregio canal forks off. Placed with its main façade on the Cannaregio canal is the 18th-century **Palazzo Labia**, which contains sumptuous frescoes by Tiepolo. The fate of the palazzo hangs in the balance: current owner, the public RAI television company, put it on the market in 2008, since when there has been little movement.

Beyond the Riva di Biasio stop, just before the rio del Megio, is the **Fondaco dei Turchi** (right bank), a 19th-century reconstruction of a Veneto-Byzantine building leased to Turkish traders in the 17th century as a residence and warehouse; it now

Grand Canal

century. The current neo-Gothic construction was built in 1907. Beyond it is the longest façade on the Grand Canal, with an endless parade of arches. This belongs to Sansovino's **Fabbriche Nuove**, built in 1554-56 for Venice's financial judiciary; it now houses the Court of Assizes.

Just before the rio dei Santi Apostoli (left bank) is **Palazzo Mangilli Valmarana**, built in 1751 for Joseph Smith, the British consul, who amassed the Canaletto paintings that now belong to Queen Elizabeth II. Beyond the *rio* is the 13th-century **Ca' da Mosto**, once the site of the Leon Bianco (white lion) Hotel. This is one of the earliest Veneto-Byzantine *palazzi* on the canal. As the vaporetto swings round the bend here, the Rialto bridge comes into view.

On the right bank, the **Fabbriche Vecchie** was designed by Scarpagnino in the early 16th century. If you're doing this trip in the morning, you'll see the crowds stocking up at the fruit and vegetable part of the Rialto markets beside the two *fabbriche*.

At the foot of the Rialto bridge is the **Fondego dei Tedeschi** (left bank), a huge residence-cum-warehouse leased to the German community from the 13th century onwards. The present building – currently being converted into a Louis Vuitton-run shopping mall – was designed by Spavento and Scarpagnino in 1505-08. The façade once had frescoes by Titian and Giorgione, fragments of which can now be seen at the Ca' d'Oro.

Opposite, the **Palazzo dei Camerlenghi** (1523-25; right bank) is built around the curve of the canal; the walls lean noticeably. It was the headquarters of the Venetian Exchequer, with a debtors' prison on the ground floor.

Under the bridge, but before the Rialto vaporetto stop, the **Palazzo Manin Dolfin** (left bank) has a

houses the **Museo di Storia Naturale**. Across the *rio*, the **Depositi del Megio** (state granaries) have a battlemented plain-brick façade.

After the San Marcuola stop is **Palazzo Vendramin Calergi** (left bank), designed by Mauro Codussi in the early 16th century, with porphyry insets in the façade. Wagner died here in 1883; it now plays host to the **Casinò**.

After the Baroque church of San Stae (right bank), with its exuberant sculpture, comes **Ca' Pesaro**, a splendid example of Venetian Baroque by Baldassare Longhena. After two smaller *palazzi* stands **Palazzo Corner della Regina**, with a rusticated ground floor featuring grotesque masks; the palazzo dates from the 1720s.

On the left bank, an uneventful stretch ends at the **Ca' d'Oro**, the most gorgeously ornate Gothic building on the Grand Canal. It has an open loggia on the piano nobile.

Just beyond, on the right bank, a covered **Pescaria** (fish market) has occupied a site here since the 14th

Palazzo Corner

Palazzo Pisani Moretta

portico straddling the *fondamenta* (canal path). The façade is by Sansovino (late 1530s); the rest was rebuilt by Ludovico Manin, the last doge of Venice. It now belongs to the Bank of Italy.

On the left after the Rialto vaporetto stop, **Palazzetto Dandolo** is a Gothic building that appears to have been squeezed in. Enrico Dandolo, the blind doge who led the ferocious assault on Constantinople in 1204, was born in an earlier palazzo here.

Palazzo Farsetti and **Palazzo Loredan** (left bank) are Veneto-Byzantine buildings that now house the city hall. Though heavily restored, these two adjoining *palazzi* are among the few surviving examples of the typical 12th-century Venetian house, with its first-floor polyforate window.

The austerely classical **Palazzo Grimani** is one of the largest *palazzi* on the Grand Canal. Its creator, Michele Sanmicheli, was famous for his military architecture, and this building is characteristically assertive.

Seven *palazzi* further on, before the rio Michiel, stands the pink **Palazzo Benzon** (left bank), home of

Countess Marina Querini-Benzon, a society figure in the late 18th century. Byron was charmed by her when she was already in her sixties.

Facing off across the canal at the Sant'Angelo vaporetto stop are the small **Palazzo Corner** (left bank), built in the last decade of the 15th century by Mauro Codussi, with a rusticated ground floor, elegant balconies and double-arched windows; and the 16th-century **Palazzo Cappello Layard** (right bank), once the home of Sir Henry Austen Layard, archaeologist and British ambassador to Constantinople.

Almost opposite the San Tomà stop stand the four **Palazzi Mocenigo** (left bank), with blue-and-white poles in the water. The central double palazzo (16th century) was where Byron lived in 1818-19.

On the right bank, **Palazzo Pisani Moretta**, a large Gothic 15th-century palazzo, is just before the San Tomà stop. After the stop, **Palazzo Balbi** (1582-90) – with obelisks, indicating that an admiral lived here – is the seat of the Veneto Regional Council.

Palazzo Franchetti

Next door, across the rio Ca' Foscari, come three magnificent mid-15th-century Gothic *palazzi*. The first and largest is **Ca' Foscari**, now the HQ of Venice University. The next two are the **Palazzi Giustinian**; Wagner stayed in one of them in the winter of 1858-59, composing part of *Tristan und Isolde*. The horn prelude to the third act was inspired by the mournful cries of the gondoliers.

Just before the San Samuele vaporetto stop is the heavy, grey-white **Palazzo Grassi** (left bank), designed by Giorgio Massari. This was the last of the great patrician *palazzi*, built in 1748-72 when the city was already in terminal decline. It now belongs to French magnate François Pinault. **Ca' Rezzonico** (right bank) is a Baroque masterpiece by Longhena, begun in 1667. Robert Browning died here. It's now the museum of 18th-century Venice.

A little further round the bend, **Ca' del Duca** (left bank) incorporates a part of the aggressively rusticated base and columns of a palace that Bartolomeo Bon was going to build for the Cornaro family; the massive project was never completed.

At the right foot of the Accademia bridge stand the **Gallerie dell' Accademia**; once the church and monastery of Santa Maria della Carità, they now boast an unrivalled collection of Venetian paintings.

Beyond the bridge, at its left foot, is **Palazzo Franchetti**, built in the 15th century but much restored and altered in the 19th; it's now used for conferences and exhibitions.

Immediately beyond this are two **Palazzi Barbaro** (left bank): part of the first – 15th-century Gothic, with a fine Renaissance water entrance – still belongs to the Curtis family, who hosted Henry James in 1870-75.

After the bridge on the right bank are four fine Renaissance *palazzi*, then campo San Vio, one of only a few squares on the Grand Canal. In the corner is the Anglican church of **St George**. To one side of the campo is the 16th-century **Palazzo Barbarigo**, with eye-catching but tacky 19th-century mosaics. Next is the pretty Gothic **Palazzo da' Mula**.

Just before one of the few Grand Canal gardens comes the bashful **Casetta delle Rose** (left bank), set behind its own small trellised garden.

Canova had a studio here. Nearby, the massive rusticated ground floor of the **Palazzo Corner della Ca' Grande** (now the Prefecture) influenced Longhena's Baroque *palazzi*. The imposing pile was commissioned in 1537 from Sansovino and built after 1545.

Work on the single-storey **Palazzo Venier dei Leoni** (right bank) ground to a halt in 1749 and never resumed. It now contains the **Peggy Guggenheim Collection**. Next but one comes the pure, lopsided charm of the Renaissance **Ca' Dario**, built in the 1470s, with decorative use of coloured marbles. Venetians say it's cursed, as many of its owner have met sticky ends. Gaudy 19th-century mosaics on **Palazzo Salviati** advertise the products of that family's glass works. Further on, the large neo-Gothic **Palazzo Genovese**, built in 1892 on the site of the abbey of San Gregorio, now houses the five-star Centurion Palace Hotel.

The new hostelry faces a Venetian classic across the way: the luxurious **Palazzo Gritti** (left bank), with its 15th-century Gothic façade; the hotel has recently undergone a multi-million-euro makeover. Three *palazzi* further on is the narrow Gothic **Palazzo Contarini Fasan**, traditionally known as Desdemona's house. The lovely balconies have wheel tracery.

Lording it over the end of the right bank is the wonderfully curvy church of **Santa Maria della Salute**, an audacious Baroque creation by Baldassare Longhena (1671). At the very tip is the **Dogana di Mare** (Customs House; 1677), with its tower, gilded ball and weathervane figure of Fortune; inside the warehouses at the Punta, stunningly renovated by architect Tadao Ando, is the Punta della Dogana contemporary art gallery.

The last notable building on the left bank is **Ca' Giustinian**, built in the late Gothic style of the 1470s, and once a hotel where Verdi, Gautier, Ruskin and Proust stayed; it's now the HQ of La Biennale (p27). At the corner of calle Vallaresso is **Harry's Bar**, the near-legendary Venetian watering hole founded in the 1930s. Just beyond the Vallaresso stop lie the pretty **Giardinetti Reali** and **piazza San Marco**.

Peggy Guggenheim Collection

Santo Stefano p39

Tintoretto's Last Suppers

No one ever accused the great Venetian colourist Tintoretto (1518-94) of being a slacker. His paintings, often on a huge scale, are to be found in many of Venice's major churches. And while other big producers – such as the monotonously ubiquitous Palma il Giovane – tend to repeat themselves unashamedly, Tintoretto always astonishes by the fertility of his imagination.

This is even more apparent if you study his variations on a theme. One subject in particular seemed to hold an unending fascination for the mystically minded Tintoretto: the Last Supper. There are seven paintings of this subject by the artist in Venice: they give a good idea of the development of his techniques and style, and also offer an insight into the deepest workings of his imagination.

The following itinerary covers much of the central, western and northern part of the city. Given how compact Venice is, you could cover the ground in a determined morning or afternoon. It would be far better, however, to stretch it out over a whole Tintoretto-packed day, perhaps pausing for a reviving lunch before or after visiting the Scuola Grande di San Rocco.

Tintoretto's earliest *Last Supper* is in the church of **San Marcuola** (p95), by the vaporetto stop of that name. In this early work, Tintoretto still organises the mainly horizontal composition in terms of symmetry and narrative clarity, adopting the same classical structure found in Leonardo's more famous version of the subject. The main innovation with respect to Leonardo is the greater dynamism: the apostles are all caught in mid movement; the action spills over to either side of the table, with busy serving women and

Scuola Grande di San Rocco

children participating in the scene. This background movement would increase in later paintings, until it almost came to dominate the scenes.

From San Marcuola, head towards the railway station and cross the Scalzi bridge; take the *calle* directly at the foot of the bridge, turn left at the end and cross a canal. Here, in the church of **San Simeone Profeta** (p120; aka San Simeone Grande), hangs a comparatively small *Last Supper*, tentatively dated 1560. The most striking elements of this painting, probably done with the help of assistants, are the spectral figure of the man who commissioned the work (probably the parish priest) in the background on the left, and the fine candelabra hanging over the table.

Some deft map-reading will be needed to get to **campo San Polo**. In the church of the same name (p114), the *Last Supper* (1568) has

the same floor of red and white squares as in the San Marcuola painting, but the composition is no longer classically symmetrical. The first thing we notice is the apostle at the centre of the painting turning away from the table to offer a crust of bread to a beggar lying on the floor in the foreground. This shadowy figure, startlingly foreshortened, serves to pull us into the painting, making us feel part of the scene. The table now slants diagonally upwards to the right, and the apostles are all in swirling movement around the central figure of Christ.

It's a short hop west from here past the great bulk of the Frari to the **Scuola Grande di San Rocco** (p126), where the *Last Supper* (1578-81) has an elevated stage setting used in an earlier painting in the church of Santo Stefano (p39); the same dog seems to stand quivering on the steps in the foreground, although here he is strangely spectral, with the lines of the stairs visible through his body. The setting appears to be a fairly grandiose 16th-century palazzo. The table is set low, with the apostles squatting or kneeling around it; Christ himself is kneeling, with his bare soles protruding from beneath his red robes. All around the table and in the background, everyday life goes on, with servants in the kitchen baking bread and clearing away dishes. This only adds to the visionary quality of what is happening in the centre of the painting.

Follow the flow southwards to **San Trovaso** (p134), which contains a *Last Supper* dated 1556. Though this is an early version, it's original in concept, with a greater emphasis on realism. The setting seems to be a tavern, and the apostles are sitting on all four sides of a square table. Each of them seems to be caught in mid move, one reaching for a flagon of wine at the very bottom of the painting, another twisting round to take the lid off a pot that a cat seems eager to inspect, another leaning forward in apparent surprise towards Christ. A chair lies overturned in the foreground, with its cane bottom and legs towards the viewer. In contrast to all this earthy realism, above Christ's head is a mysterious view beyond the tavern to a classical landscape, with diaphanous figures poised against sunlit arches and pillars.

Make your way across the nearby Accademia bridge into **campo Santo Stefano**. Hanging in the sacristy of the eponymous church (p64) is Tintoretto's first truly large-scale version of the *Last Supper* (1576). Although it contains a good deal of studio work, the design is clearly by the maestro and paves the way for the great painting in the Scuola di San Rocco. The setting is strikingly different from the earlier versions, with the

table on an elevated platform; the steps leading up to it provide the foreground of the painting, with a child sprawled across them and a dog poised expectantly, looking up at the laden table with an eager, quivering nose. The area in front of the stairs contains two figures that seem to mediate between the viewer and the miraculous scene: on the right is a half-naked beggar, lying and looking wistfully up at the table; on the left is a striking female figure, who may be a servant but whose open-armed gesture seems curiously beneficent, even benedictory. For the first time, Christ is viewed from behind, with the apostles leaning across the table towards him and the viewer.

For Tintoretto's final version, make your way through St Mark's square to the riva degli Schiavoni, and take a vaporetto to the island of San Giorgio Maggiore. The vast painting (1591) hanging to the right of the high altar in the church of **San Giorgio** (p152) is a magnificent work intended to dazzle the viewer with its bewildering mixture of lights and shadows, movement and stillness. The long table occupies the left half of the painting, and angels appear mysteriously in the swirling smoke from the oil lamps above. The right-hand side of the painting is dominated by two striking figures of servants at work: a girl kneels beside a basket (which is being investigated by another curious cat) and offers a dish to a servant in blue clothes and orange apron; he is caught in an elegant balletic pose, his head turned left to the girl while his body and right arm reach towards a table on the right. These figures provide an interesting solid counterpoint to the evanescent swirl of angelic figures floating mysteriously above and around them. The combination of earthy realism and visionary mysticism is here taken to startling new levels.

GRAN BRETAGNA

Biennale d'Architettura 2014

Modern & Contemporary

To most people, the word 'Venice' conjures up watery canalscapes, melting colours and Gothic and Renaissance glories. But since 1895, when the first **Biennale d'Arte Contemporanea** (p27) was staged here, the lagoon city has been a showcase for avant-garde art. With the addition in 1980 of the Architecture Biennale, it offered a benchmark for innovation in that field too.

While the commercial gallery scene has long been lively in Venice, recent years have seen the much-heralded arrival of collectors – Francois Pinault of the luxury goods LVHM empire, and fashion designer Miuccia Prada – making contemporary works available to the wider public. But they were simply following in the footsteps of others: from Peggy Guggenheim, who brought her collection of artworks and artist-lovers to *La Serenissima* in 1949, to the Bevilacqua la Masa Foundation, which gives space to young artists, the Stanze del Vetro gallery for modern artists working in glass at the Cini Foundation, and the modern art collection at Ca' Pesaro, this is a city that offers far more than 'just' an extravaganza of historic gems.

You could arrange a busy day around visiting exclusively 20th- and 21st-century sights. Or you could use them as a guideline around which to add attractions from other eras. In either case, this itinerary will lead you through a large part of the city.

The **Giardini della Biennale** (Biennale gardens; p83) is a good place to begin any exploration of modern Venice. At any point (except Mondays) between June and late November, the pavilions in the

Ponte della Constituzione p42

otherwise closed-off sector of the Giardini will be hopping with visitors to the Biennale d'Arte (odd years) or d'Architettura (even years; p27). What's in the exhibitions is generally fascinating; but the pavilions themselves – most created by a country or group of countries to display their national representative – are a magnificent panorama of building styles, from art deco to hyper-modern, with Australia's new pavilion, being built at the time of writing to a design by Denton Corker Marshall, the latest of the bunch. Venice's 20th-century architectural great Carlo Scarpa is responsible for details such as the former main ticket booth and the sculpture garden.

It's an easy stroll from here to the **Arsenale** (p83), the city's historic shipbuilding yard, where massive spaces have been given a clean, industrial-mod revamp to serve as the perfect foil for more Biennale exhibits.

Now take your map and your courage in your hands, and plunge westward into the backstreets towards Santa Maria Formosa. Here, the **Fondazione Querini Stampalia** (p73) has a superb small collection of classical art, a top-floor space made over by Mario Botta where contemporary shows are sometimes held, and a stunning ground floor area, complete with café and delightful garden, designed by Carlo Scarpa in the 1960s.

At this point, you might like to stroll up to the fondamenta Nuove to peer across the northern lagoon towards the cemetery island, **San Michele** (p155) with its modern eastwards extension by UK architect David Chipperfield. Or simply head straight down to piazza San Marco, where the **Negozio Olivetti** (p53) is another of Scarpa's masterpieces: note the extraordinary amount of light he managed to coax into this low, narrow space. Across the piazza, the busy **Fondazione Bevilacqua la Masa** (p51) supports young local artists and stages regular shows, both of their work and by others from around the world.

Vaporetto 2 goes from the San Zaccaria stop across to the island of San Giorgio, where exhibitions at the **Fondazione Cini**'s (p151) Le Stanze del Vetro space focus on designs by

20th- and 21st-century artists and architects for production in Venice's famed glass foundries. Don't neglect to take the lift to the top of the belltower in the church next door for the finest possible view over the city.

Get back on vaporetto 2, travel to the Zattere stop, and walk east along the canal-front Zattere to the very tip; en route is the **Fondazione Vedova** (p140) with works by modern Venetian artist Emilio Vedova and (more fascinating) exhibition mechanisms designed by Renzo Piano.

The view across to the Doge's Palace and San Marco from the easternmost point is glorious. The building right behind you is the **Punta della Dogana** (p143), a space reorganised and revamped by Japanese star architect Tadao Ando for French magnate Francois Pinault. Shows here feature many works from Pinault's own immense collection, and are relentlessly contemporary.

A short walk west alongside the Grand Canal, the **Peggy Guggenheim Collection** (p142) – Venice's third most visited attraction – seems welcoming and homely in comparison. Set in a pretty garden, Peggy's former home has works by Picasso, Duchamps, Brancusi, Ernst and many others.

From Accademia, it's one stop on vaporetto 2 to San Samuele (the walk will take you less than 15 minutes – plus time for window-shopping, refreshment and peering at traffic on the Grand Canal as you cross the Accademia bridge), where there's more of the Ando-Pinault combo at **Palazzo Grassi** (p63). This was the Frenchman's first Venetian outpost, and the shows here are of a similar bent as those at Punta della Dogana, though they also feature monographic exhibitions by big contemporary names. Tucked in behind, the Teatrino Grassi (yet another

Ando) holds screenings, conferences and performances.

Continuing upstream on the no.2 vaporetto, you could alight at San Tomà for a look at more Scarpa adjustments in the Venice university main site at Ca' Foscari. Even if you opt to skip more Scarpa, this is a good place to change from vaporetto 2 to the no.1 – the former shoots up to the railway station, whereas the latter will deposit you at San Stae for two more modern attractions. (En route, just after passing beneath the Rialto bridge, the Fondaco dei Tedeschi – once the Venetian hub for German traders – was under wraps as this guide went to press, being transformed into a luxury shopping mall to a plan by Dutch architect Rem Koolhaas.)

The collection at **Ca' Pesaro** (p118) is mainly Italian, and stops some time around the 1950s, but includes works by Giacomo Manzù, Giorgio Morandi and Medardo Rosso. There are some international names too, such as Joan Miró, Gustav Klimt and Vassily Kandinsky. A little further down the Grand Canal, the **Fondazione Prada**'s new outpost at Ca' Corner della Regina (p119) stages interesting shows examining the crossover between art, architecture and popular culture; some exhibits have involved Koolhaas and his OMA Studio.

Back on the water, vaporetto 1 trundles towards piazzale Roma, passing beneath the bit of contemporary architecture least loved by Venetians. Officially **Ponte della Costituzione** but known to all as ponte Calatrava, this bridge by the Spanish architect opened in 2008 – quietly, to avoid too many protests. Painted white, and therefore standing oddly against the city's traditional warm colours, it ferries travellers between the bus stops in piazzale Roma and the railway station.

Venice by Area

San Marco

VENICE BY AREA

Piazza San Marco, Napoleon said, is the 'drawing room of Europe'. It may not be homely, but it is a supremely civilised meeting place. At times, it appears that much of Europe's population is crammed into this great square and the pulsating shopping streets leading out of it.

Three main thoroughfares link the key points of this neighbourhood: one runs from piazza San Marco to the Rialto bridge; one from the Rialto to the Accademia bridge; and one from the Accademia back to piazza San Marco. For a respite from the crowds, wander off these routes; even in this tourist-packed *sestiere* you can find little havens of calm.

Piazza San Marco & around

In magnificent piazza San Marco, Byzantine rubs shoulders with Gothic, late Renaissance and neoclassical. The Venetians have always kept the square clear of monuments; this is typical of Venice, where individual glory always plays second fiddle to the common weal. The north side of the square dates from the early 16th century. Its arches repeat a motif suggested by an earlier Byzantine structure. Here resided the procurators of St Mark's, who were in charge of maintaining the basilica – hence the name of this whole wing, the Procuratie Vecchie. At its eastern end is the **Torre dell'Orologio**. Construction of the Procuratie Nuove, opposite, went on for most of the first half of the 17th century, to designs by Vincenzo Scamozzi. Napoleon joined the two wings at the far end – not for the sake of symmetry, but in order to create the ballroom that was lacking in the Procuratie Nuove, which had become the imperial residence. So, in 1807, down came Sansovino's

Piazza San Marco & Campanile

church of San Geminiano and up went the Ala Napoleonica, which now houses the **Museo Correr**. The **Campanile** and **Basilica di San Marco** close off the square to the east.

Between the basilica and the lagoon, the **Piazzetta** is the real entrance to Venice, defined by two free-standing columns of granite. What appears to be a winged lion on top of the eastern column is in fact a chimera from Persia, Syria or maybe China; the wings and book are Venetian additions. St Theodore, who tops the other column, was Venice's first patron saint. The area directly in front of the **Palazzo Ducale** (Doge's Palace) was known as the *broglio*, and was the place where councillors conferred and connived (hence the term 'imbroglio'). Opposite the palace stands the **Biblioteca Marciana**, now the main city library.

West of the Piazzetta are the **Giardinetti Reali** (Royal Gardens), created by the French. The dainty neoclassical coffee house by Gustavo Selva is now a tourist information office. By the San Marco Vallaresso vaporetto stop is **Harry's Bar**, the city's most famous watering hole.

Heading east from the Piazzetta, you will cross the ponte della Paglia (Bridge of Straw). If you can elbow your way to the side of the bridge, there is a photo-op view of the ponte dei Sospiri (Bridge of Sighs). From the Bridge of Straw, there is also a superb view of the Renaissance façade of the Palazzo Ducale.

Sights & museums

Basilica di San Marco

San Marco, piazza San Marco (041 522 5205, www.basilicasanmarco.it). Vaporetto San Marco Vallaresso or San Zaccaria. **Open** *Basilica, Chancel, Pala d'Oro & Treasury 9.45am-5pm Mon-Sat; 2-5pm Sun. Loggia & Museo Mariano 9.45am-3.45pm daily.* **Admission** *Basilica free. Chancel & Pala d'Oro €2. Treasury €3. Loggia & Museo Marciano €5. No credit cards.* **Map** p47 F3 ❶
Note: To skip the huge queues that form at busy times, you can book your visit (€2 fee) through www.venetoinside.com. Large bags or rucksacks must be deposited (free) in a building in calle San Basso, off the piazzetta dei Leoncini. The basilica is open for mass and private prayer from 7am to 9.45am, with entrance from the piazzetta dei Leoncini door.
Often seen as the living testimony of Venice's links with Byzantium, St Mark's basilica is also an expression of the city's independence. In the Middle Ages, any self-respecting city state had to have a truly important holy relic. So when two Venetian merchants swiped the body of St Mark from Alexandria in 828, they were going for the very best – an Evangelist, and an entire body at that. Fortunately, there was a legend (or one was quickly cooked up) that the saint had once been caught in the lagoon in a storm, and so it was fitting that this should be his final resting place.

The Venetians were traders, but they never looked askance at a bit of

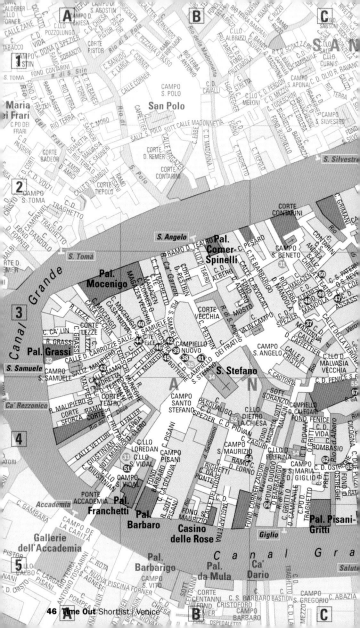

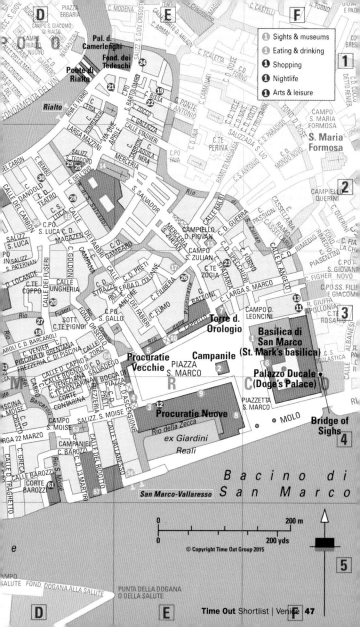

D | E | F

PIAZZA
C. MODENA   S. GIOV.   C. CASTELLI   U. FORNO

PIAZZA
CAMPO S. GIACOMO
DI RIALTO

Pal. d.
Camerlenghi

Fond. dei
Tedeschi

Ponte di
Rialto

Rialto

1	Sights & museums
1	Eating & drinking
3	Shopping
1	Nightlife
1	Arts & leisure

S. Maria
Formosa

Torre d.
Orologio

Basilica di
San Marco
(St. Mark's basilica)

Procuratie
Vecchie

Campanile

PIAZZA
S. MARCO

Palazzo Ducale
(Doge's Palace)

PIAZZETTA
S. MARCO

Procuratie Nuove

ex Giardini
Reali

MOLO

Bridge of
Sighs

San Marco-Vallaresso

Bacino di
San Marco

0   200 m
0   200 yds

© Copyright Time Out Group 2015

e

CAMPO
SALUTE FOND. DOGANA ALLA SALUTE

PUNTA DELLA DOGANA
O DELLA SALUTE

D | E

Basilica di San Marco p45

straightforward looting as well. The basilica – like the city as a whole – is encrusted with trophies brought back from Venice's greatest spoliatory exploit, the Sack of Constantinople in 1204, during the free-for-all that went under the name of the Fourth Crusade.

The present basilica is the third on the site. It was built mainly between 1063 and 1094, although the work of decoration continued until the 16th century. The church became Venice's cathedral only in 1807, ten years after the fall of the Republic; until then, the bishop exerted his authority from San Pietro in Castello. Being next door to the Palazzo Ducale, Venice's most important church was associated with political as much as spiritual power. Venetians who came to worship here were very aware that they were guests of the doge, not the pope.

Exterior

The first view of the basilica from the western end of piazza San Marco is an unforgettable experience. It is particularly impressive in the evening, when the mosaics on the façade glow in the light of the setting sun. The façade consists of two orders of five arches, with clusters of columns in the lower order; the upper arches are topped by fantastic Gothic tracery.

The only original mosaic (c1260) is the one over the northernmost door, *The Translation of the Body of St Mark to the Basilica*, which is the earliest known representation of the church. Of curiosity value is the 17th-century mosaic over the southernmost door, which shows the body of St Mark being filched from Alexandria and the Muslims reeling back in disgust because it was wrapped in pork.

The real treasures on show are the sculptures, particularly the group of three carved arches around the central portal, a Romanesque masterpiece. The inner curve of the outer arch is the liveliest, with its detailed portrayals of Venetian trades, arts, crafts and pastimes.

Visible through the doors, the narthex (covered porch) has an *opus sectile* marble floor; a small lozenge of porphyry by the central door is said to mark the spot where Frederick Barbarossa, Holy Roman Emperor, paid homage to Pope Alexander III in 1177. The influence of Islamic art comes through in the few remaining grilles that cover the wall niches where early doges were buried. Above, a series of 13th-century mosaics in the Byzantine style shows Old Testament scenes.

The south façade, towards the Palazzo Ducale, was the first side seen by visitors arriving by sea and is thus richly encrusted with trophies proclaiming *La Serenissima*'s might.

At the corner by the Doge's Palace stand the Tetrarchs, a fourth-century porphyry group of four conspiratorial-looking kings. These come from Constantinople and are usually accepted as representing Diocletian and his Imperial colleagues.

The two free-standing pillars in front of the Baptistry door, with Syrian carvings from the fifth century, come from Acre in modern-day Israel, as does the stumpy porphyry column on the corner, known as the Pietra del Bando, where official decrees were read.

The north façade, facing piazzetta dei Leoncini, is also studded with loot, including the carving of 12 sheep on either side of a throne bearing a cross, a seventh-century Byzantine work. Note the beautiful 13th-century Moorish arches of the Porta dei Fiori, which enclose a Nativity scene.

Interior

The lambent interior exudes splendour and mystery, even when bursting with tourists. The basilica is Greek cross in form, surmounted by five great 11th-century domes. The surfaces are totally covered by more than four square kilometres (1.5 square miles) of mosaics, the result of 600 years of labour. The finest pieces, dating from the 12th and 13th centuries, are the work of Venetian craftsmen influenced by Byzantine art but developing their own independent style. The chapels and Baptistry were decorated in the 14th and 15th centuries; a century later, replacements of earlier mosaics were made using cartoons by such artists as Titian and Tintoretto. However, most of these later mosaics are flawed by the attempt to achieve the three-dimensional effects of Renaissance painting.

In the apse, *Christ Pantocrator* is a 16th-century reproduction of a Byzantine original. Beneath, in what may be the oldest mosaics in the church, are four saint-protectors of Venice: Nicholas, Peter, Mark and Hermagoras. The central dome of the Ascension, with its splendidly poised angels and apostles, dates from the early 13th century. The Passion scenes on the west vault (12th century) are a striking blend of Romanesque and Byzantine styles. The Pentecost dome (near the entrance) was probably the first to be decorated; it shows the descent of the Holy Spirit. Four magnificent angels hover in the pendentives.

Over in the right transept is the *Miraculous Rediscovery of the Body of St Mark*: this refers to an episode that occurred after the second basilica was destroyed by fire, when the secret of the whereabouts of the body was lost. The Evangelist obligingly opened up the pillar where his sarcophagus had been hidden (it's just opposite and is marked by an inlaid marble panel). Notice, too, the gorgeous 12th-century marble, porphyry and glass mosaics on the floor.

Baptistry & Zen Chapel
The Baptistry contains the Gothic tomb of Doge Andrea Dandolo and some interesting mosaics, including an image of Salome dancing. In the adjoining Zen Chapel is the bronze 16th-century tomb of Cardinal Zen (a common Venetian surname). The baptistry and chapel are very rarely open.

Chancel & Pala d'Oro
The Chancel is separated from the body of the church by the iconostasis – a red marble rood screen by the Gothic sculptors Jacobello and Pier Paolo Dalle Masegne, with fine statues of the Madonna, the apostles and St George. Access to the Chancel is via the San Clemente chapel to the right, with a mosaic showing merchants Rustico di Torcello and Buono di Malamocco, apparently about to FedEx the body of St Mark to Venice. St Mark's sarcophagus is visible through the grate underneath the altar. It was moved here from the 11th-century crypt in 1835.

The indigestibly opulent Pala d'Oro (Gold Altarpiece) is a Byzantine work and, for a change, was acquired honestly. It was made in Constantinople in 976 on the orders of Doge Pietro Orseolo I and further enriched in later years with amethysts, emeralds, pearls, rubies, sapphires and topaz, topped off with a Gothic frame and resetting in 1345.

The left transept contains the chapel of the Madonna Nicopeia (the Victory Bringer), named after the tenth-century icon on the altar, another Fourth Crusade acquisition. The St Isidore chapel beyond, with its 14th-century mosaics of the life of the saint, is reserved for private prayer and confessions, as is the adjacent Mascoli chapel. The altarpiece in this chapel, featuring saints Mark and John the Evangelist with the Virgin between them, is a striking piece of Gothic statuary. The chapel's mosaics, dating from 1430 to 1450, have a definite Renaissance look to them. They are mostly by Michele Giambono, although some of the figures have been attributed to Jacopo Bellini and to the Florentine Andrea del Castagno, who was in Venice in 1432.

Loggia & Museo Marciano
Of all the pay-to-enter sections of the basilica, this is definitely the most worthwhile – and it's the only part of the church you can visit on Sunday morning. Up a narrow stairway from the narthex are the bronze horses that vie with the lion of St Mark as the city's

symbol; here, too, is Paolo Veneziano's exquisite Pala Feriale, a painted panel that was used to cover the Pala d'Oro on weekdays. The Loggia also provides a marvellous view over the square.

The original bronze horses are now kept indoors. They were among the many treasures brought back from the Sack of Constantinople, where they had stood above the city's Hippodrome. They were at first placed in front of the Arsenale, but in around 1250 were moved to the terrace of the basilica.

In 1797, it was Napoleon's turn to play looter; the horses did not return to Venice from Paris until after his defeat at Waterloo. They remained on the terrace until 1974, when they were removed for restoration. Since 1982, they have been on display inside the basilica, with exact but soulless copies replacing them outside.

Treasury

This contains a hoard of exquisite Byzantine gold and silver plunder – reliquaries, chalices, candelabra. The highlights are a silver perfume censer in the form of a church and two 11th-century icons of the archangel Michael.

Campanile

San Marco, piazza San Marco. Vaporetto San Marco Vallaresso or San Zaccaria. **Open** *Nov-Mar* 9.30am-3.45pm daily. *Mar-June, Oct* 9am-7pm daily. *July-Sept* 9am-9pm daily. **Admission** €8. No credit cards. **Map** p47 E3 ❷

At almost 99m (325ft), the Campanile is the city's tallest building, originally built between 888 and 912. Its present appearance, with the stone spire and the gilded angel on top, dates from 1514. In July 1902 it collapsed, imploding in a neat pyramid of rubble; the only victim was the custodian's cat. It was rebuilt exactly 'as it was, where it was', as the town council of the day promised.

The Campanile served both as a watchtower and a bell tower. It provided a site for public humiliations: people of 'scandalous behaviour' were hung in a cage from the top.

Holy Roman Emperor Frederick III rode a horse to the top of the original in 1451; these days, visitors take the lift. The view is superb, taking in the Lido, the whole lagoon and (on a clear day) the Dolomites in the distance. Sansovino's little Loggetta at the foot of the tower, which echoes the shape of a Roman triumphal arch, was also rebuilt using bits and pieces found in the rubble.

Fondazione Bevilacqua la Masa

San Marco 71C, piazza San Marco (041 523 7819, www.bevilacqualamasa.it). Vaporetto San Marco Vallaresso. **Open** (during exhibitions only) 10.30am-5.30pm Mon, Wed-Sun. **Map** p47 E4 ❸

The Fondazione Bevilacqua la Masa was founded more than a century ago by Duchess Felicita Bevilacqua la Masa, who left her palace of Ca' Pesaro to the city in order to give local artists a space in which to explore new trends.

This institution is very active in organising exhibitions, collaborating with the Arts and Design faculty of the IUAV (architecture university), and with other organisations working to foster new art in Italy. There are talks, performances, an archive and an artist-in-residence programme.

Museo Correr, Biblioteca Marciana & Museo Archeologico

San Marco 52, piazza San Marco, sottoportego San Geminian (041 240 5211, www.visitmuve.it). Vaporetto San Marco Vallaresso. **Open** 10am-5pm daily. **Admission** see p12 Museum Passes. **Map** p47 E4 ❹

Note: These three adjoining museums are all entered by the same doorway, which is situated beneath the Ala Napoleonica at the western end of piazza San Marco.

Museo Correr

The Museo Correr is dedicated to the history of the Republic. Based on the private collection of Venetian nobleman Teodoro Correr (1750-1830), it has treasures enough to elevate it well beyond mere curiosity.

The museum is housed in the Ala Napoleonica and in a constantly expanding area of the Procuratie Nuove. The route now leads through nine recently opened rooms that made up the suite occupied by Sissi, aka Empress Elizabeth of Austria, wife of Franz Joseph I. In fact, the beautiful, tragedy-prone Sissi spent no more than a few months here, in 1861-62, but the stuccoes and fittings faithfully reflect the decor of the period.

Passing through the pretty oval 'everyday dining room', the spirit of these same years continues in Rooms 4 and 5, dedicated to the beautiful if icy sculptures of Antonio Canova, whose first Venetian commission – the statue of *Daedalus and Icarus* displayed here – brought him immediate acclaim. Some of the works on display are Canova's plaster models rather than his finished marble statues.

From Room 6, the historical collection – which occupies most of the first floor of the Procuratie Nuove building – documents Venetian history and social life in the 16th and 17th centuries through displays of globes, lutes, coins and robes. Room 6 is devoted to the figure of the doge. Room 11 has a collection of Venetian coins, plus Tintoretto's fine *St Justine and the Treasurers*. Beyond are rooms dedicated to the Arsenale, a display of weaponry and some occasionally charming miniature bronzes.

Beyond Room 15 lies the Correr's most recent addition: the nine-room *Wunderkammer*, charmingly laid out in a style inspired by the 18th-century passion for eclectic collecting. Curators went through the Museo Correr's store rooms, dusting off and restoring a few real gems, including a couple of early works by Vittore Carpaccio, and a remarkable portrait of dashing 16th-century mercenary Ferrante d'Avalos, formerly attributed to Leonardo da Vinci – an attribution once rubbished but now being reconsidered. Other rooms contain exquisite painted china produced for the Correr family, Renaissance bronzes and ivory carvings.

Stairs lead up to the Quadreria picture gallery – one of the best places to get a grip on the development of Venetian painting between the Byzantine stirrings of Paolo Veneziano and the full-blown Renaissance storytelling of Carpaccio. Rooms 25 to 29 are dedicated to Byzantine and Gothic painters; note Veneziano's fine *St John the Baptist* in Room 25 and the rare allegorical fresco fragments from a 14th-century private house in Room 27. Room 30 fast-forwards abruptly with the macabre, proto-Mannerist *Pietà* (c.1460) of Cosmè Tura.

The Renaissance gets into full swing in Room 34 with Antonello da Messina's *Pietà with Three Angels*, haunting despite the fact that the faces have nearly been erased by cackhanded restoration. The Bellinis get Room 36 to themselves.

The gallery's most fascinating work, though, must be Vittore Carpaccio's *Two Venetian Noblewomen* – long known erroneously as *The Courtesans* – in Room 38. These two bored women are not angling for trade: they're waiting for their husbands to return from a hunt. This was confirmed when *A Hunt in the Valley* (in the Getty Museum in Los Angeles) was shown to be this painting's other half.

Back downstairs, the historical collection continues with rooms dedicated to the *Bucintoro* (state barge), festivities, trade guilds and fairground trials of strength. The atmosphere gets neo-classical again along the corridor to the exit, café and giftshop, which is lined with reliefs by Canova.

Museo Archeologico

This collection of Greek and Roman art and artefacts is interesting not so much for the individual pieces as for the light they cast on the history of collecting. Assembled mainly by Cardinal

Domenico Grimani and his nephew Giovanni, the collection is a discerning 16th-century humanist's attempt to surround himself with the classical ideal of beauty. Highlights are the original fifth-century BC Greek statues of goddesses in Room 4, the Grimani Altar in Room 6, and the intricate cameos and intaglios in Room 7. Room 9 contains a fine head of the Emperor Vespasian. Room 20 has a couple of Egyptian mummies.

**Biblioteca Marciana/
Libreria Sansoviniana**

In 1468, the great humanist scholar Cardinal Bessarion of Trebizond left his collection of Greek and Latin manuscripts to the state. Venice didn't get round to constructing a proper home for them until 1537. Jacopo Sansovino, a Florentine architect who had settled in Venice after fleeing from the Sack of Rome in 1527, was appointed to create the library, a splendid building right opposite the Doge's Palace. With this building, Sansovino brought the ambitious new ideas of the Roman Renaissance to Venice. He also appealed to the Venetian love of surface decoration by endowing his creation with an abundance of statuary. His original plan included a barrel-vault ceiling. This collapsed shortly after construction, however, and the architect was immediately thrown into prison. His rowdy friends Titian and Aretino had to lobby hard to have him released.

The working part of Venice's main library is now housed inside La Zecca (p58) and contains approximately 750,000 volumes and around 13,500 manuscripts, most of them Greek.

The main room has a magnificent ceiling, with seven rows of allegorical medallion paintings, produced by a number of Venetian Mannerist artists as part of a competition. Veronese's *Music* (sixth row from the main entrance) was awarded the gold chain by Titian. Beyond this is the anteroom, in which a partial reconstruction has

been made of Cardinal Grimani's collection of classical statues, as arranged by Scamozzi (1596). On the ceiling is *Wisdom*, a late work by Titian. Don't miss Fra Mauro's map of the world (1459), a fascinating testimony to the great precision of Venice's geographical knowledge, with surprisingly accurate depictions of China and India.

Negozio Olivetti

San Marco 101, piazza San Marco (041 522 8387, www.negoziolivetti.it). Vaporetto San Marco Vallaresso or San Zaccaria. **Open** 11am-4.30pm Tue-Sun. **Admission** €5; €2.50 reductions. No credit cards. **Map** p47 E3 **5**

Snatched back from neglect by the admirable FAI – Italy's equivalent of the UK's National Trust – this former showroom for the Olivetti business machines company was given a modernist makeover in the mid 1950s by architect Carlo Scarpa. Clean and linear, and dramatically lit by hidden natural light sources, the showroom is something special. The floor in particular, with its inlaid coloured glass tessera, is superb.

Palazzo Ducale (Doge's Palace)

San Marco 1, piazzetta San Marco (041 271 5911, bookings 041 4273 0892, www.visitmuve.it). Vaporetto San Marco Vallaresso or San Zaccaria. **Open** 8.30am-5.30pm daily. **Tours** (book at least two days in advance) 9.55am, 10.45am, 11.35am daily. **Admission** see p186 Tourist Information. **Tours** €20, €14 reductions. **Map** p47 F3 **6**

An unobtrusive side door halfway down the right wall of the nave in San Marco leads straight into the courtyard of the Palazzo Ducale (Doge's Palace). Today's visitors take a more roundabout route, but that door is a potent symbol of the entwinement of Church and State in the glory days of *La Serenissima*. If the basilica was the Venetian Republic's spiritual nerve centre, the Doge's Palace was its political and judicial hub. The present site was the seat of ducal power from the ninth century onwards, though most of what we see today dates from the mid 15th century. Devastating fires in 1574 and 1577 took their toll, but after much heated debate it was decided to restore rather than replace – an enlightened policy for the time.

The palace is the great Gothic building of the city, but is also curiously eastern in style, achieving a marvellous combination of lightness and strength. The ground floor was open to the public; the work of government went on above. This arrangement resulted in a curious reversal of the natural order. The building gets heavier as it rises: the first level has an open arcade of simple Gothic arches, the second a closed loggia of rich, ornate arcading. The top floor is a solid wall broken by a sequence of Gothic windows. Yet somehow it doesn't seem awkward.

The façade on the Piazzetta side was built in the 15th century as a continuation of the 14th-century waterfront façade. On the corner by the ponte di Paglia (Bridge of Straw) is an exquisite marble relief carving, *The Drunkenness of Noah* from the early 15th century, while on the Piazzetta corner is a statue of *Adam and Eve* from the late 14th century. The capitals of the pillars below date from the 14th to the 15th centuries, although many of them are 19th-century copies (some of the originals are on display inside the palace).

The Porta della Carta (Paper Gate – so called because this was where permits were checked), between the palace and the basilica, is a grand piece of florid Gothic architecture and sculpture (1438-42) by Bartolomeo and Giovanni Bon. The statue of Doge Francesco Foscari and the lion is a copy dating from 1885; French troops smashed the original when they occupied the city in 1797.

Behind the palace's fairy-tale exterior, the complex machinery of empire whirred away with assembly-line efficiency. Anyone really interested in the inner workings of the Venetian state should take the 90-minute Itinerari Segreti tour. This takes you into those parts of the palace that the official route does not touch: the cramped wooden administrative offices; the stark chambers of the Cancelleria Segreta, where all official documents were written up in triplicate by a team of 24 clerks; the chamber of the three heads of the Council of Ten, connected by a secret door in the wooden panelling to the Sala del Consiglio dei Dieci, and the torture chambers beyond. The tour ends up in the leads – the sweltering prison cells beneath the roof, from which Casanova staged his famous escape (probably by bribing the guard, though his own account was far more action hero) – and among the extraordinary beams and rafters above the Sala del Maggior Consiglio (p56).

Following reorganisation, the main visit – for which an audio guide is also recommended – now begins at the Porta del Frumento on the lagoon side of the palace. The Museo dell'Opera, just to the left of the ticket barrier, has the best of the 14th-century capitals from the external loggia; the ones you see outside are mostly copies.

In the main courtyard stands the Arco dei Foscari – another fine late-Gothic work, commissioned by Doge Francesco Foscari in 1438, when Venice was at the height of its territorial influence. It was built by Antonio Bregno and Antonio Rizzo. Rizzo also sculpted the figures of Adam and Eve (these too are copies; the originals are in the first-floor *liagò*), which earned him gushing accolades and led to his appointment as official architect in 1483, after one of those disastrous fires. Rizzo had time to oversee the building of the overblown Scala dei Giganti (where doges were crowned) and some of the interior before he was found to have embezzled 12,000 ducats; he promptly fled, and died soon after.

top: Biblioteca Marciana p51;
middle & bottom: Palazzo Ducale p53

The official route now leads up the ornate Scala d'Oro staircase by Jacopo Sansovino, with stuccoes by Vittoria outlined in 24-carat gold leaf.

First floor: Doge's apartments

The doge's private life was entirely at the service of *La Serenissima* and even his bedroom had to keep up the PR effort. These rooms are occasionally closed or used for temporary exhibitions; when open, the Sala delle Mappe (also known as the Sala dello Scudo) merits scrutiny. Here, in a series of 16th-century maps, is the known world as it radiated from Venice. Just to the right of the entrance is a detailed map of the New World with Bofton (Boston) and Isola Longa (Long Island) clearly marked. Further on, seek out Titian's well-hidden fresco of St Christopher (above a doorway giving on to a staircase): it took the artist a mere three days to complete.

Second floor: State rooms

This grandiose series of halls provided steady work for all the great 16th-century Venetian artists. Titian, Tintoretto, Veronese, Palma il Vecchio and Jacopo Bassano all left their mark, though the sheer acreage that had to be covered, and the subjects of the canvases – either allegories or documentary records of the city's pomp and glory – did not always spur them to artistic heights.

The Sala delle Quattro Porte was where the Collegio – the inner cabinet of the Republic – met before the 1574 fire. After substantial renovation it became an ambassadorial waiting room, where humble envoys could gaze enviously at Andrea Vicentino's portrayal of the magnificent reception given to the young King Henry III of France in 1574. The Anticollegio, restored in part by Palladio, has a spectacular gilded stucco ceiling, four Tintorettos and Veronese's blowsy *Rape of Europa*.

Beyond here is the Sala del Collegio, where the inner cabinet convened. The propaganda paintings on the ceiling are by Veronese; note the equal scale of the civic and divine players, and the way both Justice and Peace are mere handmaidens to Venice herself. But for real hubris, stroll into the Sala del Senato, where Tintoretto's ceiling centrepiece shows *The Triumph of Venice*. Here, the Senate debated questions of foreign policy, war and commerce, and heard the reports of Venetian ambassadors. Beyond again are the Sala del Consiglio dei Dieci and the Sala della Bussola, where the arcane body set up to act as a check on the doge considered matters of national security. In the former, note Veronese's ceiling panel, *Juno Offering Gifts to Venice*. By the time this was painted in 1553, the classical gods had started to replace St Mark in Venice's self-aggrandising pantheon. The itinerary continues through an armoury.

First floor: State rooms

The Sala dei Censori leads down to a *liagò* (covered, L-shaped loggia), which gives on to the Sala della Quarantia Civil Vecchia (the civil court) and the Sala del Guariento. The latter's faded 14th-century fresco of *The Coronation of the Virgin* by Guariento (for centuries hidden behind Tintoretto's *Paradiso* in the Sala del Maggior Consiglio) looks strangely innocent amid all this worldly propaganda. The shorter arm of the *liagò* has the originals of Antonio Rizzo's stylised marble sculptures of Adam and Eve from the Arco del Foscari.

Next comes the Sala del Maggior Consiglio – the largest room in the palace. This was in effect the Republic's lower house, though this council of noblemen had fairly limited powers. Before the fire of 1577, the hall had been decorated with paintings by Bellini, Titian, Carpaccio and Veronese. When these works went up in smoke, they were replaced by less exalted ones, with one or two exceptions. Tintoretto's *Paradise*, on the far wall, sketched out by the 70-year-old artist but completed after his death in

1594 by his son Domenico, is liable to induce vertigo, as much for its theological complexity as its huge scale. In the ceiling panels are works by Veronese and Palma Il Giovane; note, too, the frieze of ducal portraits carried out by Domenico Tintoretto and assistants – the black veil marks where Marin Falier's face would have appeared had he not unwisely conspired against the state in 1356.

On the left side of the hall, a balcony gives a fine view over the southern side of the lagoon. A door leads from the back of the hall into the Sala della Quarantia Civil Nuova and the large Sala dello Scrutinio, where the votes of the *maggior consiglio* were counted; the latter is flanked by vast paintings of victorious naval battles, including a dramatic *Conquest of Zara* by Jacopo Tintoretto and *Battle of Lepanto* by Andrea Vicentino.

Criminal courts & prigioni

Backtracking through the Sala del Maggior Consiglio, a small door on the left leads past the Scala dei Censori to the Sala della Quarantia Criminale – the criminal court. The room next door retains some of the original red and gold leather wall coverings. Beyond this is a small room with Flemish paintings from Cardinal Grimani's collection.

The route now leads over the Bridge of Sighs to the Prigioni Nuove, where petty criminals were kept. Lifers were sent down to the waterlogged *pozzi* (wells) in the basement of the palazzo itself. By the 19th century, most visitors were falling for the tour-guide legend that, once over the Bridge of Sighs, prisoners would 'descend into the dungeon which none entered and hoped to see the sun again,' as Mark Twain put it. But when this new prison wing was built in 1589, it was acclaimed as a paragon of comfort; in 1608, the English traveller Thomas Coryat remarked: 'I think there is not a fairer prison in all Christendom.'

Some of the cells have their number and capacity painted over the door;

one has a trompe l'œil window, drawn in charcoal by an inmate. On the lowest level is a small exercise yard, site of an unofficial tavern. Up the stairs beyond is a display of Venetian ceramics found during excavations, and more cells, one with cartoons and caricatures left by 19th-century internees. Back across the Bridge of Sighs, the tour ends on the lower floor in the Avogaria – the offices of the clerks of court. Next to this, a bookshop has been set up, with a good selection of works on Venice.

Torre dell'Orologio

San Marco 147, piazza San Marco (bookings 041 4273 0892, www. visitmuve.it). Vaporetto San Marco Vallaresso or San Zaccaria. **Open** *Guided tours* (in English) 10am, 11am Mon-Wed; 2pm, 3pm Thur-Sun. **Admission** €12; €7 reductions. **Map** p47 E3 ❼
Note: there is no lift, and the stairs are steep and narrow. The clock tower can only be visited on a tour, which can be booked at the Museo Correr (p51), online, or by phone.

The clock tower, designed by Maurizio Codussi, was built between 1496 and 1506. Above the clock face is a statue of the Madonna. During Ascension week and at Epiphany, the Magi come out and bow to her every hour, in an angelled procession. At other times of year, the hours and minutes are indicated in Roman and Arabic numerals on either side of the Madonna; this feature dates from 1858 – one of the earliest examples of a digital clock. On the roof, statues of two burly Moors, made of gunmetal and cast in 1497, strike the hour. Another Moore (Roger) sent a villain flying through the clock face in the film *Moonraker*.

After lengthy restoration, the tower reopened in 2007. The tour reveals the workings of the clock, which dates from 1753 and was a remake of the original of 1499. Until 1998, the clock was wound manually by a *temperatore* who lived in the tower. Amid controversy, the last incumbent was replaced by an electrical mechanism. The tour concludes on the roof of the tower with a fine view over piazza San Marco, the basilica and the palace.

La Zecca

San Marco 7, piazzetta San Marco (041 520 8788). Vaporetto San Marco Vallaresso or San Zaccaria. **Open** 8.10am-7pm Mon-Fri; 8.10am-1.30pm Sat. **Admission** free. **Map** p47 E4 ❽

The Mint, designed by Sansovino, was completed by 1547. It coined Venice's gold ducats – later referred to as *zecchini*, whence comes the English word 'sequins'. It is more impregnable in appearance than the neighbouring Biblioteca Marciana (p51), though the façade had to accommodate large windows on the piano nobile (for relief from the heat) and open arches on the ground floor, where the procurators of St Mark's operated a number of cheese shops. It now houses most of the contents of the civic library.

Eating & drinking

Caffè Florian

San Marco 56, piazza San Marco (041 520 5641, www.caffeflorian. com). Vaporetto San Marco Vallaresso. **Open** 9am-midnight daily. **Map** p47 E4 ❾

Caffè Florian sweeps you back to 18th-century Venice with its mirrored, stuccoed and frescoed interior. Founded in 1720 as 'Venezia Trionfante', Florian's present appearance dates from an 1859 remodelling. Rousseau, Goethe and Byron hung out here – the last in sympathy with those loyal Venetians who boycotted the Quadri (above) across the square, where Austrian officers used to meet. These days, having a drink at Florian is more bank statement than political statement, especially if you sit at one of the outside tables, where not even a humble *caffè* costs less than €10.

Gran Caffè Quadri

San Marco 120, piazza San Marco (041 522 2105, www.quadrivenice.com, www.alajmo.it). Vaporetto San Marco Vallaresso or San Zaccaria. **Open** *Café* 9am-midnight daily. *Bistro* noon-3pm, 7-10.30pm daily. *Restaurant* 12.30-2.30pm, 7.30-10.30pm Tue-Sun. €€€€. **Map** p47 E3 ❿

Marcel Proust used to bring his *maman* to eat in this Venetian classic (est. 1638), and you can still imagine the couple in the plush red upper dining room with its spectacular view across St Mark's square. But the food – the exquisite, sometimes surprising creations of star chef Massimiliano Alajmo – might surprise them (as might the bill). Since the advent of the Alajmos (brother Raffaele runs the house) in 2011, everything here is recherché, from the extraordinary coffee specially toasted for the café at piazza level, through to the marvels cooked up for what is arguably the city's finest eating experience. There are taster menus at €170, €235 and €300.

In the evening, a palm court orchestra competes out in the square with the one at Florian's opposite, and romantics pay small fortunes to sip cocktails under the stars.

Shopping

Bevilacqua

San Marco 337B, ponte della Canonica (041 528 7581, www.bevilacquatessuti. com). Vaporetto San Zaccaria. **Open** 10am-7pm Mon-Sat; 10am-5pm Sun. **Map** p47 F3 ⓫

This diminutive shop offers exquisite examples of hand- and machine-woven silk brocades, damasks and velvets. There's also a branch at San Marco 2520 (041 241 0662).

Martinuzzi

San Marco 67A, piazza San Marco (041 522 5068). Vaporetto San Marco Vallaresso. **Open** 9am-7pm Mon-Sat. **Map** p47 E4 ⓬

The oldest lace shop in Venice, Martinuzzi has exclusive designs for bobbin lace items such as place mats, tablecloths and linens. The shop is also open for business on Sundays in the summer months.

Studium

San Marco 337C, calle Canonica (041 522 2382). **Open** 9am-7.30pm Mon-Sat; 9.30am-6pm Sun. **Map** p47 F3 ⓭

This shop stocks a wide selection of books on Venice, as well as novels in English. The shop's true speciality is revealed as you step into the back room, which is filled with theology studies, icons and prayer books.

Piazza San Marco to the Rialto

Piazza San Marco is linked to the Rialto by the busiest, richest and narrowest of shopping streets: the Mercerie. The name is plural, since it is divided into five parts: the Merceria dell'Orologio; di **San Zulian** (on which stands the church of the same name); del Capitello; di **San Salvador** (with its church of the same name) and del 2 Aprile.

Mercerie means 'haberdashers', but we know from John Evelyn's 1645 account of 'one of the most delicious streets in the world' that in among the textile emporia were shops selling perfumes and medicines too. Most of the big-name fashion designers are to be found here now. The ponte dei Baretteri (Hatmakers' Bridge), in the middle of the Mercerie, is a record holder in Venice: six roads lead directly off the bridge.

The Mercerie emerge near campo San Bartolomeo, the square at the foot of the Rialto, with the statue of playwright Carlo Goldoni looking amusedly down at the milling crowds.

Sights & museums

San Salvador

San Marco, campo San Salvador (041 270 2464). Vaporetto Rialto. **Open** 9am-noon, 4-6.15pm Mon-Sat; 4-6pm Sun. **Map** p47 D2 ⓮

If you can't make it to Florence on your trip to Italy, come to San Salvador instead. Begun by Giorgio Spavento in 1506, it was continued by Tullio Lombardo and completed by Sansovino in 1534. But even though the geometrical sense of space and the use of soft-toned greys and whites exude Tuscan elegance, the key to the church's structure is in fact a combination of three domed Greek crosses, which look back to the Byzantine tradition of St Mark's. The church contains two great Titians, the *Annunciation* at the end of the right-hand aisle (with the signature '*Tizianus fecit, fecit*' – 'Titian made this, made this'; the repetition was intended either to emphasise the wonder of the artist's creativity, or is a simple mistake) and the *Transfiguration* on the high altar; note the exquisite glass water jug in the lower right hand corner of the former painting; the latter conceals a silver reredos, revealed at Christmas, Easter and 6 August (the feast of San Salvador).

There's also some splendid Veneto-Tuscan sculpture, including Sansovino's monument to Doge Francesco Venier, situated between the second and third altars on the right. At the end of the right transept is the tomb of Cristina Cornaro, the hapless Queen of Cyprus (d.1510), a pawn in a game of Mediterranean strategy that ended with her being forced into abdicating the island to Venetian rule. In the left aisle, the third altar belonged to the school of the *luganagheri* (sausage makers), and has vibrant figures of San Rocco and San Sebastiano by Alessandro Vittoria, influenced by Michelangelo's *Slaves*. The sacristy (rarely accessible) contains delightful 16th-century frescoes of birds and leafage.

Caffè Florian p58

San Zulian

San Marco, mercerie San Zulian (041 523 5383). Vaporetto San Marco Vallaresso or San Zaccaria. **Open** 9am-7pm daily. **Map** p47 E2 ⑮

The classical simplicity of Sansovino's façade (1553-55) for San Zulian is offset by a grand monument to Tommaso Rangone, a wealthy and far from self-effacing showman-scholar from Ravenna, whose fortune was made by a treatment for syphilis, and who wrote a book on how to live to 120 (he only made it to 80). He unilaterally declared his library to be one of the seven wonders of the world, and had himself prominently portrayed in all three of Tintoretto's paintings for the Scuola Grande di San Marco (now housed in the Gallerie dell'Accademia; p140).

The interior of San Zulian has a ceiling painting of *The Apotheosis of St Julian* by Palma il Giovane, and a Titianesque *Assumption* by the same painter on the second altar on the right, which also has good statues of St Catherine of Alexandria and Daniel by Alessandro Vittoria. The first altar on the right has a *Pietà* by Veronese.

Eating & drinking

Caffetteria Doria

San Marco 4578C, calle dei Fabbri (329 351 7367 mobile). Vaporetto Rialto. **Open** 6am-8.30pm Mon-Sat; 1-8.30pm Sun. No credit cards. **Map** p47 D2 ⑯

Take a page out of the locals' book and squeeze into this popular, standing-room-only bar for a delicious cup of coffee, mid-afternoon snack or one of the best *spritz* in town. Service is always friendly and welcoming. Knowledgeable owners Andrea and Riccardo stock a huge selection of wine and spirits.

Rosa Salva

San Marco 950, calle Fiubera (041 521 0544, www.rosasalva.it). Vaporetto Rialto or San Marco Vallaresso. **Open** 8am-8.30pm daily. No credit cards. **Map** p47 E3 ⑰

This long-established family-owned café and *pasticciere* makes one of the smoothest *cappuccini* in town, and some delicious cakes to go with it. If it's ice-cream you fancy, all the flavours are made on the premises. There's a good lunch spread, with sandwiches and filled rolls, as well as pastas and simple salads. The candied fruit in intriguing jars, and piles of sugared rose buds and violet leaves, are delightful. There's a branch at Castello 6778, campo Santi Giovanni e Paolo (041 522 7949).

Shopping

Araba Fenice

San Marco 1822, Frezzeria (041 522 0664). Vaporetto Giglio or San Marco Vallaresso. **Open** 9.30am-7.30pm Mon-Sat. **Map** p47 D3 ⑱

A classic yet original line of women's clothing made exclusively for this boutique, plus jewellery in ebony and mother-of-pearl.

Carteria Tassotti

San Marco 5472, calle de la Bissa (041 528 1881). Vaporetto Rialto. **Open** 10am-1pm, 2-7pm daily. **Map** p47 E1 ⑲

Carteria Tassotti holds a charming selection of greeting cards, decorative paper, diaries and notebooks.

Daniela Ghezzo Segalin Venezia

San Marco 4365, calle dei Fuseri (041 522 2115, www.danielaghezzo.it). Vaporetto Rialto or San Marco Vallaresso. **Open** 10am-1pm, 3-7pm Mon-Fri; 10am-1pm Sat. **Map** p47 D3 ⑳

The shoemaking tradition established by 'the Cobbler of Venice', Rolando Segalin, continues through his talented former apprentice Daniela Ghezzo. Check out the footwear in the window, including an extraordinary pair of gondola shoes. A pair of Ghezzo's creations will set you back anything between €650 and €1,800. Repairs are done as well.

Diesel

San Marco 5315-6, salizada Pio X (041 241 1937, www.diesel.com). Vaporetto Rialto. **Open** 10am-7.30pm Mon-Sat; 11am-7pm Sun. **Map** p47 D1 ㉑
This well-known Veneto-based company's kooky, club-wise, lifestyle-based fashion has invaded Europe and North America; its hipper-than-hip store is a landmark on the shopping scene here.

Dolceamaro

San Marco 5415, sottoportego de la Bissa (041 241 3045). Vaporetto Rialto. **Open** 10.30am-7.30pm daily. **Map** p47 E1 ㉒
Dolceamaro ('bitter-sweet') has choc delights ranging from 100% cocoa chocolate slabs for fundamentalists to a beautifully tailored man's shirt made entirely from milk chocolate. In colder weather, the hot chocolate is a must: get an espresso-sized shot of this dark gloopy delight.

Marchini Pasticceria

San Marco 676, calle Spadaria (041 522 9109). Vaporetto Rialto or San Zaccaria. **Open** 9am-8pm daily. **Map** p47 E3 ㉓
Probably Venice's most famous sweet shop, and certainly the most expensive, Marchini has exquisite chocolate, including Le Baute Veneziane – small chocolates in the form of Carnevale masks. Cakes can be ordered.

Nalesso

San Marco 5537, salizada fontego dei Tedeschi (041 522 1343). Vaporetto Rialto. **Open** 10am-7.30pm Mon-Sat; 11am-7pm Sun. No credit cards.
Map p47 E1 ㉔
Specialising in classical Venetian music, Nalesso also sells concert tickets for the Fenice and Malibran theatres as well as for concerts in various churches.

L'O.FT

San Marco 4773, calle dell'Ovo (041 522 5263, www.otticofabbricatore.com). Vaporetto Rialto. **Open** 9am-12.30pm, 3.30-7.30pm Mon-Sat; 11am-7pm Sun.
Map p47 D2 ㉕

Aka L'Ottico Fabbricatore, this ultra-modern shop specialises in designer eyewear – the kind you won't find anywhere else, with extraordinary frames in anything from buffalo horn to titanium. Pop in for a pair of sunglasses, or bring along your prescription and treat yourself. The boutique also sells gossamer-like cashmere and sensual silk apparel, plus a selection of luxurious bags.

Paropàmiso

San Marco 1701, Frezzeria (041 522 7120). Vaporetto Rialto or San Marco Vallaresso. **Open** 10.30am-7.30pm Mon-Sat; 11am-7pm Sun. **Map** p47 E3 ㉖
An overwhelming mix of beads in minerals, glass, coral and metal makes this wholesale emporium a true delight. As well as Venetian wares, Paropàmiso has imports from Africa and the Far East. You can buy ready-made jewellery or put together your own: clasps and materials for stringing are also available. There's a selection of other ethnic goods here too, including fabrics, rugs, masks and small items of furniture.

Pot-Pourrì

San Marco 1810, ramo dei Fuseri (041 241 0990, www.potpourri.it). Vaporetto San Marco Vallaresso. **Open** 3.30-7.30pm Mon; 10am-1pm, 3.30-7.30pm Tue-Sat. **Map** p47 D3 ㉗
This faux-boudoir houses designers such as Cristina Effe and Marzi as well as homewares. Clothes are draped over armchairs or hung from wardrobe doors, while charming knick-knacks cover the dressing table.

Testolini

San Marco 4744-6, calle dei Fabbri (041 522 3085, www.testolini.it). Vaporetto Rialto. **Open** 9am-7.30pm Mon-Sat.
Map p47 D2 ㉘
Testolini carries stationery, backpacks, briefcases, calendars and supplies for both art and office. The staff can be on the cool side but the choice is huge… by Venetian standards.

Arts & leisure

Scuola Grande di San Teodoro

San Marco 4810, salizzada San Teodoro (041 521 0294, www.imusiciveneziani. com). Vaporetto Rialto. **Map** p47 D2 ㉙
If your heart is set on performers in wigs, head for the Scuola Grande di San Teodoro, where the local I Musici Veneziani orchestra plays Vivaldi and a medley of opera arias.

Teatro Carlo Goldoni

San Marco 4650B, ramo Bembo (041 240 2011, www.teatrostabileveneto.it). Vaporetto Rialto. **Map** p47 D2 ㉚
The Goldoni regularly offers Venetian classics by its namesake and 20th-century classics regularly feature on the programme, as do more contemporary Italian pieces.

From the Rialto to the Accademia bridge

The route from the Rialto to the Accademia passes through a series of ever-larger squares. From cosily cramped campo San Bartolomeo, the well-marked path leads to campo San Luca, then campo Manin with its 19th-century statue of Daniele Manin, leader of the 1848 uprising against the Austrians. An alley to the left of this campo will lead you to the Scala del Bòvolo, a striking Renaissance spiral staircase (closed for renovation at the time of writing). Back on the main drag, the calle della Mandola leads to broad campo Sant'Angelo with its dramatic view of **Santo Stefano**'s leaning tower; off calle della Mandola to the right is the Gothic **Palazzo Fortuny**, once home to the Spanish fashion designer Mariano Fortuny.

Just before the Accademia bridge, campo Santo Stefano is second in size only to piazza San Marco in the *sestiere*. The tables of several bars

scarcely encroach on the space where kids play on their bikes or kick balls around the statue of Risorgimento ideologue Nicolò Tommaseo. (Poor Tommaseo is known locally as *il cagalibri*, 'the bookshitter', for reasons which become clear when the statue is viewed from the rear.) The 18th-century church of **San Vidal** lies at the Accademia bridge end of the square.

On the Grand Canal to the north-west of campo Santo Stefano is campo San Samuele, which holds a deconsecrated 11th-century church and the massive **Palazzo Grassi** exhibition centre. Leading there from the campo, calle delle Botteghe is a hotch-potch of fascinating shops. Nearby, in calle Malipiero, the 18th-century love machine Giacomo Casanova was born (though in which house exactly is not known). The neighbourhood is full of Casanova associations, including the site of the theatre where his mother performed (corte Teatro).

Sights & museums

Palazzo Fortuny

San Marco 3958, campo San Beneto (041 520 0995). Vaporetto Sant'Angelo. **Open** varies. **Admission** varies. No credit cards. **Map** p46 C3 ㉛
This charming 15th-century palazzo, which belonged to Spanish fashion designer Mariano Fortuny (1871-1949), should not be missed on the occasions when it opens for temporary exhibitions. These are often photographic – photography being one of Fortuny's interests – alongside theatrical set design, cloth dyes and some elegant silk dresses. Also on display are some of Fortuny's paintings of Middle Eastern views.

Palazzo Grassi

San Marco 3231, campo San Samuele (041 523 1680, www.palazzograssi.it). Vaporetto San Samuele. **Open** (during

exhibitions) 10am-7pm Mon, Wed-Sun.
Admission €15 (€20 Palazzo Grassi & Punta della Dogana; p143); €10 (€15 both) reductions. **Map** p46 A3 ㉜

This superbly – though boringly – regular 18th-century palazzo on the Grand Canal was bought in 2005 by French billionaire businessman François-Henri Pinault. Pinault brought in Japanese superstar-architect Tadao Ando for an expensive overhaul, which increased the exhibition space by 2,000sq m (21,000sq ft). Most of the palazzo's shows centre on Pinault's own massive contemporary art collection. Next door at no.3260, the Teatrino Grassi – another Ando makeover – shows art videos and hosts events.

San Vidal

San Marco, campo San Vidal (041 277 0561). Vaporetto Accademia. **Open** 9.30am-6pm daily. **Map** p46 B4 ㉝

This early 18th-century church, with a façade derived from Palladio, was for years used as an art gallery. It has now been restored and hosts concerts. Over the high altar is a splendid Carpaccio painting (1514) of St Vitalis riding what appears to be one of the bronze horses of San Marco. The third altar on the right has a painting by Piazzetta, *Archangel Raphael and Saints Anthony and Louis.*

Santo Stefano

San Marco, campo Santo Stefano (041 522 5061, www.chorusvenezia. org). Vaporetto Accademia or San Samuele. **Open** 10am-5pm Mon-Sat. **Admission** €3 (or Chorus; p12). **Map** p46 B3 ㉞

Santo Stefano is an Augustinian church, built in the 14th century and altered in the 15th. The façade has a magnificent portal in the florid Gothic style. The large interior, with its splendid ship's-keel roof, is a multicoloured treat, with different marbles used for the columns, capitals, altars and intarsia, and diamond-patterned walls.

On the floor is a huge plaque to Doge Morosini (best known for blowing up the Parthenon) and a more modest one to composer Giovanni Gabrieli. On the interior façade to the left of the door is a Renaissance monument by Pietro Lombardo and his sons, decorated with skulls and festoons. In the sacristy are two tenebrous late works by Tintoretto, *The Washing of the Feet* and *The Agony in the Garden (The Last Supper* is by the great man's assistants), and three imaginative works by Gaspare Diziani (*Adoration of the Magi, Flight into Egypt* and *Massacre of the Innocents*).

Eating & drinking

Bar all'Angolo

San Marco 3464, campo Santo Stefano (041 522 0710). Vaporetto Sant'Angelo. **Open** 6.30am-9pm Mon-Sat. Closed Jan. No credit cards. **Map** p46 B3 ㉟

Secure a table outside and watch the locals saunter through the campo as you enjoy a coffee or *spritz*. Inside, you have your choice of standing at the usually crowded bar or relaxing in one of the comfortable seats in the back, where you'll find locals and tourists being served good *tramezzini, panini* and salads by friendly, if hurried, staff. There are certainly bigger bars in this busy campo, but none match the quality found here.

Marchini Time

San Marco 4598, campo San Luca (041 241 3087, www.marchinitime.it). Vaporetto Rialto. **Open** 7.30am-8.30pm Mon-Sat; 9am-8.30pm Sun. No credit cards. **Map** p47 D2 ㊱

The Marchini pastry empire is the oldest in *La Serenissima*. This space lights up campo San Luca with its colourful windows displaying the latest cakes, cookies and chocolates. There's a dizzying array of *cornetti* to enjoy with your breakfast coffee – the raspberry jam-filled one is mouth-watering.

Shopping

Alberto Bertoni – Libreria
San Marco 3637B, rio terà degli Assassini
(041 522 9583, www.bertonilibri.com).
Vaporetto Sant'Angelo. **Open** 9am-1pm,
3-7.30pm Mon-Sat. **Map** p46 C3 ❸
Just off calle de la Mandola (look for
the display case marking the turn-off),
this well-hidden cavern is home to art
books, exhibition catalogues and the
like, all with significant reductions off
cover prices.

Antiquus
San Marco 2973, calle delle Botteghe
(041 520 6395). Vaporetto Sant'Angelo.
Open 10am-noon, 3-7.30pm Mon-Sat.
Map p46 B3 ❸
This charming shop has a beautiful collection of Old Master paintings, furniture, silver and antique jewellery, including Moor's-head brooches and earrings.

Arcobaleno
San Marco 3457, calle delle Botteghe
(041 523 6818). Vaporetto Sant'Angelo.
Open 9am-12.30pm, 4-7.30pm Mon-Fri;
9am-12.30pm Sat. No credit cards. **Map**
p46 B3 ❸
Arcobaleno stocks a vast assortment
of artists' pigments. As well as art supplies, it carries all the basics in hardware, light bulbs and detergents.

Chiarastella Cattana
San Marco 3357, salizada San Samuele
(041 522 4369, www.chiarastella
cattana.it). Vaporetto San Samuele or
Sant'Angelo. **Open** 10am-1pm, 3-7pm
Mon-Sat. **Map** p46 B3 ❹
Chiarastella Cattana's elegantly stylish
tablecovers, duvet and sheet covers,
bathrobes and accessories are crafted
from natural hand-loomed textiles in
gorgeously muted colours with botan-
ical motifs.

Ebrû
San Marco 3471, campo Santo Stefano
(041 523 8830, www.albertovallese-
ebru.com). Vaporetto Sant'Angelo.

Open 10am-1.30pm, 2.30-7pm Mon-
Wed; 10am-1pm, 2.30-7pm Thur-Sat;
11am-6pm Sun. **Map** p46 B3 ❹
Beautiful, marbled handcrafted paper,
scarves and ties. These are Venetian
originals, whose imitators can be
found in other shops around town.

Gaggio
San Marco 3441-51, calle delle Botteghe
(041 522 8574, www.gaggio.it).
Vaporetto San Samuele or Sant'Angelo.
Open 10.30am-1pm, 4-6.30pm Mon-Fri;
10.30am-1pm Sat. **Map** p46 B3 ❹
Emma Gaggio is a legend among seam-
stresses, and her sumptuous hand-
printed silk velvets are used to make
cushions and wall hangings as well as
bags, hats, scarves and jackets.

Galleria Marina Barovier
San Marco 3216, calle Malipiero
(041 523 6748, www.barovier.it).
Vaporetto San Samuele. **Open** (by
appt) 10am-12.30pm, 3.30-7.30pm Mon-
Sat. No credit cards. **Map** p46 A3 ❹
Marina Barovier hosts a collection of
masterpieces of Venetian 20th-century
works in glass and represents numerous renowned artists (local and international) working in glass. It stages a
few shows a year.

Galleria Venice Design
San Marco 3146, salizada San Samuele
(041 520 7915, www.venicedesignart
gallery.com). Vaporetto San Samuele.
Open 10am-1pm, 3-7pm daily. **Map**
p46 B3 ❹
As one of the historical landmarks of
contemporary art in Venice, this gallery deals especially in sculpture by
established artists, both Italian and
international. It also focuses on artists'
jewellery pieces and interior design.

L'Isola – Carlo Moretti
San Marco 2970, calle delle Botteghe
(041 5233 1973, www.carlomoretti.
com). Vaporetto San Samuele or
Sant'Angelo. **Open** 10am-7.30pm
daily. **Map** p46 B3 ❹

This long-established family firm produces and sells high-class, exquisitely coloured contemporary glasses, bowls, vases, light fixtures and much else. The showroom closes some Sundays in August and all Sundays from January to March.

Laura Crovato

San Marco 2995, calle delle Botteghe (041 520 4170). Vaporetto Sant'Angelo. **Open** 4-7.30pm Mon; 11am-1pm, 4-7.30pm Tue-Sat. **Map** p46 B3 ㊻

Nestling between expensive galleries and antique shops, Laura Crovato offers a selection of used clothes and a sprinkling of new items, including raw-silk shirts and scarves, costume jewellery and sunglasses.

Ottica Carraro Alessandro

San Marco 3706, calle della Mandola (041 520 4258, www.otticacarraro.it). Vaporetto Sant'Angelo. **Open** 9.30am-1pm, 3-7.30pm Mon-Sat. **Map** p46 C3 ㊼

Get yourself some unique and funky eyewear – the frames are exclusively produced and guaranteed for life. OCA offers extraordinary quality at reasonable prices.

Perle e Dintorni

San Marco 3740, calle della Mandola (346 588 1618). Vaporetto Sant'Angelo. **Open** 9.30am-7.30pm Mon-Sat; noon-7pm Sun. **Map** p46 C3 ㊽

Here you can buy bead jewellery or assemble your own unique pieces, choosing from a vast assortment of glass beads, most of which are new versions based on antique designs.

Wellington BooKs

San Marco 4000, salizada de la Chiesa (041 523 4964, 331 712 9641, www.wellingtonbooks.weebly.com). Vaporetto Sant'Angelo. **Open** 10.30am-8.30pm Mon-Sat; 2-8pm Sun. **Map** p46 C3 ㊾

Wellington BooKs (the capital is intentional, the reference is to *acqua alta* and rubber boots) offers an intelligent choice of titles in English, many of them in pretty cloth-bound editions. Check the Facebook page (wellingtonbooks.venice) for the occasional literary event and/or book club meeting.

Arts & leisure

Multisala Rossini

San Marco 3997A, salizada de la Chiesa o del Teatro (041 241 7274). Vaporetto Rialto or Sant'Angelo. No credit cards. **Map** p46 C3 ㊿

The three-screen Rossini reopened in 2012 to the delight of Venice's film-lovers. Besides a mix of big hits, smaller productions and retrospectives (and occasional screenings in the *versione originale*), the very centrally located Rossini has a bar run by the Marchini dynasty (p64), a restaurant and even an in-house supermarket.

San Vidal

San Marco 2862B, campo San Vidal (041 277 0561, www.interpreti veneziani.com). Vaporetto Accademia. **Map** p46 B4 (51)

For highly professional renditions of Vivaldi and other mainly Baroque favourites, visit the church of San Vidal (p64), where the no-frills Interpreti Veneziani play. Tickets can be purchased on the door, or at the Museo della Musica (p69).

The Accademia bridge to piazza San Marco

The route from campo Santo Stefano back to piazza San Marco zigzags at first, passing through small squares, including campo San Maurizio, with its 19th-century church now transformed into the **Museo della Musica**, and **campo Santa Maria del Giglio** (aka Santa Maria Zobenigo). It winds past banks, hotels and top-dollar antique shops, to end in wide via XXII Marzo, with an intimidating view of the Baroque statuary of **San Moisè**.

Vivaldi variations

Where to hear the music of the great Baroque composer.

With its superb venues and unique atmosphere, Venice lends itself magnificently to early music – though in Venice this is all too often reduced to a quick romp through Vivaldi's *The Four Seasons*. If you're going to indulge in a concert – and this is an indulgence, with few outfits offering tickets at less than €25, whatever the technical standard – you'll need to examine your priorities.

   If you really want the whole costumed shebang, try **I Musici Veneziani**, who perform in the **Scuola Grande di San Teodoro** (p63); if you're a true music buff, however, you may feel you're paying for the 'experience' rather than any musical finesse.

   Performing in the church of **San Vidal** (p64), the **Interpreti Veneziani** is a serious musical ensemble, playing to a high standard. There's quite a bit of showmanship here too, with lots of camaraderie and high-fiving among performers at the end of movements.

   To avoid disappointment, serious music aficionados should check out the programme at **La Fenice** (p71) and the **Teatro Malibran** (p98): besides the opera season at the former, there are numerous symphony and chamber music concerts throughout the year. And though getting tickets for these still requires forethought, it is easier than acquiring opera places.

   If you're happier to experience your early music while exploring Venice's *calli* in your own head-phoned world, opt for a recording by the **Venice Baroque Orchestra** (www.venicebaroqueorchestra.it).

Interpreti Veneziani

Once upon a time, lucky music-lovers could catch this award-winning, globetrotting ensemble at the Scuola Grande di San Rocco. Nowadays, you're more likely to catch them in the US or the Far East.

   Formed in 1997 by conductor, harpsichordist, organist and Baroque scholar Andrea Marcon, the ensemble rediscovers neglected works of the Venetian Baroque, and performs them on period instruments. The group has won acclaim for its performances of previously unpublished works by Claudio Monteverdi and Antonio Vivaldi, and for its revival of lost operas including Handel's *Siroe* (in 2000), *L'Olimpiade* by Baldassare Galuppi (in 2006) and the Venetian *Serenata Andromeda Liberata* (2004), which was composed at least in part by Vivaldi.

   The orchestra's revolutionary playing technique does away with the mechanical, tinkly, so-called 'sewing machine' style that is usually the norm for Baroque music: you feel as if you're hearing *The Four Seasons* for the very first time.

VENICE BY AREA

SOCIETAS
MDCCXCII

Teatro La Fenice

Off to the left (as you make your way towards San Marco) is the opera house, **La Fenice**, and more streets of supersmart shops, in the Frezzeria district.

Press on and you will be ready for what is arguably the greatest view anywhere in the world: piazza San Marco from the west side.

Sights & museums

Museo della Musica

San Marco 2601, campo San Maurizio (041 241 1840, www.interpretiveneziani. it). Vaporetto Giglio. **Open** 9.30am-7.30pm daily. **Admission** free. **Map** p46 B4 ⊕

This small private museum, set up in the former church of San Maurizio, is run by the Interpreti Veneziani concert concern. Serving partly as a sales and promotion outlet, the museum contains an interesting collection of period instruments. But it also presents an opportunity to appreciate the neoclassical interior of the church, designed by Giannantonio Selva, the architect of the Fenice theatre (below). The Museo della Musica puts on concerts, mainly Vivaldi and other Baroque favourites, at the church of San Vidal (p64); tickets can be bought at the museum.

San Moisè

San Marco, campo San Moisè (041 528 5840). Vaporetto San Marco Vallaresso. **Map** p47 D4 ⊕

The Baroque façade of San Moisè has been lambasted by just about everybody as one of Venice's truly ugly pieces of architecture. Inside, an extravagant Baroque sculpture occupies the high altar, representing not only Moses receiving the stone tablets but also Mount Sinai itself. Near the entrance is the grave of John Law, author of the disastrous Mississippi Bubble scheme that almost sank the French central bank in 1720.

Santa Maria del Giglio

San Marco, campo Santa Maria Zobenigo (041 275 0462, www. chorusvenezia.org). Vaporetto Giglio. **Open** 10am-5pm Mon-Sat. **Admission** €3 (or Chorus; p12). No credit cards. **Map** p46 C4 ⊕

This church's façade totally lacks any Christian symbols (give or take a token angel or two). Built between 1678 and 1683, it's a huge exercise in defiant self-glorification by Admiral Antonio Barbaro, who was dismissed by Doge Francesco Morosini for incompetence in the War of Candia (Crete). On the plinths of the columns are relief plans of towns where he served; his own statue (in the centre) is flanked by representations of Honour, Virtue, Fame and Wisdom.

The interior is more devotional. You may not have heard of the painter Antonio Zanchi (1631-1722), but this is his church. Particularly interesting is *Abraham Teaching the Egyptians Astrology* in the sacristy, while the Molin chapel has *Ulysses Recognised by his Dog* (an odd subject for a church). The chapel also contains a *Madonna and Child*, which is proudly but erroneously attributed to Rubens. Behind the altar there are two paintings of the Evangelists by Tintoretto, formerly organ doors.

Teatro La Fenice

San Marco 1983, campo San Fantin (041 2424, 041 786 511, www.teatro lafenice.it). Vaporetto Giglio. **Open** 9.30am-6pm daily. **Admission** €9; €6.50 reductions. No credit cards. **Map** p46 C4 ⊕

Venice's principal opera house – aptly named 'the phoenix' – has a long history of fiery destruction and rebirth. The theatre (1792) designed by Giannantonio Selva replaced the Teatro San Benedetto, which burnt down in 1774. Selva's building was destroyed in 1836, and was rebuilt by the Meduna brothers, recreating the style of Selva. In 1996, a massive blaze broke out, courtesy of two electricians. After years of legal wrangling, the theatre was rebuilt and inaugurated in December 2003. Hidden away from view behind the ornate gilding and faux-Baroque plush are state-of-the-art technological innovations. The tour with audio guide lasts roughly 45 minutes. For information on performances at La Fenice, see p71.

Eating & drinking

Harry's Bar

San Marco 1323, calle Vallaresso (041 528 5777, www.cipriani.com). Vaporetto San Marco Vallaresso. **Open** 10.30am-11pm daily. **Map** p47 E4 ⑥⑥

This historic watering hole, founded by Giuseppe Cipriani in 1931, has changed little since the days when Ernest Hemingway came here to work on his next hangover… except for the prices and the numbers of tourists. But despite the crush, a Bellini (peach juice and sparkling wine) at the bar is as much a part of the Venetian experience as a gondola ride. At mealtimes, diners enjoy Venetian-themed international comfort food at steep prices (€140-plus for three courses). Stick with a Bellini, and don't even think of coming in here wearing shorts or ordering a *spritz*.

L'Ombra del Leone

Ca' Giustinian, San Marco 1364, calle del Ridotto (041 241 3519). Vaporetto San Marco Vallaresso. **Open** 9am-9pm daily. **Map** p47 D4 ⑥⑦

Located inside the Grand Canal-side Ca' Giustinian, the headquarters of the Biennale (p27), this sleek modern café-restaurant offers a superb panorama from its terrace on the water as well as good (and reasonably affordable) light lunches and a hopping evening *aperitivo* scene, especially in the warmer months. Incongruously for this hyper-cool venue, the Kids' Space right next to the café has small children's playthings, along with nappy-changing and breast-feeding areas.

Osteria San Marco

San Marco 1610, Frezzeria (041 528 5242, www.osteriasanmarco.it). Vaporetto San Marco Vallaresso. **Meals served** 12.30-11pm Mon-Sat. Closed 2wks Jan. €€€. **Map** p47 D3 ⑥⑧

This smart, modern *osteria* on a busy shopping street is a breath of fresh air in this touristy area. The guys behind the operation are serious about food and wine, and their attention to detail shows through both in the selection of bar snacks and wines by the glass, and in the sit-down menu, based on the freshest of local produce. Prices are high, but you're paying for the area as well as the quality. This is one of the few places in Venice where you can eat a proper meal throughout the day.

Shopping

Antichità Marciana

San Marco 1864, campo San Fantin (041 523 5666, www.antichita marciana.it). Vaporetto San Marco Vallaresso. **Open** 3.30-7.30pm Mon; 9.30am-1pm, 3.30-7pm Tue-Sat. **Map** p47 D3 ⑥⑨

Primarily a purveyor of (minor) Old Master paintings, this shop also has a tasteful selection of antique baubles and a range of soft furnishings made from richly painted velvets created by the owner in her workshop. A favourite among interior designers.

Bugno Art Gallery

San Marco 1996D, campo San Fantin (041 523 1305, www.bugnoartgallery.it). Vaporetto San Marco Vallaresso. **Open** 4-7.30pm Mon, Sun; 10.30am-7.30pm Tue-Sat. **Map** p47 D3 ⑥⓪

Large windows overlooking the Fenice opera house reveal a space devoted to artists working in all types of media. Well-known local artists are also included in the gallery's collection. So packed is the exhibition calendar that shows often spill over into a smaller exhibition space nearby.

Caterina Tognon

*San Marco 2158, Palazzo Treves, Corte
Barozzi, (041 520 7859, www.caterina
tognon.com). Vaporetto San Marco
Vallaresso.* **Open** 10am-1pm, 3-7pm
Tue-Sat. **Map** p47 D4 ⑥①

Following the success of her first gallery, which opened in Bergamo
in 1992, renowned curator Caterina
Tognon brought her expertise to
Venice. Contemporary art in glass
is her greatest love, but also shows
work in other media if they meet her
super-high standards. Various shows
take place each year by emerging and
renowned artists.

Cristina Linassi

*San Marco 2434, ponte delle Ostreghe
(041 241 7532, www.cristinalinassi.it).
Vaporetto Giglio.* **Open** 9.30am-1pm,
2.30-7.30pm Mon-Sat; 9.30am-1pm,
2.30-7pm Sun. **Map** p46 C4 ⑥②

This boutique sells gorgeous hand-embroidered nightgowns, towels and
sheets made in its own workshop. The
catalogue has designs for made-to-order items.

Galerie Bordas

*San Marco 1994B, calle dietro la Chiesa
(041 522 4812, www.galerie-bordas.
com). Vaporetto San Marco Vallaresso.*
Open 11am-1pm, 4.30-7.30pm Mon-Sat.
Map p47 D3 ⑥③

The only gallery dealing in serious
graphics by internationally renowned
masters. The space is small but the collection of artists' books held at Galerie
Bordas is huge.

Trois Antichità

*San Marco 2666, campo San Maurizio
(041 522 2905). Vaporetto Giglio.*
Open 4-7.30pm Mon; 10am-1pm,
4-7.30pm Tue-Sat. No credit cards.
Map p46 C4 ⑥④

This is one of the best places in *La
Serenissima* to buy original Fortuny
fabrics – and at considerable savings
on the prices you'd find in the UK
and the US (though note that this still

doesn't make them particularly cheap).
Made-to-order bead-work, masks and
accessories are also available from
Trois Antichità.

Venetia Studium

*San Marco 2425, calle delle Ostreghe
(041 523 6953, www.venetiastudium.
com). Vaporetto Giglio.* **Open** 9.30am-
7.40pm Mon-Sat; 10.30am-6pm Sun.
Map p46 C4 ⑥⑤

Venetia Studium is the sole author-ised manufacturer of the distinctive
Fortuny lamps. It also stocks splendid
silk pillows, scarves, handbags and
other accessories in a marvellous range
of colours. They're certainly not cheap,
but they do make perfect gifts. There's
a new shop based at Dorsoduro 180,
calle del Bastion.

Arts & leisure

Palazzo Barbarigo Minotto

*San Marco 2504, fondamenta Duodo
o Barbarigo (340 971 7272, www.
musicapalazzo.com). Vaporetto Giglio.*
Map p46 C4 ⑥⑥

In the beautiful surroundings of a
17th-century palazzo, performances
include a variety of classic opera arias,
Neapolitan songs and complete operas
with few instruments and a piano to
accompany the singers. During the
evening, the small audience follows the
performers around the salons of the
palazzo, from the frescoed Sala Tiepolo
on to the bedroom for the more intimate
'love duets'.

Teatro La Fenice

*San Marco 1965, campo San Fantin
(041 2424, 041 786 654, www.teatro
lafenice.it). Vaporetto Giglio.* **Map** p46
C4 ⑥⑦

La Fenice's world-class opera, ballet
and concert seasons run through most
of the year. You'll need to book well
ahead to secure tickets. For more information about La Fenice, and details of
tours of the theatre, see p69.

VENICE BY AREA

Campo Santa Maria Formosa

Castello

VENICE BY AREA

Castello is not only Venice's largest *sestiere,* it's also the most remarkably varied, stretching from the bustle and splendour in the north-west around Santa Maria Formosa and Santi Giovanni e Paolo, to the homely, washing-festooned stretches around and beyond wide via Garibaldi. Castello is also where the Biennale takes place.

Northern & western Castello

The canal dividing the Doge's Palace from the prison marks the end of the *sestiere* of San Marco. This means that the **Museo Diocesano di Arte Sacra** and stately **San Zaccaria**, although closely associated with San Marco, actually belong to Castello. But the heart of northern and western Castello lies inland: **campo Santa Maria Formosa**, a large, bustling,

irregular-shaped square on the road to just about everywhere.

Southward from Santa Maria Formosa runs the busy shopping street of ruga Giuffa, named after either a community of Armenian merchants from Julfa, or a band of thugs – *gagiuffos* in 13th-century dialect – who used to terrorise the area. The first turn to the left off this street leads to the grandiose 16th-century **Palazzo Grimani**.

For more grandeur, head north to **campo Santi Giovanni e Paolo**. The Gothic red brick of the Dominican church is beautifully set off by the glistening marble on the trompe l'œil façade of the **Scuola Grande di San Marco** – now housing the civic hospital, but with a series of magnificent rooms recently open to the public – and the bronze of the equestrian monument to Bartolomeo Colleoni gazing down contemptuously. It's a short walk through narrow *calli* from Santi

Giovanni e Paolo to the fondamenta Nuove, where the northern lagoon comes into view.

Sights & museums

Museo della Fondazione Querini Stampalia

Castello 5252, campo Santa Maria Formosa (041 271 1411, www.querini stampalia.it). Vaporetto Rialto. **Open** 10am-8pm Tue-Sun. **Admission** €10; €8 reductions. **Map** p74 A2 ①

This Renaissance palazzo and its art collection were bequeathed to Venice by Giovanni Querini, a 19th-century scientist, man of letters and silk producer from one of the city's most ancient families. The ground floor and gardens, redesigned in the 1960s by Carlo Scarpa, offer one of Venice's few successful examples of modern architecture. On the second floor, the gallery contains some important paintings, including a marvellous *Presentation in the Temple* by Giovanni Bellini and a striking *Judith and Holofernes* by Vincenzo Catena. On the top floor is a gallery designed by Mario Botta, which hosts exhibitions of contemporary art.

Museo Diocesano di Arte Sacra

Castello 4312, ponte della Canonica (041 522 9166, www.veneziaubt.org). Vaporetto San Zaccaria. **Open** 10am-5.30pm Tue-Sun. **Admission** €5; €2.50 reductions. No credit cards. **Map** p74 A3 ②

This museum is situated in the ex-monastery of Sant'Apollonia, whose Romanesque cloisters are unique in Venice. The museum contains a number of works of art and clerical artefacts (reliquaries, chalices, missals, crucifixes) from suppressed churches and monasteries. The *quadreria* is notable for two energetic paintings by Luca Giordano (*Christ and the Money-Lenders, Massacre of the Innocents*) and for three recently acquired works by Venice's great colourist Tintoretto.

Palazzo Grimani

Castello 4858, ramo Grimani (041 520 0345, www.palazzogrimani.org). Vaporetto San Zaccaria. **Open** 8.15am-2pm Mon; 8.15am-7.15pm Tue-Sun. **Admission** €8.50; €4.50-€6.50 reductions. No credit cards. **Map** p74 B2 ③

Inaugurated in December 2008 after a restoration process lasting 27 years, this magnificent palazzo has an original nucleus built by Antonio Grimani, doge of Venice, in the 1520s. However, it is most closely associated with his nephew Giovanni Grimani, cardinal and collector of antiquities. He enlarged and extended the palace, calling artists from central Italy, including Francesco Salviati and Federico Zuccari, to decorate it. Film buffs may remember the palace as the setting for the final gory scenes of Nicholas Roeg's film, *Don't Look Now*.

San Francesco della Vigna

Castello, campo San Francesco della Vigna (041 520 6102). Vaporetto Celestia. **Open** 8am-12.30pm, 3-7pm Mon-Sat; 3-6.30pm Sun. **Map** p74 C2 ④

San Francesco may be off the beaten track, but it's worth a detour. In 1534, Jacopo Sansovino was asked to design this church for the Observant Franciscan order. The Tuscan architect opted for a deliberately simple style to match the monastic rule of its inhabitants. The façade (1568-72) was a later addition by Andrea Palladio; it is the first example of his system of superimposed temple fronts.

The dignified, solemn interior consists of a single broad nave with side chapels. The many works of art include Paolo Veronese's first Venetian commission, the stunning *Holy Family with Saints John the Baptist, Anthony the Abbot and Catherine* (c1551).

San Zaccaria

Castello, campo San Zaccaria (041 522 1257). Vaporetto San Zaccaria. **Open** 10am-noon, 4-6pm Mon-Sat; 4-6pm Sun. **Map** p74 B3 ⑤

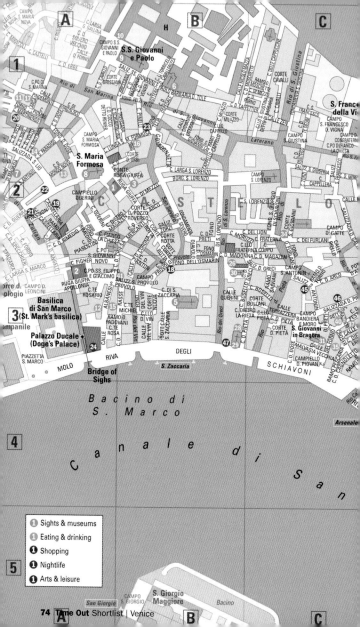

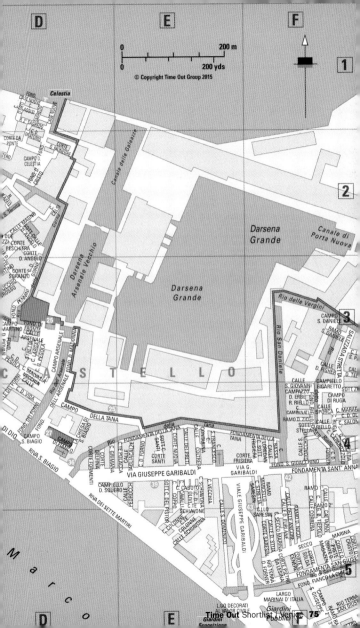

Founded in the ninth century, this church has always had close ties with the Doge's Palace. Eight Venetian rulers were buried in the first church on the site, one was killed outside and another died while seeking sanctuary inside. The body of St Zacharias, the father of John the Baptist, was brought to Venice in the ninth century; it still lies under the second altar on the right. The current church was begun in 1444 but took decades to complete, making it a curious combination of Gothic and Renaissance. The interior is built on a Gothic plan – the apse, with its ambulatory and radiating cluster of tall-windowed chapels, is unique in Venice – but the architectural decoration is predominantly Renaissance. The façade is a happy mixture of the two styles.

Inside, every inch is covered with paintings – of varying quality. Giovanni Bellini's magnificent *Madonna and Four Saints* (1505), on the second altar on the left, leaps out of the confusion.

Santa Maria dei Derelitti (Ospedaletto)

Castello 6691, barbarie delle Tole (041 271 9012). Vaporetto Fondamente Nove. **Open** *Church* 3.30-6.30pm Thur-Sun. *Hospice* by appt. **Admission** (incl guided tour) €2. No credit cards. **Map** p74 B1 **6**

The church was built in 1575 within the complex of the Ospedaletto, a hospice for the poor and aged. There is still an old people's home here. Between 1668 and 1674 Baldassare Longhena gave the church its staggering façade, complete with bulging telamons (architectural supports in the shape of male figures) and leering faces. The interior contains interesting 18th-century paintings, including one of Giambattista Tiepolo's earliest works, *The Sacrifice of Isaac*.

Santa Maria della Fava

Castello, campo della Fava (041 522 4601). Vaporetto Rialto. **Open** 9.30-11.30am, 4.30-7pm Mon-Sat; 4.30-7pm Sun. **Map** p74 A2 **7**

St Mary of the Bean – the name is said to refer to a popular bean cake produced by a bakery that stood nearby – is on one of the quieter routes between the Rialto and San Marco. This 18th-century church is worth visiting for two paintings by the city's greatest artists of that period: Tiepolo's *Education of the Virgin* and Giovanni Battista Piazzetta's *Virgin and Child with St Philip Neri*.

Santa Maria Formosa

Castello, campo Santa Maria Formosa (041 275 0462, www.chorusvenezia.org). Vaporetto Rialto or San Zaccaria. **Open** 10am-5pm Mon-Sat. **Admission** €3 (or Chorus; see p12). No credit cards. **Map** p74 A2 **8**

St Magnus, Bishop of Oderzo, had a vision in which the Virgin appeared as a buxom (*formosa*) matron, and a church was built in this bustling square to commemorate this. The present church was designed by Mauro Codussi in 1492 and has two façades: one on the canal (1542); the other on the campo (1604). The Baroque campanile has a grotesque mask, now recognised as a portrait of a victim of the disfiguring Von Recklinghausen's disease.

The first chapel in the right aisle has a triptych painted by Bartolomeo Vivarini, *Madonna of the Misericordia* (1473), which includes a realistic *Birth of the Virgin*. Half-hidden by the elaborate high altar is one of the few works on show in Venice by a woman artist: an 18th-century *Allegory of the Foundation of the Church, with Venice, St Magnus and St Maria Formosa* by Giulia Lama.

Santi Giovanni e Paolo (San Zanipolo)

Castello, campo Santi Giovanni e Paolo (041 523 5913, www.basilica santigiovanniepaolo.it). Vaporetto Fondamente Nove or Ospedale. **Open** 9am-6pm Mon-Sat; noon-6pm Sun. **Admission** €2.50; €1.25 reductions. No credit cards. **Map** p74 B1 **9**

Scuola Grande di San Marco p78

Santi Giovanni e Paolo was founded by the Dominican order in 1246 but not finished until 1430. Between 1248 and 1778, 25 doges were buried here. The vast interior – 101m (331ft) long – is a single spatial unit, and is packed with monuments to Venetian heroes as well as doges. The right transept has a painting of *St Antonine Distributing Alms* (1542) by Lorenzo Lotto. Above are splendid stained-glass windows, to designs by such Renaissance artists as Bartolomeo Vivarini and Cima da Conegliano (1470-1520).

The ceiling paintings in the rosary chapel (*The Annunciation*, *Assumption* and *Adoration of the Shepherds*) are by Paolo Veronese, as is another *Adoration* to the left of the door.

Scuola Grande di San Marco

Castello, campo Santi Giovanni e Paolo (041 529 4111, www.scuolagrande sanmarco.it). Vaporetto Fondamente Nove or Ospedale. **Open** 9.30am-1pm, 2-7pm Tue-Sun. **Admission** free. **Map** p74 B1 ⑩

Once home to one of the six *scuole grandi* – the confraternities of Venice – this is now occupied mainly by the city hospital. But late in 2013 some of the finest of the *scuola* rooms were opened to the public, beautifully restored.

Eating & drinking

See also p81 **I Tre Mercanti**.

Al Portego

Castello 6015, calle Malvasia (041 522 9038). Vaporetto Rialto. **Open** 10.30am-3pm, 5.30-10pm daily. **€€**. No credit cards. **Map** p74 A1 ⑪

With its wooden decor and happy drinkers in the calle outside, this rustic *osteria* is every inch the traditional Venetian *bàcaro*. Alongside a big barrel of wine, the bar is loaded down with a selection of *cicheti*, from meatballs and stuffed squid to *nervetti* stewed with onions. In a second room, simple pasta dishes and soups, and *secondi* such as *fegato alla veneziana*, are served for early lunch and dinner.

Alla Basilica

Castello 4255, calle degli Albanesi (041 522 0524, www.allabasilicavenezia.it). Vaporetto San Zaccaria. **Meals served** noon-3pm Tue-Sun. **€**. **Map** p74 A3 ⑫

Run by the diocese of Venice, Alla Basilica has all the charm of a company canteen, and the solid home cooking will win no prizes. But it's just €14 for a full meal (wine is extra), and it's brilliantly central, located (as the name implies) right behind St Mark's basilica. Groups can eat here in the evenings too if they book ahead.

Alle Testiere

Castello 5801, calle del Mondo Novo (041 522 7220, www.osterialletestiere.it). Vaporetto Rialto. **Meals served** noon-2pm, 7-10.30pm Tue-Sat. Closed late Dec-mid Jan & late July-Aug. **€€€**. **Map** p74 A2 ⑬

This tiny restaurant is today one of the hottest culinary tickets in Venice. There are so few seats that staff do two sittings each evening; booking for the later one (at 9pm) will ensure a more relaxed meal. Bruno, the chef, offers creative variations on Venetian seafood; *caparossoli* (local clams) sautéed in ginger, and John Dory fillet sprinkled with aromatic herbs in citrus sauce, are two mouth-watering examples. The desserts, too, are spectacular.

Boutique del Gelato

Castello 5727, salizzada San Lio (041 522 3283). Vaporetto Rialto. **Open** Feb-May, Oct, Nov 10am-8.30pm daily. June-Sept 10am-11.30pm daily. Closed Dec-Jan. No credit cards. **Map** p74 A2 ⑭

Be prepared to be patient at this tiny outlet on busy salizzada San Lio because there's always a crowd waiting to be served. The choice of flavours is limited but the quality is high. And though the staff at peak times are not always charming, it's worth the wait.

Da Bonifacio

Castello 4237, calle degli Albanesi (041 522 7507). Vaporetto San Zaccaria. **Open** 6.30am-7.30pm Mon-Wed, Fri; 7.30am-7.30pm Sat, Sun. No credit cards. **Map** p74 A3 ⓯

A firm favourite with Venetians, whom you'll find outside the entrance in great numbers, waiting to squeeze inside for a coffee, drink and something from the cake cabinet. As well as a tempting array of snacks and traditional cakes such as *mammalucchi* (deep-fried batter cakes with candied fruit), Da Bonifacio is famous for its creative *fritelle* (with wild berry, chocolate, almond or apple fillings), which appear in January and remain through Carnevale.

La Mascareta

Castello 5183, calle lunga Santa Maria Formosa (041 523 0744, www.oste maurolorenzon.it). Vaporetto Rialto. **Open** 7pm-2am daily. **Map** p74 B2 ⓰

Genial, bow-tied Mauro Lorenzon keeps hundreds of wines – including some rare vintages – in his cellars, serving them up by the bottle or glass along with plates of cheeses, seafood, cold meats or crostini. At mealtimes, the pressure will be on to sit down and eat a proper meal, but though the food here is good, it's not exceptional and prices are high.

Osteria di Santa Marina

Castello 5911, campo Santa Marina (041 528 5239, www.osteriasantamarina. com). Vaporetto Rialto. **Meals served** 7.30-9.30pm Mon; 12.30-2.30pm, 7.30-9.30pm Tue-Sat. Closed 2wks Jan. €€€. **Map** p74 A1 ⓱

This upmarket *osteria* in pretty campo Santa Marina has the kind of professional service and standards that are too often lacking in Venice – and the ambience and the high level of the seafood-oriented cuisine justify the price tag. The joy of this place is in the detail: the bread is all home-made; a taster course turns up just when you were about to ask what happened to the *branzino* (sea bass). Book ahead.

Spritz

Venice's favourite fizz.

It's difficult to avoid *spritz* in Venice: before lunch, early evening, after dinner – just about any time, in fact, you'll find crowds outside Venetian bars, glasses of amber-orange liquid in hand. But despite its jaunty hue and party-fun flavour, *spritz* comes in varying degrees of danger.

The origins of this ubiquitous drink are as obscure as its 'real' recipe. Perhaps invented by Venice's Austrian occupiers in the 19th century (they couldn't take the strength of local wines, one story goes, and so ordered it watered down), a classic version calls for one part prosecco, one part bitters and one part sparkling seltzer, with a slice of orange and some ice.

It's quite normal these days to find mineral water being used instead of the more carbonated seltzer; and, often, still white wine replaces prosecco, making it altogether less sparkling.

The real threat to navigation comes from your choice of bitter. When ordering, you can specify *spritz all'*Aperol (11% ABV), with the very Venetian Select (14%) or with Campari (20%+). Whatever version you choose, a generous glass will cost somewhere between €2 and €3.50 in all but the swishest bars.

Al Portego p78

Shopping

Anticlea Antiquariato
Castello 4719A, calle San Provolo (041 528 6946). Vaporetto San Zaccaria. **Open** 10am-1.30pm, 2-7pm Mon-Sat. **Map** p74 B3 ⑱
Packed with curious antique treasures, as well as an outstanding selection of Venetian glass beads.

Filippi Editore Venezia
Castello 5284, calle Casseleria (041 523 6916, www.libreriaeditricefilippi.com). Vaporetto San Zaccaria. **Open** 9am-12.30pm, 3-7.30pm Mon-Sat. **Map** p74 A2 ⑲
Venice's longest-running publishing house has over 400 titles on Venetian history and folklore – all limited editions in Italian. The beautiful tomes can also be ordered online.

Giovanna Zanella
Castello 5641, calle Carminati (041 523 5500, www.giovannazanella.it). Vaporetto Rialto. **Open** 9.30am-1pm, 3-7pm Mon-Sat. **Map** p74 A1 ⑳
Venetian designer-cobbler Giovanna Zanella creates a fantastic line of handmade shoes in an extraordinary variety of styles and colours. A pair of shoes costs between €450 and €1,000. There are bags and other accessories also on sale.

I Tre Mercanti
Castello 5364, ponte alla Guerra (041 522 2901, www.itremercanti.it). Vaporetto Rialto. **Open** 11am-7.30pm daily. **Map** p74 A2 ㉑
There's an interesting selection here of seriously good Italian food and wine, some of it from local producers but some from further afield. Stock includes excellent olive oils, preserved vegetables, pastas and rices. At a street-side window, passersby can pick up sandwiches and rolls: a choice of locally made breads with 30-odd fillings. And there are gourmet variations on tiramisù to go as well.

Kalimala
Castello 5387, salizada San Lio (041 528 3596, www.kalimala.it). Vaporetto Rialto. **Open** 9.30am-7.30pm Mon-Sat. **Map** p74 A2 ㉒
A Venetian cobbler whose shoes are stylish without being quirky, and whose prices start at about €80. Handmade in beautiful Tuscan leather, in a wonderful array of colours, the range covers boots, loafers and sandals, plus bags and tablet holders.

Papier Mâché
Castello 5174B, calle lunga Santa Maria Formosa (041 522 9995, www.papier mache.it). Vaporetto Rialto. **Open** 9am-7.30pm Mon-Sat; 10am-7pm Sun. **Map** p74 B1 ㉓
This workshop uses traditional techniques to create masks inspired by the works of Klimt, Kandinsky, Tiepolo and Carpaccio. It stocks ceramics and painted mirrors too.

Arts & leisure

Palazzo delle Prigioni
Castello 4209, ponte della Paglia (041 984 252, www.collegiumducale.com). Vaporetto San Zaccaria. **Map** p74 A3 ㉔
Just over the Bridge of Sighs from the Doge's Palace, the Palazzo delle Prigioni hosts concerts by the Collegium Ducale Orchestra – which performs its Venetian Baroque and German Romantic repertoires several times a week – and also jazz evenings courtesy of the Venice Jazz Quartet.

Southern & eastern Castello

The low-rise, clustered buildings of working-class eastern Castello housed the employees of the **Arsenale** – Venice's docklands. Also here were Venice's foreign communities, as local churches testify: there's **San Giorgio dei Greci** (Greeks) and the **Scuola di**

Sestieri

Dividing up Venice.

Most of the towns and cities of the Italian mainland were happy to follow the example of the ancient Romans, slicing themselves into *quartieri* (quarters), which would have been delineated by the main axis roads – the *cardo* and *decumanus* – that intersected each other at the city centre. Ever original, Venice opted to set itself apart with *sestieri* (sixths) – topological divisions that still characterise the city today.

Historians squabble about who was responsible for the breakdown. Some say that the *sestieri* date from the very earliest settlements in these marshy lagoon islands – unlikely, given that the inhabitants were few and that power, when it stabilised, lay in Torcello (see p162) and the vanished town of Malamocco, only shifting to what we now call Venice in the ninth century.

Some argue that ninth-century Doge Orso Partecipazio created the *sestieri* as soon as he had moved his base to Rivoalto – now known as Rialto. Still others say it was the need to raise taxes for waging war on the Byzantine Emperor Manuel Komnenus that led Doge Vitale Michiel II to carve the city into more manageable, dunnable administrative divisions in 1171.

Unwieldy and difficult to pin down, the *sestieri* nonetheless reflect Venice's largely impenetrable topography. To make orientation even more difficult, street names are considered decorative or descriptive – many, for example, are called *calle drio la chiesa*

(street behind the church) or *calle forner* (bakery street) – and house numbers relate to the *sestiere* and not to the street. In Castello, the largest *sestiere*, numbers begin at one and go up almost to 7,000, often with inexplicable leaps from one front door to the next. If this seems complicated, you have to wonder how they managed before 1798, when the Austrians arrived to instill 'order' into the vanquished city-state: until then, there had been no numbers at all.

Locals and guidebooks will tell you that the *sestieri* are symbolised in each gondola's *ferro* (prow decoration), where six prongs – the six *sestieri* – point forward and a seventh – Giudecca (part of the *sestiere* of Dorsoduro) – points back. There's no historic documentation for this... but why doubt a good story?

San Giorgio degli Schiavoni (Slavs), with its captivating cycle of paintings by Vittorio Carpaccio. The great promenade along the lagoon – the riva degli Schiavoni – was named after the same community.

Inland from the *riva* is the quaint Gothic church of **San Giovanni in Bragora** in the square of the same name. Antonio Vivaldi was born on this campo on 4 March 1678, and was choir master at the church of **La Pietà**. In calle della Pietà, alongside the church, is the **Piccolo Museo della Pietà**, dedicated to the Pietà (a foundling home) and the composer.

Crossing the bridge over the rio dell'Arsenale, you can see the grand Renaissance entrance to the Arsenale shipyard. Once a hive of empire-building industry, it's now an expanse of empty warehouses and docks, though parts have been beautifully restored and are used for Biennale-related events.

The *riva* ends in the sedately residential district of Sant'Elena. This, in Venetian terms, is a 'modern' district. In 1872, work began to fill in the *barene* (marshes) that lay between the edge of the city and the ancient island of Sant'Elena, with its charming Gothic church. Also tucked away here is Venice's football stadium, Stadio PL Penzo – though fans are hoping for a new mainland ground sometime in the not-too-distant future.

Sights & museums

Arsenale

Castello, campo dell'Arsenale (www.arsenaledivenezia.it). Vaporetto Arsenale. **Map** p75 D4 ㉓
The word 'arsenale' derives from the Arabic *dar sina'a*, meaning 'house of industry'. The industry, and efficiency, of Venice's Arsenale was legendary: the *arsenalotti* could assemble a galley in just a few hours. Shipbuilding

activities began here in the 12th century; at the height of the city's power, 16,000 men were employed.

The imposing land gateway by Antonio Gambello (1460) in campo dell'Arsenale is the first example of Renaissance classical architecture to appear in Venice, although the capitals of the columns are 11th-century Veneto-Byzantine. The winged lion gazing down from above holds a book without the traditional words *Pax tibi Marce* (Peace to you, Mark) – unsuitable in this military context.

Shipbuilding activity ceased in 1917, after which the complex remained largely unused navy property until 2013 when much of it returned to town council hands. It is destined, authorities say, to become a scientific and cultural hub. Exhibitions and performances will continue to be held in some of the cavernous spaces within its walls.

In campo della Tana, on the other side of the rio dell'Arsenale, is the entrance to the *Corderia* (rope factory), an extraordinary building 316m (1,038 ft) long. This vast space is used to house large swathes of the Biennale. In May, the Mare Maggio sea-, boat- and travel-themed festival (www.maremaggio. it) opens up much of the Arsenale to the curious.

Museo dell'Istituto Ellenico

Castello 3412, ponte dei Greci (041 522 6581). Vaporetto San Zaccaria. **Open** 9am-5pm daily. **Admission** €4; €2 reductions. No credit cards. **Map** p74 B3 ㉖
There have been a Greek church, college and school at this location since the end of the 15th century. The oldest piece in the museum's collection is the 14th-century altar cross behind the ticket desk. The icons on display mainly follow the dictates of the Cretan school, with no descent into naturalism. The best pieces are those that are resolute in their hieratic (traditional-style Greek) flatness, such

as *Christ in Glory among the Apostles* and the Great Deesis from the first half of the 14th century. Also on display are priestly robes and other Greek-rite paraphernalia.

Museo Storico Navale

Castello 2148, campo San Biagio (041 244 1399). Vaporetto Arsenale. **Open** 8.45am-1.30pm Mon-Fri; 8.45am-1pm Sat. **Admission** €5; €3.50 reductions. No credit cards. **Map** p75 D4 ㉗

This museum dedicated to ships and shipbuilding continues an old tradition: under the Republic, the models created for shipbuilders in the final design stages were kept in the Arsenale. Some of the models on display are from that collection. The ground floor has warships, cannons, explosive speedboats and dodgy looking manned torpedoes, plus a display of ships through the ages. On the first floor are ornamental trimmings and naval instruments, plus a series of impressive models of Venetian ships. Here, too, is a richly gilded model of the *Bucintoro*, the doges' state barge.

The second floor has uniforms, more up-to-date sextants and astrolabes, and models of modern Italian navy vessels. On the third floor, there are models of Chinese, Japanese and Korean junks, cruise ships and liners, and a series of fascinating naïve votive paintings, giving thanks for shipwrecks averted or survived. A room at the back has a display of gondolas, including the last privately owned covered gondola in Venice, which belonged to the larger-than-life art collector and bon vivant Peggy Guggenheim.

Piccolo Museo della Pietà 'Antonio Vivaldi'

Castello 3701, calle della Pietà (041 522 2171, www.pietavenezia.org). Vaporetto Arsenale or San Zaccaria. **Open** by appt. **Admission** €3. No credit cards. **Map** p74 B3 ㉘

This museum chronicles the activities of the Ospedale della Pietà, the orphanage where Antonio Vivaldi was violin teacher and choir master. Numerous documents recount such details as the rules for admission of children and the rations of food allotted them. There is also a selection of period instruments.

La Pietà (Santa Maria della Visitazione)

Castello, riva degli Schiavoni (041 523 1096). Vaporetto San Zaccaria. **Open** for services only. **Map** p74 B3 ㉙

By the girls' orphanage of the same name, the church of La Pietà was famous for its music. Antonio Vivaldi, violin and choir master here from 1703 until 1740, wrote some of his finest music for his young charges. The ceiling has a *Coronation of the Virgin* (1755) by Giambattista Tiepolo.

San Giorgio dei Greci

Castello, fondamenta dei Greci (041 523 9569). Vaporetto San Zaccaria. **Open** 9am-12.30pm, 2.30-4.30pm Mon, Wed-Sat. **Map** p74 B3 ㉚

By the time the church of San Giorgio was begun in 1539, the Greeks were well established in Venice and held a major stake in the city's scholarly printing presses. Designed by Sante Lombardo, the church's interior is fully Orthodox in layout, with its women's gallery, and high altar behind the iconostasis. The campanile is decidedly lopsided.

San Giovanni in Bragora

Castello, campo Bandiera e Moro (041 270 2464). Vaporetto Arsenale. **Open** 9am-noon, 3.30-5pm Mon-Sat. **Map** p74 C3 ㉛

San Giovanni in Bragora (the meaning of 'bragora' is obscure) is an intimate Gothic structure. The church where composer Antonio Vivaldi was baptised (a copy of the entry in the register is on show), San Giovanni also contains some very fine paintings. Above the high altar is the recently restored *Baptism of Christ* (1492-95) by Cima da Conegliano. A smaller Cima, on

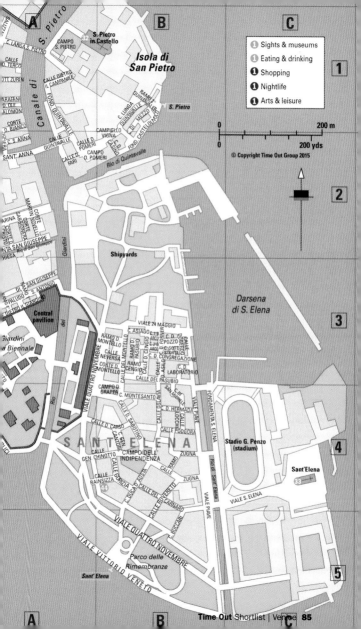

the right of the sacristy door, shows *Constantine Holding the Cross and St Helen* (1502). On the same wall, just before the second altar, is a triptych by Bartolomeo Vivarini, *Madonna and Child and Two Saints*, dated 1478.

San Pietro di Castello

Castello, campo San Pietro (041 275 0462, www.chorusvenezia.org). Vaporetto San Pietro. **Open** 10am-5pm Mon-Sat. **Admission** €3 (or Chorus; see p12). No credit cards. **Map** p85 A1 ⓷²

Until 1807, San Pietro in Castello was the cathedral of Venice, and its remote position testifies to the determination of the Venetian government to keep the clerical authorities far from the centre of temporal power. There has probably been a church here since the seventh century, but the present building was constructed in 1557 to a design by Palladio.

The body of the first patriarch of Venice, San Lorenzo Giustiniani, is preserved in an urn elaborately supported by angels above the high altar, a magnificent piece of Baroque theatricality designed by Baldassare Longhena (1649). In the right-hand aisle is the so-called 'St Peter's Throne', a delicately carved marble work from Antioch containing a Muslim funerary stele and verses from the Koran.

Sant'Elena

Castello 3, Servi di Maria, campo Chiesa Sant' Elena (041 520 5144). Vaporetto Sant'Elena. **Open** 5-7pm Mon-Sat. **Map** p85 C4 ⓷³

The red-brick Gothic church of Sant'Elena contains no great works of art (the church was deconsecrated in 1807, turned into an iron foundry, and not opened again until 1928) but its austere Gothic nakedness is a relief after all that Venetian ornament. In the chapel to the right of the entrance lies the body of St Helen, the irascible mother of the Emperor Constantine and finder of the True Cross. (Curiously enough, her body is also to be found in the Aracoeli church in Rome.)

Scuola di San Giorgio degli Schiavoni

Castello 3259A, calle dei Furlani (041 522 8828). Vaporetto Arsenale or San Zaccaria. **Open** 2.45-6pm Mon; 9.15am-1pm, 2.45-6pm Tue-Sat; 9.15am-1pm Sun. **Admission** €3; €2 reductions. No credit cards. **Map** p74 C2 ⓷⁴

The *schiavoni* were Venice's Slav inhabitants, who had become so numerous and influential by the end of the 15th century that they could afford to build this *scuola* (or meeting house) by the side of their church, San Giovanni di Malta. The *scuola* houses one of Vittore Carpaccio's two great Venetian picture cycles. In 1502, eight years after completing his St Ursula cycle (now in the Accademia), Carpaccio was commissioned to paint a series of canvases illustrating the lives of the Dalmatian saints George, Tryphone and Jerome. There is a wealth of incidental detail, such as the little dog in the painting of *St Augustine in his Study* – with its paraphernalia of humanism (astrolabe, shells, sheet music, archaeological fragments).

Eating & drinking

Al Covo

Castello 3968, campiello della Pescaria (041 522 3812, www.ristorantealcovo. com). Vaporetto Arsenale. **Meals served** 12.45-2pm, 7.30-10pm Mon, Tue, Fri-Sun. Closed mid Dec-mid Jan & 2wks Aug. €€€. **Map** p74 C3 ⓷⁵

Though Al Covo is hidden in an alley, it's very much on the international gourmet map. Its reputation is based on a dedication to serving the best seafood, including a sashimi of Adriatic fish and crustaceans, and *paccheri* pasta with pistachio pesto, mussels and aubergines. The restaurant's decor should make it ideal for a romantic dinner, but in fact it's more for foodies than lovers, and service can be prickly. Chef/owner Cesare Benelli's American wife Diane talks English-speakers through the menu. Desserts are delicious.

Angiò

Castello 2142, ponte della Veneta Marina (041 277 8555). Vaporetto Arsenale. **Open** 7am-9pm Mon, Wed-Sun. **Map** p75 D4 ⑯

Angiò is the finest stopping point along one of Venice's most tourist-trafficked spots – the lagoon-front riva degli Schiavoni. Tables stretch towards the water's edge, with a stunning view across to San Giorgio Maggiore; ultra-friendly staff serve pints of Guinness, freshly made sandwiches and inter-esting selections of cheese and wine. Closing time is pushed back to midnight or later in summer months, when music events are held on Saturday evenings.

Corte Sconta

Castello 3886, calle del Pestrin (041 522 7024, www.cortescontavenezia.it). Vaporetto Arsenale. **Meals served** 12.30-2.30pm, 7-10pm Tue-Sat. Closed Jan & mid July-mid Aug. €€€€. **Map** p74 C3 ⑰

This trailblazing seafood restaurant is such a firm favourite on the well-informed tourist circuit that it's a good idea to book ahead. The main act is a procession of seafood *antipasti*. The pasta is own-made and the warm *zabaione* dessert is a delight. Decor is of the modern bohemian trattoria vari-ety, the ambience loud and friendly. In summer, try to secure one of the tables in the pretty, vine-covered courtyard.

Dai Tosi

Castello 738, secco Marina (041 523 7102, www.trattoriadaitosi.com). Vaporetto Giardini. **Meals served** noon-2pm Mon, Tue, Thur; noon-2pm, 7-9.30pm Fri-Sun. Closed 2wks Aug. €-€€. **Pizzeria. Map** p75 F5 ⑱

In one of Venice's most working-class areas, this pizzeria is a big hit with locals. Beware of another restaurant of the same name on the street: this place (at no.738) is better. The cuisine is humble but filling, the pizzas are tasty, and you can round the meal off nicely with a killer *sgropin* (a post prandial refresher made with lemon sorbet, vodka and prosecco). In summer, angle for one of the garden tables.

El Refolo

Castello 1580, via Garibaldi (no phone). Vaporetto Giardini. **Open** *During Biennale* 10.30am-12.30am Tue-Sun. *Rest of year* 5.30pm-12.30am Tue-Sun. No credit cards. **Map** p75 E4 ⑲

If you want to settle at one of the high stools on the pavement outside this tiny bar, be prepared to wait. Because friendly El Refolo, with its well-priced wine (from €2.50 a glass), ever-chang-ing selection of filled rolls and excel-lent salami and/or cheese platters is everybody's favourite, especially when the area throngs with Biennale-goers. Over summer weekends, owner Massimiliano doesn't pull down the shutters until very late indeed.

Il CoVino

Castello 3829, calle del Pestrin (041 241 2705, www.covinovenezia.com). Vaporetto Arsenale. **Meals served** 12-3pm, 9.15-10pm Mon, Tue, Fri-Sun. €€€. **Map** p74 C3 ⑳

Venice's newest hot gastronomic ticket in 2014, the relaunched Il CoVino has a lot to like about it. In one corner of the tiny room, Dmitri juggles pots and pans in his open-to-view kitchen, while affable Andrea sees to the very few tables. The inventive dishes (meat, fish – no pasta) on the ever-changing menu are market-fresh and very tasty. But the fact that diners are obliged to pay a set price of €36, even if they don't want all three included courses, will put some off; with wine and extras, the bill is unlikely to be much less than €50 a head. The wine list has mainly natural unfiltered wines.

Il Ridotto

Castello 4509, campo Santi Filippo e Giacomo (041 520 8280, www.ilridotto. com). Vaporetto San Zaccaria. **Meals served** noon-2pm, 7-11pm Mon, Tue, Fri-Sun; 7-10pm Thur. €€€€. **Map** p74 B3 ㉑

VENICE BY AREA

Corte Sconta p87

Gianni Bonaccorsi's restaurant is a natural stopover for upcoming chefs passing through the lagoon city. Though expertise flows in both directions, Gianni's policy of using the freshest and best of local ingredients in unfussy ways to produce something remarkably sophisticated is adhered to with memorable results. The five-course taster menu (€70) gives the best scope for experiencing Il Ridotto's range, but there's a good lunch deal too – €28 for a selection of *cicheti* plus a fish or meat main. The place – two narrow rooms – is tiny, the decor is ultra-simple and the service is warm and professional.

Across the campo (no.4357), Gianni's trattoria L'Aciugheta serves decent pizzas and good *cicheto* snacks.

Pasticceria Melita

Castello 1000-4, fondamenta Sant'Anna (no phone). Vaporetto Giardini or San Pietro. **Open** 8am-2pm, 3.30-8.30pm Tue-Sun. No credit cards. **Map** p75 F4 ㊷

The welcome in this family café-bakery is not always sunny, but the quality of the pastries behind the old-fashioned bar counter will compensate. There's no sitting down for a languorous coffee and cake session: it's a 'stand-up or takeaway only' kind of place, but it's a favourite with locals.

Serra dei Giardini

Castello 1254, viale Garibaldi, giardini pubblici (041 296 0360, www.serradeigiardini.org). Vaporetto Giardini. **Open** 10am-9.30pm Tue-Fri, Sun; 10am-midnight Sat. **Map** p75 F4 ㊸

This gorgeous greenhouse has stood inside the giardini pubblici since 1894. Restored and run by a local cooperative, it now houses a plant shop and a café/tea shop with garden tables. The setting is charming, and the coffee, juices and light meals on offer are good. The idyll can be slightly marred by less-than-charming staff.

Vincent Bar

Sant'Elena, viale IV Novembre 36 (041 520 4493). Vaporetto Sant'Elena. **Open** 7am-10pm Tue-Sun. No credit cards. **Map** p85 B4

Sant'Elena is surely the only place in Venice you'll find more residents, trees and grassy expanses than tourists and churches. Grab a seat – and a drink – outside this bar and join the locals gazing across the lagoon at passing boats. The big mixed salads served at lunch make a great light meal, and there are huge helpings of competently prepared pasta dishes too. Ice-cream is made on the premises.

Shopping

Banco Lotto N°10

Castello 3478B, salizada Sant'Antonin (041 522 1439, www.ilcerchiovenezia.it). Vaporetto Arsenale. **Open** 3.30-7.30pm Mon; 10am-1pm, 3.30-7.30pm Tue-Sat. **Map** p74 C3 ㊺

The quirky dresses, bags and accessories sold in this little outlet all hail from the workshops of Venice's women's prison on the Giudecca island. Many of the designs are one-offs, and there's a strong vintage flavour.

Vino e... Vini

Castello 3566, salizada Pignater (041 521 0184). Vaporetto Arsenale. **Open** 9am-1pm, 5-8pm Mon-Sat. **Map** p74 C3 ㊻

Vino e... Vini stocks a wide-ranging selection of major Italian wines, as well as French, Spanish, Californian and even Lebanese vintages.

Arts & leisure

La Pietà

Castello, riva degli Schiavoni (041 522 1120, www.chiesavivaldi.it). Vaporetto San Zaccaria. **Map** p74 B3 ㊼

I Virtuosi Italiani perform early music concerts in what must surely be the easiest sell in Venice: Vivaldi in the Vivaldi church. See also p67.

Santa Lucia station

Cannaregio

VENICE BY AREA

Step out of Santa Lucia station and be prepared to be dazzled by the stunning sight of the Grand Canal. The walk to the centre along busy lista di Spagna, Cannaregio's main thoroughfare, is less grand. Concealed beyond, however, is a blissfully calm area of long canalside walks. The only big surprise of the area comes in the Ghetto, where a thriving Jewish community creates a sudden burst of activity amid the quiet of this second-largest *sestiere*.

From Santa Lucia station to the Rialto

Heading away from the railway station towards the Rialto, the tourist-tack-filled *lista* leads to the large campo San Geremia, overlooked by the church of the same name. Once you've crossed the Cannaregio Canal – by way of ponte delle Guglie, a grandiose bridge with obelisks – the route assumes more character, taking in lively street markets.

Off to the right, in a square giving on to the Grand Canal, is the church of **San Marcuola**. A bit further on, the more picturesque church of La Maddalena, inspired by the Pantheon in Rome, stands in the small campo della Maddalena. Beyond this, wide strada Nuova begins. Off to the left is the church of **San Marziale**, with whimsical ceiling paintings; on the strada Nuova itself stands the church of Santa Fosca, another mainly 18th-century creation. Down a *calle* to the right is the entrance to the **Ca' d'Oro**, Venice's most splendid Gothic palazzo.

The strada Nuova ends by the church of **Santi Apostoli**; the route to the Rialto soon becomes narrow and crooked, passing the church of **San Giovanni Crisostomo** and the adjacent courtyard of the corte Seconda del Milion, where Marco Polo was born in 1256. Some of the Veneto-Byzantine-style houses in the courtyard date from that time. There's a plaque commemorating Marco Polo on the rear of the

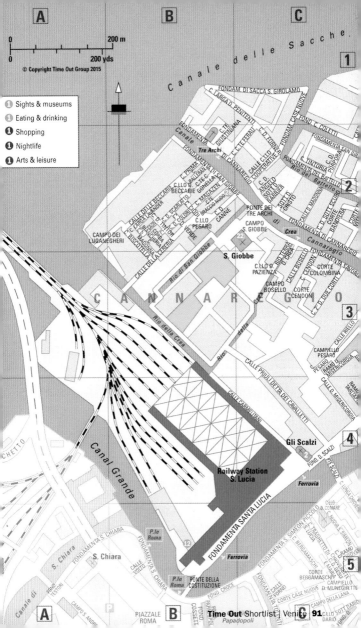

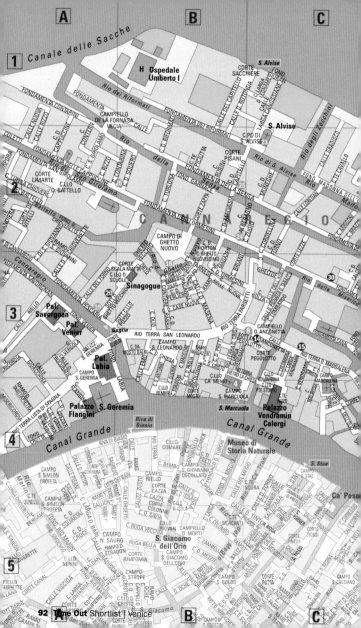

top: Santi Apostoli p96;
bottom: Ca' d'Oro

Teatro Malibran, formerly the Teatro di San Giovanni Crisostomo, one of Venice's earliest theatres.

Ca' d'Oro (Galleria Franchetti)

Cannaregio 3932, calle Ca' d'Oro (041 523 8790, www.cadoro.org). Vaporetto Ca' d'Oro. **Open** 8.15am-2pm Mon; 8.15am-7.15pm Tue-Sat; 10am-6pm Sun. **Admission** €6; €3 reductions. Price varies during special exhibitions. No credit cards. **Map** p93 D5 **1**

In its 15th-century heyday, the façade of this pretty townhouse had a colour scheme of light blue and burgundy, with 24-carat gold highlights. Though the colour has worn off, the Grand Canal frontage of Ca' d'Oro – built for merchant Marin Contarini between 1421 and 1431 – is still the most elaborate example of the florid Venetian Gothic style besides the Doge's Palace.

Inside, little of the original structure and decor has survived. The pretty courtyard was reconstructed with its original 15th-century staircase and well-head a century ago by Baron Franchetti; the mosaic floor is a 19th-century imitation of the floors in San Marco. The baron also assembled the collection of paintings, sculptures and coins that is exhibited inside. The highlight of the collection is Mantegna's *St Sebastian*, a powerful late work.

Gli Scalzi

Cannaregio, fondamenta degli Scalzi (041 715 115) Vaporetto Ferrovia. **Open** 7-11.50am, 4-7pm daily. **Map** p91 C4 **2**

Officially Santa Maria di Nazareth, this church is better known as Gli Scalzi after the order of Carmelitani *scalzi* (Barefoot Carmelites) to whom it belongs. They bought the plot in 1645 and subsequently commissioned Baldassare Longhena to design the church. The fine façade (1672-80) is the work of Giuseppe Sardi.

The interior is striking for its coloured marble and massively elaborate baldachin over the high altar. There are many fine Baroque statues, including the *St John of the Cross* by Giovanni Marchiori in the first chapel on the right and the anonymous marble crucifix and wax effigy of Christ in the chapel opposite. An Austrian shell that plummeted through the roof in 1915 destroyed the church's greatest work of art, Tiepolo's ceiling fresco, but spared his *Angels of the Passion*, *Agony in the Garden* and *St Theresa in Glory*.

San Giovanni Crisostomo

Cannaregio, campo San Giovanni Crisostomo (041 522 7155). Vaporetto Rialto. **Open** 8.15am-12.15pm, 3-7pm Mon-Sat; 3-7pm Sun. **Map** p93 E5 **3**

This small Greek-cross church by Mauro Codussi contains two great paintings. On the right-hand altar is *Saints Jerome, Christopher and Louis of Toulouse*, signed by Giovanni Bellini and dated 1513. On the high altar hangs *Saints John the Baptist, Liberale, Mary Magdalene and Catherine* (c1509) by Sebastiano del Piombo. On the left-hand altar is *Coronation of the Virgin*, a fine relief (1500-02) by Tullio Lombardo.

San Marcuola

Cannaregio, campo San Marcuola (041 713 872). Vaporetto San Marcuola. **Open** 10am-noon, 5-6pm Mon-Sat. **Map** p92 B3 **4**

The church, designed by 18th-century architect Giorgio Massari, has been beautifully restored – its gleaming interior comes as a surprise after the unfinished brick façade. It contains some vigorous statues by Gianmaria Morlaiter and, in the chancel, a *Last Supper* (1547) by Tintoretto. Opposite is a 17th-century copy of another Tintoretto (*Christ Washing the Feet of His Disciples*).

San Marziale

Cannaregio, campo San Marziale (041 719 933). Vaporetto Ca' d'Oro or San

Marcuola. **Open** 4-6.30pm Mon-Sat; 8.30-10am Sun. **Map** p93 D3 ⑤

The real joy of this church is its ceiling, with its four luminous paintings (1700-05) by the vivacious colourist Sebastiano Ricci. Two of them depict *God the Father with Angels* and *St Martial in Glory*; the other two recount the miraculous story of the wooden statue of the *Madonna and Child* that resides on the second altar on the left – apparently, it made its own way here by boat from Rimini. The high altar is a Baroque extravaganza.

Santi Apostoli

Cannaregio, campo Santi Apostoli (041 523 8297). Vaporetto Ca' d'Oro. **Open** 8.30am-noon, 5-7pm Mon-Sat; 4-7pm Sun. **Map** p93 E5 ⑥

The campanile of this 17th-century church, crowned by an onion dome, is a Venetian landmark. The Cappella Corner, off the right side of the nave, is a century older than the rest of the structure. On the altar is a splendidly theatrical *Communion of St Lucy* by Giambattista Tiepolo. The chapel to the right of the high altar has remnants of 14th-century frescoes while the one to the left has a dramatically stormy painting of *The Guardian Angel* by Francesco Maffei.

Eating & drinking

Antica Adelaide

Cannaregio 3728, calle larga Doge Priuli (041 523 2629, www.antica adelaide.it). Vaporetto Ca d'Oro. **Open** 7am-midnight daily. **Meals served** noon-2.30pm, 7.30-10.30pm daily. €€. **Map** p93 D4 ⑦

This historic bar-*osteria* reopened in 2006, after painstaking restoration, with dynamic restaurateur and wine buff Alvise Ceccato at the helm. Popular around *aperitivo* time, it has also made a splash on the culinary front, with its unusual menu of revisited traditional dishes from the Veneto. Vegetarians are well catered for.

Boscolo

Cannaregio 1818, campiello dell'Anconeta (041 720 731). Vaporetto San Marcuola. **Open** 6.40am-8.40pm daily. No credit cards. **Map** p92 C3 ⑧

The bar at Boscolo's *pasticceria* is always packed; locals flock to enjoy an extra-strong *spritz al bitter* with one of the home-made *pizzette*. There is also an excellent assortment of Venetian sweets: *frittelle* during Carnevale, as well as *zaleti* and *pincia* (made with cornflour and raisins). Boscolo's range of chocolates in the form of interesting (and graphic) *Kama Sutra* positions has made this confectioner famous.

La Bottega ai Promessi Sposi

Cannaregio 4367, calle dell'Oca (041 241 2747). Vaporetto Ca' d'Oro. **Meals served** 12.30-2.30pm, 8-11pm Mon, Tue, Thur-Sun. €€. No credit cards. **Map** p93 E5 ⑨

This pared-back *osteria* has a wooden counter groaning with excellent *cicheti* and a good selection of wines by the glass. In the back rooms are a few tables where diners can sample simple dishes – mainly fish or not exclusively seafood – such as fried *schie* (tiny grey prawns) on rocket with balsamic vinegar.

Ca' d'Oro (Alla Vedova)

Cannaregio 3912, ramo Ca' d'Oro (041 528 5324). Vaporetto Ca' d'Oro. **Meals served** 11.30am-2.30pm, 6.30-10.30pm Mon-Wed, Fri, Sat; 6.30-11pm Sun. Closed Aug. €€. No credit cards. **Map** p93 D4 ⑩

Officially Ca' d'Oro, this place is known by locals as Alla Vedova – the Widow's Place. The widow has joined her *marito*, but her family still runs the show. The traditional decor remains, though the warmth of the welcome can vary. Tourists head for the tables, where tasty pasta dishes (such as spaghetti in cuttlefish ink) and *secondi* are served; locals stay at the bar snacking on classic *cicheti*, including the best *polpette* (meatballs) in Venice.

Eat like a Venetian

Making sense of the city's hostelries.

Venice's uniqueness extends into many unexpected spheres – eating and drinking included. Take, for example, the all-day bar. Unassuming places such as **Da Lele** (see p127) or **Alla Ciurma** (see p111) open their doors at around 6am. But you'll search in vain for a coffee machine: market traders or workers arriving from the mainland drop by at sunrise for their first (alcoholic) drink of the day. It keeps – they'll tell you – the damp out of your bones. This kind of central heating comes cheap: in a city where everything seems to cost over the odds, a small glass of wine (*un'ombra*) costs anything from Lele's ridiculous 60c to around €1.50. And in all but the smartest bars, the ubiquitous *spritz* (see p79) comes in at €2.

Or, rather, it does when consumed standing. The traditional Venetian eaterie, known as a *bàcaro* – **Al Portego** (p78), **Ca' d'Oro** (p96), **All'Arco** (p111) and **Bottega ai Promessi Sposi** (p96) are fine examples – has a back room out the back with a few tables in it. But dominating the front of the premises you'll find a high glass-fronted bar counter inside which there will be shelves piled with tapas-like snacks called *cicheti*. From creamed cod (*baccalà mantecato*) to meatballs, to sardines stewed in onion (*sarde in saor*), to tiny stuffed peppers, you'll find a huge selection, to be eaten one at a time, or piled on to a plate to make what can add up to a pretty full meal. But this is on-the-hoof food: the proper tables are for proper diners.

Al Portego

Cicheti are charged individually – anything between €1.50 and €3 is normal, depending on what you choose. So a well-filled plate can cost €10 or less.

Cichetando (dining on *cicheti*) may be a (rare) cheap option for eating out in Venice but in the more traditional places you'll have to dine early to take advantage. *Bàcari* that consider themselves old-school generally close the kitchen by 9pm or so. A newer generation places its emphasis more on food than on drinking-with-snacks, and keeps on cooking until 10pm or 10.30pm.

At the higher end of Venice's dining scene, *trattorie* and *ristoranti* function much as in the rest of Italy, the difference being that their prices tend to be higher than elsewhere. Between the two comes the trap that many visitors fall into: the hostelry catering only to the easily-ripped-off tourist horde. So avoid anything with a *menu turistico* in several languages and a determined enticer at the door. Pay for the best, or seek out some dark *bàcaro*: anything else will not be the real Venetian thing.

La Cantina

Cannaregio 3689, campo San Felice (041 522 8258). Vaporetto Ca' d'Oro. **Open** 11am-10pm Mon-Sat. €€. **Map** p93 D4 ⓫

The service here can verge on the rude. But the *aperitivo* snack offerings – including *crostini* made on the spot with whatever's in season – are so substantial that a quick drink can easily turn into a full meal; seafood platters and the occasional hot dish are delicious; and outside tables are the perfect place for watching the world bustle by. Around 30 wines are available by the glass.

F30

Cannaregio, Santa Lucia railway station (041 525 6154). Vaporetto Ferrovia. **Open** 7am-11pm Mon-Thur, Sun; 7am-3am Fri, Sat. **Meals served** 11am-10.30pm daily. €-€€€. **Map** p91 B5 ⓬

Part of the Santa Lucia station upgrade, this is a light-filled, modern café-restaurant with a view over the Grand Canal. Eat excellent *tramezzini* or cakes perched at the bar, or put away a decent pizza, large mixed salad or classic pasta dish at restaurant tables. F30 is a one-off run by locals, with musicians from 9pm on Saturday nights and 'Soul Fridays' with a DJ set from 10pm.

Vini da Gigio

Cannaregio 3628, fondamenta San Felice (041 528 5140, www.vinidagigio. com). Vaporetto Ca' d'Oro. **Meals served** noon-2.30pm, 7-10.30pm Wed-Sun. Closed 3wks Jan-Feb. €€€. **Map** p93 D4 ⓭

Vini da Gigio is strong on Venetian antipasti, including raw seafood; there are also a number of decent meat and game options. As the name suggests, wine is another forte, with good international and by-the-glass selections. The only drawback in this highly recommended restaurant is the unhurried service. Book well ahead.

Shopping

Cibele

Cannaregio 1823, campiello dell'Anconeta (041 524 2113). Vaporetto San Marcuola (041 524 2113). **Open** 8.30am-12.45pm, 4-7.45pm Mon-Sat. **Map** p92 C3 ⓮

Natural health foods, cosmetics and medicines are on sale here. Staff also prepare blends of herbal teas and remedies.

Mori & Bozzi

Cannaregio 2367, rio terà Maddalena (041 715 261). Vaporetto San Marcuola. **Open** 9.30am-7.30pm daily. Closed Sun in July & Aug. **Map** p92 C3 ⓯

Women's shoes for the coolest of the cool: whatever the latest fad, it's here. Beautiful bags, clothes, hats and accessories are also sold.

Nightlife

Santo Bevitore

Cannaregio 2393A, campo Santa Fosca (041 717 560, www.ilsantobevitore pub.com). Vaporetto Ca' d'Oro or San Marcuola. **Open** 9.30am-1.30am Mon-Sat. No credit cards. **Map** p92 C3 ⓰

This friendly pub-café is popular for *cicheti* during the day or a beer or a glass of wine in the evening.

Arts & leisure

Teatro Malibran

Cannaregio 5873, calle dei Milion (041 786 603, www.teatrolafenice.it). Vaporetto Rialto. **Map** p93 E5 ⓱

Inaugurated in 1678 as Teatro San Giovanni Crisostomo, this 900-seater was built on the site where Marco Polo's family palazzo once stood. The theatre now shares the classical music, ballet and opera season with La Fenice; in addition, it has its own chamber music season.

Il Ghetto

The word 'ghetto' is one that Venice has given to the world. It originally meant an iron foundry, a place where iron was *gettato* (cast). Until 1390, when the foundry was transferred to the Arsenale, casting was done on a small island in Cannaregio. In 1516, it was decided to confine the city's Jewish population to this island; here they remained until 1797. Venetian treatment of the Jews was by no means as harsh as in many European countries, but neither was it benevolent – restrictions were many and tough.

With the arrival of Napoleon in 1797, Jews gained full citizenship rights; many chose to remain in the Ghetto. In the deportations during the Nazi occupation of Italy in 1943, 202 Venetian Jews were sent to the death camps. The Jewish population of Venice and Mestre now stands at about 500 (see www.jvenice.org for information). Only around a dozen Jewish families still live in the Ghetto, but it remains the centre of spiritual, cultural and social life for the Jewish community. Most of the city, including the Ghetto, is an eruv.

Sights & museums

Museo Ebraico

Cannaregio 2902B, campo del Ghetto Nuovo (041 715 359, www.museo ebraico.it). Vaporetto Guglie or San Marcuola. **Open** 10am-5.30pm Mon-Fri, Sun. *Guided tours* (hourly) 10.30am-4.30pm Mon-Thur, Sun; 10.30am-2.30pm Fri. **Admission** *Museum only* €4; €3 reductions. *Museum & synagogues* €10; €8 reductions. **Map** p92 B3 ⓭

This well-run museum and cultural centre has been spruced up over recent years, with a bookshop and a new section dedicated to the history and traditions of the various 'nations' that make up Venice's Jewish community, its relationship with the city after the 1797 opening of the Ghetto, some of its famous personages and the role of usury. In the older rooms there are ritual objects in silver, sacred vestments and hangings, and a series of marriage contracts. The museum is best visited as part of a guided tour. This takes in three synagogues – the Scuola Canton (Ashkenazi rite), the Scuola Italiana (Italian rite) and the Scuola Levantina (Sephardic rite). Tours of the Jewish cemetery on the Lido also set out from here.

Eating & drinking

Gam Gam Kosher Restaurant

Cannaregio 1122, fondamenta di Cannaregio (041 275 9256, http:// gamgamkosher.com). Vaporetto Guglie. **Open** noon-10pm Mon-Thur, Sun. **€€**. **Jewish**. **Map** p92 A3 ⓭

Gam Gam livens up evenings in the Ghetto with its tables out on the Cannaregio Canal and its friendly staff coping with the hungry crowds. As the name implies, the food (and wine) is kosher, and there's a range of traditional options including latkes, gefilte fish and falafel. But there's a definite Venetian twist to the cooking. And the non-meat, non-dairy range makes this a favourite for vegetarians and vegans. You are advised to book.

Shopping

Kosher Tevà

Cannaregio 1242, campo del Ghetto Vecchio (041 524 4486). Vaporetto Guglie. **Open** 10am-6.30pm Mon-Fri, Sun. No credit cards. **Map** p92 A3 ⓴

Tevà produces excellent breads, biscuits and cakes... all kosher.

North & west

There's no better place for getting away from it all than the north-western areas of Cannaregio. Built around three long parallel canals, it has no large animated squares and (with the exception of the Ghetto) no sudden surprises – just views over the northern lagoon. And, at night, a lively scene around a handful of restaurants and bars.

The area does, however, have its landmarks, such as the *vecchia* (old; 14th-century) and *nuova* (new; 16th-century) Scuole della Misericordia, the 'new' one being a huge pile designed by Sansovino, its façade never completed. It has long awaited conversion into a cultural institute.

Out on a limb in the far west, Renaissance **San Giobbe** was the first Venetian work of master mason Pietro Lombardo. On the northern-most canal (the rio della Madonna dell'Orto) are the churches of **Sant'Alvise** and **Madonna dell'Orto**, plus many fine *palazzi*.

Sights & museums

Madonna dell'Orto

Cannaregio, campo Madonna dell'Orto (041 719 933, www.madonnadellorto. org). Vaporetto Orto. **Open** 10am-5pm Mon-Sat; noon-6pm Sun. **Admission** €2.50. No credit cards. **Map** p93 D2 ㉑

The 'Tintoretto church' was originally dedicated to St Christopher, the patron saint of the gondoliers. However, a cult developed around a supposedly miraculous statue of the Madonna and Child that stood in a nearby garden. In 1377, the sculpture was transferred into the church (it's now in the chapel of San Mauro), and the church's name changed to the Madonna dell'Orto – of the Garden.

The false gallery at the top of the beautiful Gothic façade is unique in Venice; the sculptures are all fine 15th-century works. But it is the works by Tintoretto that have made the church famous. Two colossal paintings dominate the side walls of the chancel. On the left is *The Israelites at Mount Sinai*. Opposite is a gruesome *Last Judgement*. His paintings in the apse include *St Peter's Vision of the Cross* and *The Beheading of St Paul*. On the wall of the right aisle is the *Presentation of the Virgin in the Temple*. The Contarini chapel contains the artist's beautiful *St Agnes Reviving the Son of a Roman Prefect*. Tintoretto,

his son Domenico and his artistically gifted daughter Marietta are buried in a chapel off the right aisle.

Also take a look at Cima da Conegliano's masterpiece *Saints John the Baptist, Mark, Jerome and Paul* (1494-95) over the first altar on the right. The second chapel on the left contains a painting by Titian of *The Archangel Raphael and Tobias* (and dog).

San Giobbe

Cannaregio, Campo San Giobbe (041 524 1889, www.chorusvenezia.org). Vaporetto Crea or Tre Archi. **Open** 10am-1.30pm Mon-Sat. **Admission** €3 (or Chorus; p12). **Map** p91 C2 ㉒

The first Venetian creation of Pietro Lombardo, the interior of San Giobbe is unashamedly Renaissance in style. Most of the church's treasures – altarpieces by Giovanni Bellini and Vittore Carpaccio – are now in the Accademia (p140). An atmospheric *Nativity* by Gerolamo Savoldo remains, as does an *Annunciation with Saints Michael and Anthony* triptych by Antonio Vivarini in the sacristy. The Martini chapel, the second on the left, is a little bit of Tuscany. The terracotta medallions of Christ and the four Evangelists are by the Della Robbia studio – the only examples of its work in Venice.

Sant'Alvise

Cannaregio, campo Sant'Alvise (041 275 0462, www.chorusvenezia.org). Vaporetto Sant'Alvise. **Open** 10am-5pm Mon-Sat. **Admission** €3 (or Chorus; p12). No credit cards. **Map** p92 C2 ㉓

A simple 14th-century Gothic building, Sant'Alvise's interior was remodelled in the 1600s with extravagant trompe l'œil effects on the ceiling. On the inner façade is a *barco*, a hanging choir of the 15th century with elegant wrought-iron gratings. Beneath are eight charmingly naïve biblical paintings in tempera, attributed to Lazzaro Bastiani. On the right wall of the church are two paintings by Tiepolo, *The Crowning with Thorns* and *The Flagellation*.

Il Ghetto p98

Walk like a Venetian

Pedestrian etiquette.

Acqua alta

With their unique transport situation, Venetians have developed a particular etiquette for getting around on foot, with clear rules depending on the particular weather conditions.

In general, 'traffic' tends to flow in lanes (keep to the right) with potential for passing: a quick acceleration to the left with a polite '*permesso*' will get you past those in front. Locals take a dim view of anyone stopping in narrow alleyways or on busy bridges to gawp. Pull off well to the side or into a quiet side-street to consult a map or admire a building. Be adventurous and explore remoter districts if you want to avoid the high-season all-day-long traffic jams clogging the main arteries of the city, especially those near San Marco and Rialto.

Acqua alta (high water) presents other problems. Except in truly exceptional cases, all this means is that a couple of inches of water laps into the lowest parts of the city for an hour or two, then recedes. As the water rises, sirens sound five ten-second blasts two hours before the tide's high point. During the *acqua alta* season (September to April), trestles and wooden planks are stacked up along flood-prone thoroughfares, ready to be transformed into raised walkways. Venetians caught out by the rising water without wellies wait their turn patiently, then proceed slowly but surely. They expect tourists to do the same, or risk a telling-off.

Pedestrian etiquette extends beyond the walkways. The streets may be waterlogged, but they continue to function as a municipal road network; locals are understandably peeved if tourists doing Gene Kelly impersonations prevent them from reaching their destination dry. Remember, too, that during *acqua alta* you can't see where the pavement stops and the canal begins. Maps posted at vaporetto stops show flood-prone areas; if you don't want to get your feet wet, stick to higher ground or sit out those damp hours in your hotel room or a bar.

To see if you'll be facing this challenge, go to www.comune. venezia.it and click on '*previsione maree*' for tide forecasts. Anything over 80cm means that low-lying areas, such as piazza San Marco, will be submerged.

A larger and livelier work by the same painter, *Road to Calvary*, hangs on the right wall of the chancel.

Eating & drinking

Al Timon

Cannaregio 2754, fondamenta dei Ormesini (041 524 6066). Vaporetto Ca' d'Oro or San Marcuola. **Open** 6pm-1am daily. **Map** p92 B2 ㉔

Steak house, *cichetteria* but most popularly *aperitivo* hang-out, Al Timon is buzzing, with tables spilling out from a tiny inside space on to the lovely canalside pavement and even on to the canal itself: there's a boat where *spritz*-sippers can enjoy a water-borne drink. You can eat until late here, while occasional lunch-time openings are announced on their Facebook page. Book ahead to be sure of a table.

Anice Stellato

Cannaregio 3272, fondamenta della Sensa (041 720 744). Vaporetto Guglie or Sant'Alvise. **Meals served** 12.30-2pm, 7.30-10pm Wed-Sun. **€€**. **Map** p92 B2 ㉕

The bar in this friendly *bàcaro* fills up with *cichetari* (snacking locals) in the hour before lunch and dinner. Tables take up two simply decorated rooms, as well as the canalside walk. From the kitchen come Venetian classics such as *bigoli in salsa*, some given a novel twist.

Bea Vita

Cannaregio 3082, fondamenta delle Cappuccine (041 275 9347). Vaporetto Santa Marta or Tre Archi. **Meals served** noon-2.30pm, 7.30-10.30pm Mon-Sat. **€€**. **Map** p92 B2 ㉖

On the long canalside promenade just north of the Ghetto, Bea Vita attracts locals with its ample portions and decent prices. After a single *antipasto* from the creative menu, you're likely to feel full – but desserts are mouth-watering. The small wine list includes a decent by-the-glass selection. There's a good €28 taster menu.

Da Rioba

Cannaregio 2553, fondamenta della Misericordia (041 524 4379, www.da rioba.com). Vaporetto Orto. **Meals served** 12.30-2.30pm, 7.30-10.30pm Tue-Sun. Closed 3wks Jan & 3wks Aug. **€€**. **Map** p92 C3 ㉗

A pleasant spot for lunch on warm days, when tables are laid out along the canal. This nouveau-rustic *bàcaro* attracts a Venetian clientele; the menu includes local standards such as *schie con polenta* as well as more modern Italian dishes.

Dalla Marisa

Cannaregio 652B, fondamenta San Giobbe (041 720 211). Vaporetto Crea or Tre Archi. **Meals served** noon-2.30pm Mon, Wed, Sun; noon-2.30pm, 8-9.15pm Tue, Thur-Sat. Closed Aug. **€€**. No credit cards. **Map** p91 B2 ㉘

Signora Marisa is a culinary legend in Venice, with locals calling up days in advance to ask her to prepare ancient recipes such as *risotto con le secoe* (risotto made with a cut of beef from around the spine). Book well ahead – and note, serving times are rigid: turn up late and you'll go hungry. There's a €15 lunch menu.

L'Orto dei Mori

Cannaregio 3386, fondamenta dei Mori (041 524 3677, www.osteriaortodeimori. com). Vaporetto Orto. **Meals served** 12.30-3.30pm, 7-10.30pm Mon, Wed-Sun. Closed 3wks Jan. **€€€**. **Map** p93 D3 ㉙

The cook may be Sicilian but there's a Venetian feel to this welcoming *osteria*, especially when tables are out on the picturesque *fondamenta*. Venetian dishes include a light *baccalà mantecato* (creamed cod) and a tasty *risotto al nero di seppia* (risotto with squid ink).

Shopping

Nicolao Atelier

Cannaregio 2590, fondamenta della Misericordia (041 520 7051, www. nicolao.com). Vaporetto Guglie. **Open** 9am-1pm, 2-6pm Mon-Fri. **Map** p92 C3 ㉚

Santa Maria dei Miracoli

A simple carnival costume can be hired from €150 per day; the more elaborate ones can go up to as much as €300 a day. Costumes are also for sale.

East

Behind the straight edge of the fondamenta Nuove, eastern Cannaregio is more intriguingly closed in, with many narrow alleys (including the Venetian record holder: calle Varisco, which is 52 centimetres/20 inches wide at its narrowest point), charming courtyards and well-heads, but no major sights, with the exception of the spectacularly ornate church of **I Gesuiti**, the **Oratorio dei Crociferi** and the miniature marvel of **Santa Maria dei Miracoli**.

Sights & museums

I Gesuiti

Cannaregio, salizada dei Spechieri (041 523 1610). Vaporetto Fondamente Nove. **Open** 10am-noon, 4-6pm daily. **Map** p93 F4 ③①
The Jesuits were never very popular in Venice, and it wasn't until 1715 that they felt secure enough to build a church here. Local architect Domenico Rossi was given explicit instructions to dazzle. The exterior, with a façade by Gian Battista Fattoretto, is conventional enough; the interior is anything but. All that tassled, bunched, overpowering drapery is not the work of a rococo set designer gone berserk with luxurious brocades: it's green and white marble. Titian's *Martyrdom of St Lawrence* (1558-59) is over the first altar on the left side.

Oratorio dei Crociferi

Cannaregio 4905, campo dei Gesuiti (041 271 9012). Vaporetto Fondamente Nove. **Open** by appt. **Admission** €6. **Map** p93 E4 ③②
Founded in the 13th century by Doge Renier Zeno, the oratory is a sort of primitive *scuola*, with the familiar square central meeting hall but without the quasi-masonic ceremonial trappings. Palma il Giovane's colourful cycle of paintings shows Pope Anacletus instituting the order of the Crociferi (cross-bearers), and dwells on the pious life of Doge Pasquale Cicogna, who was a fervent supporter of the order.

Santa Maria dei Miracoli

Cannaregio, campo Santa Maria dei Miracoli (041 275 0462, www.chorus venezia.org). Vaporetto Fondamente Nove or Rialto. **Open** 10am-5pm Mon-Sat. **Admission** €3 (or Chorus; p12). No credit cards. **Map** p93 E5 ③③
One of the most exquisite churches in the world, Santa Maria dei Miracoli was built in the 1480s to house a miraculous image of the Madonna. The building is the work of the Lombardo family, and there is an almost painterly approach to the use of multicoloured marble in the four sides of the church, each of which is of a slightly different shade. The sides have more pilasters than necessary, making the church appear longer than it really is.

Inside, the 50 painted ceiling panels by Pier Maria Pennacchi (1528) are almost impossible to distinguish without using binoculars. Instead, turn your attention to the carvings by the Lombardos on the columns, steps and balustrade, with their delicate, lifelike details.

Eating & drinking

Algiubagiò

Cannaregio 5039, fondamenta Nuove (041 523 6084, www.algiubagio.net). Vaporetto Fondamente Nove. **Open** 7am-midnight Mon, Wed-Sun. Closed Jan. **Meals served** noon-3pm, 7-10.30pm Mon, Wed-Sun. €€€. **Map** p93 F4 ③④
This busy spot has morphed from bar to full-on restaurant, now with a vast waterside terrace. The wide-ranging menu has something for everyone, including vegetarians (though steak is the house speciality). There's a small but well-chosen wine list.

Alla Frasca

Cannaregio 5176, campiello della Carità (041 528 5433, www.osteriavinialla frasca.com). Vaporetto Fondamente Nove. **Meals served** noon-2.30pm, 7-10.30pm Tue-Sat; noon-2.30pm Sun. **€€. Map** p93 F4 ③⑤

A pleasant trattoria with a good seafood menu: the fish soup and spaghetti with lobster are excellent. The tables on a tiny square are ridiculously scenic.

Boccadoro

Cannaregio 5405A, campiello Widman (041 521 1021, www.boccadorovenezia. it). Vaporetto Fondamente Nove. **Meals served** noon-3pm, 7-11pm daily. **€€€. Map** p93 F5 ③⑥

Boccadoro has modern decor and very good food, with a focus on fresh fish – such as tuna tartare or *cozze pepate* (peppery mussels).

Da Alberto

Cannaregio 5401, calle Giacinto Gallina (041 523 8153). Vaporetto Rialto. **Meals served** noon-3pm, 6.30-9.30pm Mon-Sat. **€€. Map** p93 F5 ③⑦

This *bácaro* has a well-stocked bar counter, at which you can snack. The wide-ranging menu – served at tables in the back – is rigidly Venetian, offering the likes of *seppie in umido* (stewed cuttlefish). Book ahead for a table.

Trattoria Storica

Cannaregio 4858, salizada Sceriman (041 528 5266). Vaporetto Ca' d'Oro. **Meals served** 12.30-2.30pm, 6.30-10pm Mon-Sat. **€€. Map** p93 E4 ③⑧

This family restaurant is good value for hearty servings of traditional Venetian fare. At lunch, there's a generous €15 set menu.

Shopping

Gianni Basso Stampatore

Cannaregio 5306, calle del Fumo (041 521 4681). Vaporetto Fondamente Nove. **Open** 9am-1pm, 2.30-6pm Mon-Sat. **Map** p93 F4 ③⑨

Come here to choose the perfect motif for your hand-printed business cards, ex libris or stationery.

Libreria Marco Polo

Cannaregio 5886A, calle del Teatro Malibran (041 522 6343, www.libreria marcopolo.com). Vaporetto Rialto. **Open** 9.30am-7.30pm Mon-Thur, Sat; 9.30am-11.30pm Fri. **Map** p93 E5 ④⓪

Claudio Moretti's quirky bookshop sells remainders and second-hand books. Travel is a speciality.

Vittorio Costantini

Cannaregio 5311, calle del Fumo (041 522 2265, www.vittoriocostantini.com). Vaporetto Fondamenta Nove. **Open** 9.15am-1pm, 2.15-5.30pm Mon-Fri. **Map** p93 F4 ④①

Vittorio is internationally renowned as one of the most original Venetian glass workers. His intricate animals, insects, fish and birds are instantly recognisable for their fine workmanship.

Nightlife

Irish Pub

Cannaregio 3847, corte dei Pali già Testori (041 099 0916, www.theirish pubvenezia.com). Vaporetto Ca' d'Oro. **Open** 10am-2am daily. **Map** p93 D4 ④②

Expats, locals and tourists of all ages come to Venice's oldest Irish pub (previously known as the Fiddler's Elbow). Party-pooping neighbours have put a stop to the music nights, but regulars still pack the place out for the sports events shown on four plasma screens.

Arts & leisure

Teatro Fondamenta Nuove

Cannaregio 5013, fondamenta Nuove (041 522 4498, www.teatrofondamenta nuove.it). Vaporetto Fondamente Nove. No credit cards. **Map** p93 E4 ④③

Opened in 1993 in an old joiner's shop, this theatre stages contemporary dance and avant-garde drama, as well as quality experimental music performances.

Ponte di Rialto p111

San Polo &
Santa Croce

Within the bulge created by the great bend in the Grand Canal lie the *sestieri* of San Polo and Santa Croce. Working out where one stops and the other begins is an arduous task. The area ranges from the eastern portion, tightly clustered around the Rialto market – which was the city's ancient heart and where, despite the stalls selling trashy tourist-trinkets, you can still feel its steady throb, particularly in the bustling morning market – to a quieter, residential, more down-at-heel area in the far west, extending to the university zone by San Nicolò da Tolentino. Between the two extremes come the large open space of campo San Polo, the great religious complex of the Frari and the *scuole* of San Rocco and San Giovanni Evangelista.

The Rialto markets

'Rialto', most experts agree, derives from 'Rivoaltus' (high bank). It was on this point of higher ground at the midpoint along the Grand Canal that one of the earliest settlements was founded, in the fifth century. The district has been the commercial centre of the city since the market was placed here in 1097.

Near the foot of the **Rialto bridge,** the small church of **San Giacomo di Rialto** is generally agreed to be the oldest of the city's churches. All around it stretch the markets – the best places to buy your fruit, veg and seafood. In recent years, this area has taken on a new lease of life as a centre of Venetian nightlife, with a number of bars opening under the porticoes of the Renaissance Fabbriche Vecchie (Scarpagnino, 1520-22).

The ruga degli Speziali leads to the Pescaria (fishmarket; open Tue-Sat mornings). Beyond the market extends a warren of medieval low-rent housing interspersed with proud *palazzi*.

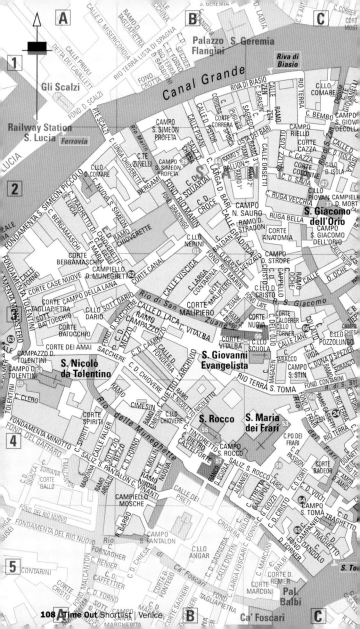

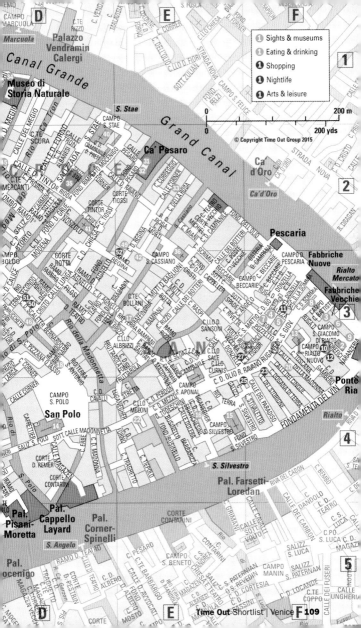

Marcuola

Palazzo
Vendramin
Calergi

Canal Grande

Museo di
Storia Naturale

S. Stae

CAMPO
S. STAE

Ca' Pesaro

Grand Canal

Ca'
d'Oro

Ca'd'Oro

Pescaria

Fabbriche
Nuove

Rialto
Mercato

Fabbriche
Vecchie

Ponte
Ria

Rialto

San Polo

S. Silvestro

Pal. Farsetti
Loredan

Pal.
Pisani-
Moretta

Pal.
Cappello
Layard

S. Angelo

Pal.
Corner-
Spinelli

Pal.
ocenigo

Legend:
- ❶ Sights & museums
- ❷ Eating & drinking
- ❶ Shopping
- ❶ Nightlife
- ❶ Arts & leisure

0   200 m
0   200 yds

© Copyright Time Out Group 2015

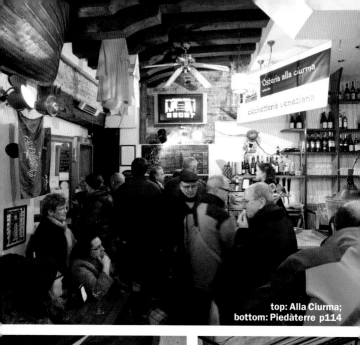

top: Alla Ciurma;
bottom: Piedàterre p114

Ponte di Rialto (Rialto bridge)

Map p109 F3 ❶

The Ponte di Rialto was built in 1588-92, to a design by aptly named Antonio Da Ponte. Until the 19th century, it was the only bridge over the Grand Canal. It replaced a wooden one, which can be seen in Carpaccio's painting of *The Miracle of the True Cross* in the Accademia (p140). After the decision was taken to build it, 60 years passed, during the course of which designs by Michelangelo, Vignola, Sansovino and Palladio were rejected. Da Ponte's simple but effective project eventually went ahead, probably because it kept the utilitarian features of the previous structure, with its double row of shops. The bridge thus acts as a continuation of the market at its foot.

San Giacomo di Rialto

San Polo, campo San Giacomo (041 522 4745). Vaporetto Rialto or Rialto Mercato. **Open** 9.30am-noon, 4-6pm Mon-Sat. **Map** p109 F3 ❷

The traditional foundation date for this church is that of the city itself: 25 March 421. It has undergone several radical reconstructions since then, the last in 1601. Nonetheless, the original Greek-cross plan was always preserved, as were its minuscule dimensions.

Eating & drinking

Al Mercà

San Polo 213, campo Cesare Battisti già Bella Vienna (347 100 2583 mobile). Vaporetto Rialto or Rialto Mercato. **Open** 9am-3pm, 6-9pm Mon-Sat; 6-9pm Sun. No credit cards. **Map** p109 F3 ❸

Quite literally a hole in the wall, with standing room only, Al Mercà (or Al Marcà – the spelling varies) has been serving Rialto marketgoers since 1918. Today's owners offer the usual choice of wine, and a decent *spritz*, plus snacks – meatballs, artichoke hearts and mini-sandwiches, in addition to numerous options for panino toppings.

All'Arco

San Polo 436, calle Ochialera (041 520 5666). Vaporetto Rialto or Rialto Mercato. **Open** 8am-2.30pm Mon-Sat. No credit cards. **Map** p109 F3 ❹

A hugely popular *bàcaro*. Throughout the day, friendly bar staff serve *ombre* (glasses of wine), stiffer stuff and wonderfully fresh *cicheti* to an enthusiatic and varied clientele. At €1.50 a *cicheto*, you can have a delicious meal for very little, but note – it's standing room only.

Alla Ciurma

San Polo 406, calle Galeazza (041 523 9514). Vaporetto Rialto or Rialto Mercato. **Open** 8am-3pm, 5.30-9pm Mon-Sat. No credit cards. **Map** p109 F3 ❺

Packed, loud and casually friendly, Alla Ciurma mixes market stallholders with locals and tourists in a happy confusion around a high counter packed with *cicheti* of all kinds, including skewers of deep-fried seafood and – their speciality – king prawns wrapped in bacon. Most people drop by for a glass of wine or a *spritz*. There are a couple of tables: if you can bag a seat at lunch you can enjoy good salads and an excellent *baccalà mantecato* (creamed cod).

Bancogiro

San Polo 122, campo San Giacomo di Rialto (041 523 2061). Vaporetto Rialto Mercato. **Meals served** noon-11pm Tue-Sun. €€€. **Map** p109 F3 ❻

The location of this updated *bàcaro* is splendid: the main entrance gives on to the busy Rialto square of San Giacomo, while the back door leads to a prime bit of Grand Canal frontage, with (hotly contested) tables. Bancogiro dispenses excellent wines and *cicheti* to an appreciative crowd downstairs; upstairs, the restaurant has creative seafood dishes.

Do Mori

San Polo 429, calle dei Do Mori (041 522 5401). Vaporetto Rialto, Rialto Mercato or San Silvestro. **Open** 8am-8pm Mon-Sat. No credit cards. **Map** p109 F3 ❼

VENICE BY AREA

Wines of north-east Italy

The best tastes of the region.

The wine-growing area that stretches from the Veneto north-east to Friuli is, after Tuscany and Piedmont, one of Italy's strongest: even in Venice's humbler establishments, the house wine is often surprisingly refined.

The grape-growing area is divided into two regions, the Veneto and Friuli-Venezia Giulia. The latter has the strongest reputation, mostly centred on the Collio and Colli Orientali appellations. This pair of appellations can be confusing. The names Collio and Colli Orientali don't tell you what you're getting in the glass: they are umbrella affairs. You might order a Colli Orientali tocai friuliano, or refosco; or a Collio merlot, or sauvignon.

The Veneto region is coming on, too. Long considered good only for full-bodied red Amarone and Valpolicella, the region is undergoing an image makeover, thanks to energetic winemakers who use local grape varieties such as corvina and garganega to turn out some fine and complex reds. The Veneto is also home to Italy's favourite fizz, prosecco.

RED

Cabernet: When Venetians ask for a glass of cabernet, they generally mean cabernet franc. A staple of the Veneto's upland wine enclaves, the grape yields an honest, more-ish red. For Veneto area cabernets, look out for Mattiello, Costozza and Cavazza. In Friuli, cabernet sauvignon and cabernet franc have a foothold. Russiz Superiore and La Boatina make some of the best.

Raboso: The classic Venetian winter-warming red, raboso is rough, acidic and tannic. The best kind is served from a huge demijohn in your local *bàcaro*.

Refosco: A ruby-red with hints of grass and cherries, locals like to keep this variety to themselves. Try the one produced by Dorigo.

Valpolicella, Recioto della Valpolicella & Amarone: The best Valpolicella, bottled as Valpolicella classico or Valpolicella superiore, can be very good. Amarone and Recioto, the area's two famous passito wines, are made from partially dried Valpolicella grapes. Recioto is the sweet version, Amarone the dry. The best producers include Allegrini (Recioto), Bussola, Cantina Sociale Valpolicella, Corte Sant'Alda, Dal Forno, Masi (Amarone), Quintarelli (Amarone), Viviani and Zenato.

WHITE & SPARKLING

Soave & Recioto di Soave: In the Soave classico area, a few winemakers are showing that this blend of garganega and trebbiano is capable of great things: look out for Pieropan's La Rocca or Calvarino selections. In the 1980s, a few producers revived the tradition of Recioto di Soave, a dessert wine made from raisinised garganega grapes. The best producers include Anselmi, Ca' Rugate, Gini, Inama, Pieropan and Suavia.

Friulian whites: The Collio and Colli Orientali appellations turn out some of Italy's most graceful white wines. Four varietals dominate: sauvignon (the Ronco delle Mele cru produced by Venica & Venica is great); pinot bianco; pinot grigio; and tocai friuliano (a dry summery white). Good producers include Ascevi, Castello di Spessa, Collavini, Dorigo, Gravner, Humar, Jermann, Kante, Keber, Le Vigne di Zamò, Livio Felluga, Marco Felluga, Miani, Pecorari, Polencic, Primosic, Princic, Puiatti, Rodaro, Ronco dei Tassi, Ronco del Gelso, Ronco del Gnemiz, Russiz Superiore, Schioppetto, Scubla, Toros, Venica & Venica, Villa Russiz and Volpe Pasini. Other white varieties grown in these areas include chardonnay and ribolla gialla, a local grape that makes for fresh and lemony wines. Finally, there is Picolit, the expensive Italian take on Sauternes, made from partially dried grapes.

Prosecco di Conegliano & Valdobbiadene: The classic Veneto dry white fizz, prosecco comes from vineyards around Valdobbiadene and Conegliano. The most highly prized version of prosecco is known as Cartizze. A more rustic, unfizzy version – known as *prosecco spento* or simply *spento* – is served by the glass in *bàcari*. The best producers include Bortolomiol, Bisol, Col Vetoraz, Le Colture, Nino Franco and Ruggeri & Co.

Do Mori claims to be the oldest *bàcaro* in Venice, dating back to 1462. Copper pans hang from the ceiling, and at peak times the narrow bar is a heaving mass of bodies lunging for the excellent mini-sandwiches and fine wines. Don't point to a label at random, as prices can sometimes be in the connoisseur bracket. You won't go far wrong if you stick to a glass of the classic *spento* – prosecco minus the bubbles.

Muro Rialto

San Polo 222, campo Cesare Battisti già Bella Vienna (041 241 2339, www. murovenezia.com). Vaporetto Rialto. **Open** 9am-3pm, 4pm-2am Mon-Sat; 4pm-2am Sun. **€€. Map** p109 F3 ❽
Sleek, stylish Muro attracts throngs of sophisticated *spritz*-seekers. There's something for everyone here – from *aperitivi* and *cicheti* at the spacious downstairs bar and outside tables, to eclectic fine dining on the first floor. Staff are friendly. Branches Muro San Stae (Santa Croce 2048, campiello dello Spezier, 041 524 1629) and Muro Frari (San Polo 2604B-C, 041 524 5310) serve pizza plus mainly seafood fare.

Naranzaria

San Polo 130, Erbaria (041 724 1035, www.naranzaria.it). Vaporetto Rialto or Rialto Mercato. **Open** noon-2am Tue-Sun. Closed 10 days Jan. **Map** p109 F3 ❾
From a superb location – one side gives on to campo San Giacomo, the other on to the market and the Grand Canal – this *nouveau-bàcaro* offers a selection of fine wines, many of them produced by co-owner Brandino Brandolini. There's also a restaurant but you're best opting for liquid refreshment and moving on: prices are high and the vibe is not always friendly.

Shopping

Attombri

San Polo 65, sottoportego degli Orafi (041 521 2524, www.attombri.com). Vaporetto Rialto or Rialto Mercato.

VENICE BY AREA

Open 9am-1.30pm Mon, Fri; 9am-1.30pm, 2-6.30pm Tue-Thur; 10am-6.30pm Sat. **Map** p109 F3 ➓
Underneath the arches of the Rialto bridge, jewellers Stefano and Daniele Attombri peddle their sumptuous creations. Intricate, unique pieces combine metal wire and antique Venetian glass beads, or blown glass cameos of their own design. They also produce homewares, including mirrors and lamps.

Drogheria Mascari
San Polo 381, ruga degli Spezieri (041 522 9762, www.imascari.com). Vaporetto Rialto Mercato. **Open** 8am-1pm, 4-7.30pm Mon-Sat. No credit cards. **Map** p109 F3 ⓫
This wonderful old-fashioned grocery shop is the best place to find exotic spices, nuts, dried fruit and mushrooms, as well as oils and wines from different regions in Italy. Coffee, loose-leaf tea and infusions are also stocked.

Piedàterre
San Polo 60, sottoportego degli Orafi (041 528 5513, www.piedaterre-venice.com). Vaporetto Rialto or Rialto Mercato. **Open** 10am-12.30pm, 2.30-7.30pm Mon-Sat. **Map** p109 F3 ⓬
Furlane (or *friulane*) are the traditional slipper-like shoes that you'll see on the feet of many gondoliers. In this little shop, brilliantly coloured bundles of them line the walls. The design is traditional, as is the use of recycled materials such as old tyres to make the soles. But the colours and textiles are eye-catchingly modern. There are shoes here for adults and children.

West from the Rialto
The route to campo San Polo traverses a series of busy shopping streets, passing the church of **San Giovanni Elemosinario** and the deconsecrated church of Sant'Aponal, which has fine Gothic sculpture on its façade. To the south of this route, towards the Grand Canal, stands **San Silvestro**, while to

the north is a fascinating network of little-visited alleys and courtyards.

After the shadowy closeness of these *calli*, the open expanse of **campo San Polo** – home to the church of the same name – comes as a sunlit surprise. It's the largest square on this side of the Grand Canal.

The curving line of *palazzi* on the east side of the square is explained by the fact that these buildings once gave on to a canal, which was subsequently filled in. From the south-west of the square, salizada di San Polo leads to Palazzo Centani, the birthplace of the prolific Venetian playwright Carlo Gondoli, which contains a small theatre studies museum and library: the Casa di Carlo Goldoni (San Polo 2794, calle dei Nomboli, 041 275 9325, www.visitmuve.it).

Sights & museums

San Giovanni Elemosinario
San Polo, ruga vecchia San Giovanni (041 275 0462, www.chorusvenezia.org). Vaporetto Rialto, Rialto Mercato or San Silvestro. **Open** 10am-5pm Mon-Sat. **Admission** €3 (or Chorus; p12). No credit cards. **Map** p109 F3 ⓭
This small Renaissance church – a Greek cross within a square – was founded in the ninth or tenth century but rebuilt after a fire in 1514, probably to a design by Scarpagnino. On the high altar is a painting by Titian of the titular saint, *St John the Alms Giver*.

San Polo
San Polo, campo San Polo (041 275 0462, www.chorusvenezia.org). Vaporetto San Silvestro or San Tomà. **Open** 10am-5pm Mon-Sat. **Admission** €3 (or Chorus; p12). No credit cards. **Map** p109 D4 ⓮
The church of San Polo (Venetian for Paolo, or Paul) faces away from the square, towards the canal, although later buildings have deprived it of its façade and water entrance. The campanile (1362) has two 12th-century lions

at the base, one brooding over a snake and the other toying with a human head. Paintings include a *Last Supper* by Tintoretto, to the left of the entrance, and a Tiepolo: *The Virgin Appearing to St John of Nepomuk*. Giambattista Tiepolo's son, Giandomenico, is the author of a brilliant cycle of *Stations of the Cross* in the Oratory of the Crucifix.

San Silvestro

San Polo, campo San Silvestro (041 523 8090). Vaporetto San Silvestro. **Open** 7.30am-noon, 4-6pm Mon-Sat. Closed some afternoons. **Map** p109 E4 ⑮

San Silvestro was rebuilt in the neo-classical style between 1837 and 1843. The church contains a *Baptism of Christ* (c1580) by Tintoretto, over the first altar on the right. Opposite is *St Thomas à Becket Enthroned* (1520) by Girolamo da Santacroce. Facing the church is the house (no.1022) where the artist Giorgione died in 1510.

Eating & drinking

All'Amarone

San Polo 1131, calle del Luganegher (041 5223 1184, www.allamarone.com). Vaporetto Rialto Mercato or San Silvestro. **Meals served** 10am-10pm Mon, Tue, Thur-Sun. **€€**. **Map** p109 E4 ⑯

A recent addition to the Venetian eating and drinking scene, this low-key wine bar-restaurant has a friendly feel and a very interesting wine list. Run by an Italo-French couple, Amarone offers all the usual Venetian bar snacks, plus sit-down meals of well-prepared and reasonably priced pan-Italian staples, and some good salads at lunch. The wine list leans heavily towards the north-east but also includes some kosher wines.

Antiche Carampane

San Polo 1911, rio terà delle Carampane (041 524 0165, www.antichecarampane. com). Vaporetto San Silvestro. **Meals served** 12.30-2.30pm, 7.30-11pm Tue-Sat. Closed Aug. **€€€**. **Map** p109 E3 ⑰

Fiendishly difficult to find, Antiche Carampane is a Venetian classic. But be warned: there are a lot of tables packed into a very small space; and demand is so great that there are two evening sittings – at 7.30pm and 9.30pm. Arrive late for your slot and your table will have been given away. Diners come for fine seafood that goes beyond the standards, with recherché local specialities such as spaghetti in *cassopipa* (a spicy sauce of shellfish and crustaceans). Leave room for an unbeatable *fritto misto* (mixed seafood fry-up) and the delicious desserts. Inside is cosy; outside is better.

Birraria La Corte

San Polo 2168, campo San Polo (041 275 0570, www.birrarialacorte.it). Vaporetto San Silvestro or San Tomà. **Meals served** noon-2.30pm, 6-10.30pm daily. **€-€€**. **Pizzeria**. **Map** p109 D3 ⑱

The outdoor tables of this huge, no-nonsense pizzeria are a great place to observe life in the campo. The restaurant occupies a former brewery, and beer still takes pride of place over wine. Besides pizza, there are decent pasta options and good grilled-meat *secondi*.

Bar ai Nomboli

San Polo 2717C, rio terà dei Nomboli (041 523 0995). Vaporetto San Tomà. **Open** 7am-9pm Mon-Fri. Closed 3wks Aug. No credit cards. **Map** p108 C4 ⑲

This bar, much loved by Venice's students, has expanded its already impressive repertoire of sandwich combos to more than 100 sandwiches and almost 50 *tramezzini*: try the 'Serenissima' (tuna, peppers, peas, onions); or the 'Appennino' (roast beef, broccoli, pecorino) – or fashion your own creation with their fresh ingredients.

Caffè del Doge

San Polo 609, calle dei Cinque (041 522 7787, www.caffedeldoge.com). Vaporetto Rialto Mercato or San Silvestro. **Open** 7am-7pm Mon-Sat; 7am-1pm Sun. No credit cards. **Map** p109 F4 ⑳

Italians scoff at the idea of drinking cappuccino after 11am, but rules go by the board at the Caffè del Doge, where any time is good for indulging in the richest, creamiest, most luscious cup of coffee in Venice. Two signature blends and a variety of single-origin coffees are available to consume or purchase. Don't overlook the pastries.

Da Ignazio
San Polo 2749, calle dei Saoneri (041 523 4852). Vaporetto San Tomà. **Meals served** noon-3pm, 7-10pm Mon-Fri, Sun. **€€€. Map** p108 C4 ㉑
The big attraction of this tranquil, no-frills restaurant is its pretty, pergola-shaded courtyard. The cooking is safe, traditional Venetian: mixed seafood antipasti might be followed by a good rendition of *spaghetti con caparossoli* or *risi e bisi* (risotto with peas), and grilled fish *secondi*.

Rizzardini
San Polo 1415, campiello dei Meloni (041 522 3835). Vaporetto San Silvestro. **Open** 7am-8.30pm Mon, Wed-Sun. Closed Aug. No credit cards. **Map** p109 E4 ㉒
An eye-catching *pasticceria* with pastries, biscuits and snacks to go with your caffè, cappuccino or aperitivo. When owner Paolo is behind the bar, there's never a dull moment. It's especially good for traditional Venetian pastries, cookies, coffee, *frittelle* during Carnevale… if you can manoeuvre up to the counter and place your order.

Shopping

Aliani Gastronomia
San Polo 654, ruga Rialto/ruga vecchia San Giovanni (041 522 4913). Vaporetto Rialto Mercato or San Silvestro. **Open** 8am-1pm, 5-7.30pm Tue-Sat. **Map** p109 F3 ㉓
This traditional family grocery stocks a selection of cold meats and cheeses from every part of Italy, plus prepared dishes and roast meats.

Atelier Pietro Longhi
San Polo 2608, rio terà dei Frari (041 714 478, www.pietrolonghi.com). Vaporetto San Tomà. **Open** 9am-1pm, 2-6pm Mon-Fri. **Map** p108 C4 ㉔
This atelier makes exquisite period costumes and accessories for rent or purchase. Staff also organise private events and stage historical re-enactments.

Francis Model
San Polo 773A, ruga Rialto/ruga del Ravano (041 521 2889). Vaporetto Rialto Mercato or San Silvestro. **Open** 10am-7pm daily. **Map** p109 F4 ㉕
Beautifully coloured and crafted handbags, belts and briefcases are produced by hand in this tiny *bottega* by a father-and-son team.

Gilberto Penzo
San Polo 2681, calle II dei Saoneri (041 719 372, www.veniceboats.com). Vaporetto San Tomà. **Open** 8.30am-12.30pm, 3-6pm Mon-Sat. **Map** p108 C4 ㉖
Astonishingly detailed models of gondolas, *sandolos*, *topos* and *vaporetti*.

Il Bottegon
San Polo 806, calle del Figher (041 522 3632). Vaporetto San Silvestro. **Open** 9am-12.45pm, 4-7.30pm Mon-Sat. **Map** p109 E3 ㉗
Il Bottegon is one of those 'everything you could possibly need or want' shops: crammed into this tiny space are cosmetics and toiletries, pots, pans, rugs and general hardware. If you don't see what you're looking for, ask: they'll probably pull it out from somewhere.

Sabbie e Nebbie
San Polo 2768A, calle dei Nomboli (041 719 073). Vaporetto San Tomà. **Open** 10am-12.30pm, 4-7.30pm Mon-Sat. **Map** p109 D4 ㉘
A beautiful selection of Italian ceramic pieces are sold alongside refined Japanese works. The shop also sells handmade objects (such as lamps and candlesticks) by Italian designers.

Tragicomica p118

Tragicomica

San Polo 2800, calle dei Nomboli (041 721 102, www.tragicomica.it). Vaporetto San Tomà. **Open** 10am-7pm daily. **Map** p108 C4 ㉙

A spellbinding collection of masks: mythological subjects, Harlequins, Columbines and Pantaloons, as well as 18th-century dandies and ladies.

ZaZú

San Polo 2750, calle II dei Saoneri (041 715 426). Vaporetto San Tomà. **Open** 9.30am-1.30pm, 2.30-7.30pm Mon-Sat. **Map** p108 C4 ㉚

Clothing and jewels from the East that are very wearable in the West. There are handbags and other accessories too.

North-west from the Rialto

Yellow signs pointing to 'Ferrovia' mark the zigzagging north-western route from the Rialto, past the fish market, and on past **campo San Cassiano**. The plain exterior of the church here gives no clue as to its heavily decorated interior.

Across a bridge is **campo Santa Maria Mater Domini** with its Renaissance church. Before entering the campo, stop on the bridge to admire the view of the curving Grand Canal-facing marble flank of **Ca' Pesaro**, the seat of the Museo Orientale and Galleria d'Arte Moderna. On the far side of the square, which contains a number of fine Byzantine and Gothic buildings, the yellow road sign indicates that the way to the station is to the left and to the right. Take your pick.

The quieter route to the right curls parallel to the Grand Canal. Many of the most important sights face on to the Grand Canal, including the 18th-century church of **San Stae** and the Fondaco dei Turchi (Warehouse of the Turks), home to the **Museo di Storia Naturale**.

On the wide road leading towards San Stae is **Palazzo Mocenigo**, with its collection of perfumes, textiles and costumes. Nearby is the quiet square of **San Zan Degolà** (San Giovanni Decollato), with a well-preserved 11th-century church. From here, a series of narrow roads leads past the church of **San Simeone Profeta** to the foot of the Scalzi bridge across the Grand Canal.

Leave campo Santa Maria Mater Domini by the route to the left, on the other hand, and you'll make your way past the near-legendary **Da Fiore** restaurant to the house (no. 2311) where Aldus Manutius set up the Aldine Press in 1490, and where the humanist Erasmus came to stay in 1508. To the right, the rio terà del Parrucchetta leads to the large leafy **campo San Giacomo dell'Orio**.

Sights & museums

Ca' Pesaro – Galleria Internazionale d'Arte Moderna

Santa Croce 2076, fondamenta Ca' Pesaro (041 524 0695, www.visitmuve. it). Vaporetto San Stae. **Open** 10am-5pm Tue-Sun. **Admission** (incl Museo Orientale) €10.50; €8 reductions. See also p12 Museum Passes. **Map** p109 E2 ㉛

This grandiose palazzo passed through many hands until its last owner, Felicita Bevilacqua La Masa, bequeathed it to the city. Into it went the city's collection of modern art. The museum now covers a century of mainly Italian art, from the mid 19th century to the 1950s. There are also pieces by international artists, including Gustav Klimt, Vassily Kandinsky, Joan Mirò and Giorgio De Chirico.

Ca' Pesaro – Museo Orientale

Santa Croce 2070, fondamenta Ca' Pesaro (041 524 1173, www.visitmuve. it). Vaporetto San Stae. **Open** 10am-5pm Tue-Sun. **Admission** (incl Galleria

Internazionale d'Arte Moderna) €10.50; €8 reductions. See also p12 Museum Passes. **Map** p109 E2

If Japanese art and weaponry of the Edo period (1600-1868) are your thing, you'll love this eclectic collection, put together by Count Enrico di Borbone.

Fondazione Prada

Santa Croce 2215, calle de Ca' Corner (041 810 9161, www.prada.com). Vaporetto San Stae. **Open** 10am-6pm Mon, Wed-Sun during exhibitions. **Admission** €10; €8 reductions. **Map** p109 E2

Ca' Corner della Regina is an imposing late 18th-century palace, restored with funds stumped up by fashion designer (and art collector) Miucci Prada. In return she gets to stage contemporary art shows here under the Fondazione Prada banner. Exhibitions explore the relationship between art, architecture and contemporary culture, and include joint initiatives with major museums around the world.

Museo di Storia Naturale

Santa Croce 1730, salizada del Fondaco dei Turchi (041 275 0206, www.visit muve.it). Vaporetto San Stae. **Open** 10am-6pm Tue-Sun. **Admission** €8; €5.50 reductions. See also p12 Museum Passes. **Map** p109 D1

The Fondaco dei Turchi, a Venetian-Byzantine building, houses this natural history museum – now back in business after restoration. Sections include the Acquario delle Tegnue, which is is devoted to the aquatic life of the northern Adriatic, and the Sala dei Dinosauri, which has a state-of-the-art exhibition chronicling the Ligabue expedition to Niger (1973).

Palazzo Mocenigo

Santa Croce 1992, salizada San Stae (041 721 798, www.visitmuve.it). Vaporetto San Stae. **Open** 10am-4pm Tue-Sun. **Admission** €8; €5.50 reductions. See also p12 Museum Passes. No credit cards. **Map** p109 D2

Reopened late in 2013 after a major makeover, Palazzo Mocenigo is now a splendid showcase for the life of the aristocracy in 18th-century Venice. This predominantly 17th-century palazzo was the home of the Mocenigo family, which provided the Republic with seven doges. The contents include paintings, friezes and frescoes; a collection of period costumes; fine furniture and fittings; and a fascinating section on perfumes and perfumery.

San Cassiano

San Polo, campo San Cassiano (041 721 408). Vaporetto Rialto Mercato or San Stae. **Open** 9am-noon, 5-7.30pm Mon-Sat. **Map** p109 E3

San Cassiano's singularly dull exterior contains a heavily decorated interior, with a striking ceiling by Constantino Cedini. The chancel contains three major Tintorettos: *Crucifixion*, *Resurrection* and *Descent into Limbo*. On the wall opposite the altar is a painting by Antonio Balestra, which at first glance looks like a dying saint surrounded by putti. On closer inspection it transpires that the chubby children are, in fact, hacking the man to death: the painting represents *The Martyrdom of St Cassian*, a teacher who was murdered by his pupils with their pens.

San Giacomo dell'Orio

Santa Croce, campo San Giacomo dell'Orio (041 275 0462, www.chorus venezia.org). Vaporetto Riva di Biasio. **Open** 10am-5pm Mon-Sat. **Admission** €3 (or Chorus; p12). No credit cards. **Map** p108 C2

The interior of San Giacomo dell'Orio is a fascinating mix of architectural and decorative styles. Most of the columns have 12th- or 13th-century Veneto-Byzantine capitals. Note, too, the fine 14th-century ship's-keel roof.

The Sacrestia Nuova has five gilded compartments on the ceiling with paintings by Veronese: an *Allegory of the Faith* surrounded by four *Doctors of the Church*. Among the paintings

VENICE BY AREA

in the room is *St John the Baptist Preaching* by Francesco Bassano, which includes a portrait of Titian (in the red hat). Behind the high altar is a *Madonna and Four Saints* by Lorenzo Lotto. There is a good work by Giovanni Bonconsiglio at the end of the left aisle: *St Lawrence, St Sebastian and St Roch*. St Lawrence also has a chapel all to himself in the left transept, with a central altarpiece by Veronese and two fine early works by Palma il Giovane.

San Giovanni Decollato (San Zan Degolà)

Santa Croce, campo San Giovanni Decollato (041 524 0672). Vaporetto Riva di Biasio. **Open** 10am-noon Mon-Sat. **Map** p108 C1 ㊳

The church of Headless Saint John – or San Zan Degolà in Venetian dialect – is a good building to visit if you want a relief from Baroque excesses and ecclesiastic clutter. Restored and reopened in 1994, it preserves much of its original 11th-century appearance. The interior has Greek columns with Byzantine capitals supporting ogival arches, and an attractive ship's-keel roof. During the restoration, a splendidly heroic 14th-century fresco of *St Michael the Archangel* came to light in the right apse. The left apse has some of the earliest frescoes in Venice: Veneto-Byzantine works of the early 13th century. The church is used for Russian Orthodox services.

San Simeone Profeta

Santa Croce, campo San Simeone Profeta (041 718 921). Vaporetto Ferrovia. **Open** 9am-noon, 5-6.30pm Mon-Sat. **Map** p108 B2 ㊳

More usually known as San Simeone Grande, this small church of possibly tenth-century foundation underwent numerous alterations in the 18th century. The interior retains its ancient columns with Byzantine capitals. To the left of the entrance is Tintoretto's *Last Supper.* The other major work is the stark, powerful statue of a recumbent St Simeon.

San Stae

Santa Croce, campo San Stae (041 275 0462, www.chorusvenezia.org). Vaporetto San Stae. **Open** 10am-5pm Mon-Sat. **Admission** €3 (or Chorus; p12). No credit cards. **Map** p109 D2 ㊵

Stae is the Venetian version of Eustachio or Eustace, a martyred saint who was converted to Christianity by the vision of a stag with a crucifix between its antlers. This church has a dramatic late-Baroque façade (1709) by Swiss-born architect Domenico Rossi. The interior is a temple to Venice's last great blaze of artistic glory. All the leading painters operating in Venice in 1722 were asked to pick an apostle. The finest of these are: Tiepolo's *Martyrdom of St Bartholomew* and Sebastiano Ricci's *Liberation of St Peter,* perhaps his best work (both left wall chancel, lower row); Pellegrini's *Martyrdom of St Andrew* and Piazzetta's *Martyrdom of St James* (both right wall, lower row).

Santa Maria Mater Domini

Santa Croce, calle della Chiesa (041 721 408). Vaporetto San Stae. **Open** 10am-noon daily. **Map** p109 D2 ㊶

This church was built in the first half of the 16th century. The façade is attributed to Jacopo Sansovino; the harmonious Renaissance interior alternates grey stone with white marble. *The Vision of St Christine,* on the second altar on the right, is by Vincenzo Catena, a spice merchant who painted in his spare time. In the left transept hangs *The Invention of the Cross,* a youthful work by Tintoretto.

Eating & drinking

Al Nono Risorto

Santa Croce 2338, sottoportico di Siora Bettina (041 524 1169). Vaporetto San Stae. **Meals served** noon-2.30pm, 7-11pm Mon, Tue, Fri-Sun; 7-11pm Thur. €-€€. No credit cards. **Pizzeria.** **Map** p109 E3 ㊷

You don't come to this spit and sawdust trattoria-pizzeria for culinary excellence,

top: Museo di Storia Naturale
p119; bottom: San Stae

but if you're looking for a pleasant courtyard in which to sit among noisy diners tucking into decent pizzas, then it might be for you. Traditional Venetian trattoria fare is also offered.

Al Prosecco

Santa Croce 1503, campo San Giacomo dell'Orio (041 524 0222, www.al prosecco.com). Vaporetto San Stae. **Open** 9am-10pm Mon-Sat. **Map** p108 C2 ④③
Prosecco – whether sparkling or still (aka *spento*) – is second only to *spritz* in terms of daily Venetian consumption, and (as the name suggests) this bar is a good place for consuming it. But you can also drop by here for morning coffee or a light lunch. The shaded outdoor tables are a fantastic vantage point. Exceptional wines are served by the glass, accompanied by a first-rate choice of cheeses, cold meats, marinated fish and oysters. Note that it closes around 8pm in winter.

Alaska Gelateria-Sorbetteria

Santa Croce 1159, calle larga dei Bari (041 715 211). Vaporetto Riva di Biasio. **Open** *Apr-Oct* 11am-midnight daily. *Feb-Mar & Nov* noon-9pm daily. Closed Dec-Jan. No credit cards. **Map** p108 B2 ④④
There are tried and true choices here, such as hazelnut, pistachio or yoghurt, and seasonally changing exotic flavours, such as artichoke, fennel, asparagus or ginger. To those who appreciate the eccentric flavours, Carlo Pistacchi's ice-cream is some of Venice's best.

Alla Zucca

Santa Croce 1762, ponte del Megio (041 524 1570, www.lazucca.it). Vaporetto San Stae. **Meals served** 12.30-2.30pm, 7-10.30pm Mon-Sat. **€€**. **Map** p109 D2 ④⑤
One of Venice's first 'alternative' *trattorie* and still one of the best – not to mention one of the best-value. By a pretty bridge, the vegetarian-friendly Pumpkin offers a break from all that seafood. The menu is equally divided between meat (ginger pork with pilau

rice) and vegetables (pumpkin and seasoned ricotta quiche). Book ahead, especially for one of the few outside tables.

Da Fiore

San Polo 2202, calle dello Scaleter (041 721 308, www.dafiore.net). Vaporetto San Stae or San Tomà. **Meals served** 7.30-10.30pm Mon; 12.30-2.30pm, 7.30-10.30pm Tue-Sat. **€€€€**. **Map** p109 D3 ④⑥
Da Fiore is considered by many to be Venice's best restaurant. Host Maurizio Martin treats his guests with egalitarian courtesy, while his wife Mara concentrates on getting the food right. Raw fish and seafood is a key feature of the antipasti; *primi* are equally divided between pasta dishes and a series of faultless risottos. *Secondi* are all about bringing out the flavour of the fish without smothering it in sauce. It's a classic, rather than a superlative, dining experience; but that's Venice for you.

Il Refolo

Santa Croce 1459, campiello del Piovan (041 524 0016, www.rist-refolo.it). Vaporetto Riva di Biasio or San Stae. **Meals served** 7-11pm Tue; noon-3pm, 7-11pm Wed-Sun. **€€**. **Pizzeria**. **Map** p108 C2 ④⑦
The pizzeria offshoot of Michelin-starred Da Fiore (above), Il Refolo (the sea breeze) serves up a small, daily-changing selection of well crafted pizzas to a less moneyed demographic than its expensive parent. Fresh-from-Naples ingredients top thick-crust pizzas; Mara Martin, chef at Da Fiore, oversees a selection of pasta and fish dishes. The indoor space is tiny (book to be sure of getting a table), but there are tables out on a lively campo.

Majer

Santa Croce 1658, campo San Giacomo dell'Orio (041 710 677, www.majer.it). Vaporetto San Stae. **Open** 7.30am-10pm daily. **Map** p108 C2 ④⑧
Everywhere you look in Venice, a sleek new branch of this hyperactive

café-store seems to be luring in passersby with the smell of freshly made *cornetti* and loaves: there's another on this same campo at no.1630. Most of the outlets have tables at which to consume an excellent cappuccino with a delicious pastry. Most also serve light lunches and snacks throughout the day. But there are also wine, bread, cakes and their own-brand coffee to take away.

Vecio Fritolin

Santa Croce 2262, calle della Regina (041 522 2881, www.veciofritolin.it). Vaporetto San Stae. **Meals served** 7-10.30pm Tue; noon-2.30pm, 7-10.30pm Wed-Sun. **€€€. Map** p109 E2 ㊾

Wooden beams, sturdy tables and the long bar at the back of the main dining room set the mood in this old-style *bàcaro*. But the seasonally changing menu is more creative than the decor might lead you to expect, with dishes such as turbot in a crust of black rice with sautéed baby artichokes.

Shopping

Laberintho

San Polo 2236, calle del Scaleter (041 710 017, www.laberintho.it). Vaporetto San Stae or San Tomà. **Open** 10.30am-1pm, 3-6.30pm Mon, Sat; 9.15am-1pm, 3-7.15pm Tue-Fri. **Map** p109 D3 ㊿

The pair of goldsmiths who work in this tiny *bottega* produce startling retro and contemporary designs in gold, plus some (less expensive lines) in silver.

Monica Daniele

San Polo 2235, calle Scaleter (041 524 6242, www.monicadaniele.com). Vaporetto San Silvestro or San Stae. **Open** 9am-1pm, 2.30-6pm Mon-Sat. **Map** p109 D3 (51)

Monica Daniele has single-handedly brought the *tabarro* – that sweeping cloak seen in many an 18th-century Venetian print – back into vogue: a heavy woollen one will cost €500 or more. There's also a range of hats.

Rialto Biocenter

San Polo 2264, calle della Regina (041 523 9515, www.rialtobiocenter.it). Vaporetto Rialto Mercato or San Stae. **Open** 8.30am-1pm, 4.30-8pm Mon-Thur; 8.30am-8pm Fri, Sat. **Map** p109 E3 (52)

A little bit of just about everything can be found in this health-food shop, from wholemeal pasta, grains, organic fruit and veg, and freshly baked breads to natural cosmetics and incense.

From the Frari to piazzale Roma

At the heart of the western side of the two *sestieri* of San Polo and Santa Croce lies the great gothic bulk of **Santa Maria Gloriosa dei Frari** (aka I Frari), with its 70-metre (230-foot) campanile, matched by the Renaissance magnificence of the *scuola* and church of **San Rocco**. These buildings contain perhaps the greatest concentration of influential works of art in the city outside piazza San Marco and the Accademia. Beyond the Frari is the **Scuola di San Giovanni Evangelista**, one of the six *scuole grandi*.

North of here runs rio Marin, a canal with *fondamente* on both sides, lined by some fine buildings; these include the late 16th-century Palazzo Soranzo Capello (no.770), with a small rear garden that figures in Henry James's *The Aspern Papers*; and the 17th-century Palazzo Gradenigo (no.768), the garden of which was once large enough to host bullfights.

South-west of the Frari is the quiet square of San Tomà, with a church on one side and the Scuola dei Calegheri ('of the cobblers') opposite.

Heading west from the Frari, past the church and *scuola* of San Rocco (both treasure troves for Tintoretto-lovers), the route ends in a bland area of 19th-century housing. At the edge of this stands the Baroque church of **San Nicolò dei Tolentini**.

I Frari

Sights & museums

I Frari

San Polo, campo dei Frari (041 522 2637, www.chorusvenezia.org). Vaporetto San Tomà. **Open** 9am-6pm Mon-Sat; 1-6pm Sun. **Admission** €3 (or Chorus; p12). No credit cards. **Map** p108 C4 ⊗

This gloomy Gothic barn, known officially as Santa Maria Gloriosa dei Frari, is one of the city's most significant artistic storehouses. It's also one of the best places for catching high-standard performances of scared music. The church is 98m (320ft) long, 48m (158ft) wide at the transept and 28m (92ft) high – just slightly smaller than the Dominicans' Santi Giovanni e Paolo (p76) – and has the second highest campanile in the city.

Right aisle

In the second bay, on the spot where Titian is believed to be buried (the only victim of the 1575-76 plague who was allowed a city burial), is a loud monument to the artist. On the third altar is a finer memorial, Alessandro Vittoria's statue of St Jerome.

Right transept

To the right of the sacristy door is the tomb of the Blessed Pacifico, attributed to Nanni di Bartolo and Michele da Firenze (1437); the sarcophagus is surrounded by a splendidly carved canopy in the florid Gothic style. The third chapel on the right side of this transept has an altarpiece by Bartolomeo Vivarini, in its original frame, while the Florentine Chapel, next to the chancel, contains the only work by Donatello in the city: a striking wooden statue of a stark, emaciated St John the Baptist.

Sacristy

This contains one of Giovanni Bellini's greatest paintings: the *Madonna and Child with Saints Nicholas, Peter, Benedict and Mark* (1488), still in its original frame.

Chancel

The high altar is dominated by Titian's *Assumption*, a work that seems to open the church up to the heavens. The left wall hosts one of the finest Renaissance tombs in Venice, the monument to Doge Niccolò Tron, by Antonio Rizzo (1473).

Monks' choir

The choir has wooden stalls carved by Marco Cozzi (1468), inlaid with superb intarsia decoration.

Left transept

In the third chapel, with an altarpiece by Bartolomeo Vivarini and Marco Basaiti, a slab on the floor marks the grave of composer Claudio Monteverdi. The Corner chapel, at the end, contains a mannered statue of St John the Baptist by Sansovino.

Left aisle

Another magnificent Titian hangs to the right of the side door: the *Madonna di Ca' Pesaro*. This work celebrates victory in a naval expedition against the Turks in 1502, and it revolutionised altar paintings in Venice. Titian dared to move the Virgin from the centre of the composition; but the real innovation was the rich humanity of the work.

The whole of the next bay, around the side door, is occupied by the mastodontic mausoleum of Doge Pesaro (d.1659), attributed to Longhena, with sculptures by Melchior Barthel of Dresden. The penultimate bay has a monument to Canova; his body is buried in his native town of Possagno, but his heart is here.

San Nicolò da Tolentino

Santa Croce, campo dei Tolentini (041 710 806). Vaporetto Piazzale Roma. **Open** 8.30am-noon, 4.30-6.30pm Mon-Sat; 4.30-6.30pm Sun. **Map** p108 A3 ⊗

This church (1591-95), usually known as I Tolentini, was designed by Vincenzo Scamozzi. Its unfinished façade has a massive Corinthian portico (1706-14) by Andrea Tirali. The interior is a riot of Baroque decoration. On the wall outside the chancel to the left is *St Jerome Succoured by an Angel* by Flemish artist Johann Liss. Outside the chapel in the left transept is *The Charity of St Lawrence* by the Genoese Bernardo Strozzi, while in the chancel hangs an *Annunciation* by Neapolitan Luca Giordano.

San Rocco

San Polo, campo San Rocco (041 523 4864). Vaporetto San Tomà. **Open** 9.30am-5.30pm daily. **Map** p108 B4 ⑮

Built in Venetian Renaissance style (1489-1508) by Bartolomeo Bon, but radically altered by Giovanni Scalfarotto in 1725, the church has various paintings by Tintoretto, or his school. Nearly all are connected with the life of St Roch; the best is probably *St Roch Cures the Plague Victims* (chancel, lower right).

Scuola Grande di San Giovanni Evangelista

San Polo 2454, campiello della Scuola (041 718 234, www.scuolasangiovanni. it). Vaporetto San Tomà. **Open** 9.30am-5pm daily. Closed during conferences; see website. **Admission** €5; €3 reductions. No credit cards. **Map** p108 C3 ⑯

The Scuola Grande di San Giovanni Evangelista is one of the six *scuole grandi* (devotional lay brotherhoods); founded in 1261, it is the most ancient of the still-existing *scuole* and one of Venice's most magnificent structures.

The *scuola* stands in a small courtyard, at the entrance of which is a screen with a superb eagle pediment carved by Pietro Lombardo. The ground-floor, with the large Sala delle Colonne, mostly maintains its medieval aspect.

The upper floor is accessed by a magnificent double staircase, a masterpiece by Renaissance architect Mauro Codussi. The decoration in the Sala Capitolare is mainly 18th century. The floor is especially fine, with its geometrical patterns of multi-coloured marbles that mirror the arrangement of the ceiling paintings. The walls are hung with 17th- and 18th-century paintings recounting the life of St John the Evangelist, by Domenico Tintoretto and others.

The Sala dell'Albergo contains a series of paintings by Palma il Giovane. The most spirited of these is *St John's Vision of the Four Horsemen.*

Scuola Grande di San Rocco

San Polo 3054, campo San Rocco (041 523 4864, www.scuolagrandesan rocco.it). Vaporetto San Tomà. **Open** 9.30am-5.30pm daily. **Admission** €10; €8 reductions. **Map** p108 B4 ⑰

The Archbrotherhood of St Roch was the richest of the six *scuole grandi* in 15th-century Venice. It was dedicated to Venice's other patron saint, the French plague protector and dog-lover St Roch (also known as St Rock or San Rocco), whose body was brought here in 1485.

The architecture, by Bartolomeo Bon and Scarpagnino, is far less impressive than the interior decoration, which was entrusted to Tintoretto in 1564. In three intensive sessions spread out over the following 23 years, San Rocco became his epic masterpiece. To follow the development of Tintoretto's style, pick up the free explanatory leaflet and the audio guide and begin in the smaller upstairs hall – the Albergo. Here, filling up the whole of the far wall, is the *Crucifixion* (1565).

Tintoretto began work on the larger upstairs room in 1575, with Old Testament stories on the ceiling and a Life of Christ cycle around the walls.

Finally, in the ground-floor hall – which the artist decorated between 1583 and 1587, when he was in his sixties – the paintings reach a visionary pitch. *The Annunciation*, with its domestic Mary surprised while sewing, and *Flight into Egypt*, with its verdant landscape, are among the painter's masterpieces.

Eating & drinking

Caffè Dersut

San Polo 3014, campo dei Frari (041 303 2159). Vaporetto San Tomà. **Open** 6am-8pm Mon-Sat; 8am-2pm Sun. No credit cards. **Map** p108 C4 ㉝

An outlet for the Treviso-based coffee roasters of the same name, the café serves excellent breakfast coffee and pastries, good fresh fruit juices and smoothies, plus sandwiches.

Da Lele

Santa Croce 183, campo dei Tolentini (no phone). Vaporetto Piazzale Roma. **Open** 6am-8pm Mon-Fri; 6am-2pm Sat. No credit cards. **Map** p108 A4 ⑤⑨

Gabriele's (Lele's) place is the first authentic *osteria* for those arriving in Venice – or the last for those leaving. Look for the two barrels outside – and the crowds of people milling – and you've found this Venetian institution. It's very small – but there are local wines from Piave, Lison and Valdobbiadene, as well as rolls that are filled to order with meat and/or cheese. A basic but good glass of chardonnay costs just 60c, a mini panino 90c. Don't bother asking for coffee: there's no room for a machine.

Frary's

San Polo 2559, fondamenta dei Frari (041 720 050). Vaporetto San Tomà. **Meals served** noon-3pm, 6-11pm Mon, Wed-Sun. €€. **Middle Eastern**. **Map** p108 C4 ⑥⓪

A friendly, reasonably priced spot specialising in Arab cuisine, though there are some Greek and Kurdish dishes too, plus gluten-free options. Couscous comes with a variety of sauces: vegetarian, mutton, chicken or seafood. The *mansaf* (rice with chicken, almonds and yoghurt) is good.

Pasticceria Rio Marin

Santa Croce 784, rio Marin (041 718 523). Vaporetto Riva di Biasio. **Open** 6.30am-8pm Mon, Tue, Thur-Sun. Closed Aug. **Map** p108 B2 ⑥①

Bianca and Dario's delicious cakeshop offers a world of choice, for consumption with a coffee or drink at one of the tables along the rio Marin, or to take away.

Shopping

Ceramiche La Margherita

Santa Croce 659, corte Canal (393 210 0272, www.lamargheritavenezia.com). Vaporetto San Stae. **Open** 9.30am-1pm, 3.30-7pm Mon-Sat. **Map** p108 B2 ⑥②

A delightful collection of hand-painted terracotta designed by the owner.

Coop

Santa Croce 506A, piazzale Roma (041 296 0621). Vaporetto Piazzale Roma. **Open** 8.30am-8pm daily. **Map** p108 A3 ⑥③

Coop and InCoop cornershops are dotted all over; most are open Monday to Saturday; if you need to restock on Sunday, you'll need to make your way to piazzale Roma. This is good supermarket food at good prices (for Venice). This branch caters to tourists, with a salad bar, snacks and Venetian specialities.

Guarinoni

San Polo 2861, calle del Mandoler (041 522 4286). Vaporetto San Tomà. **Open** 9am-noon, 3-7pm Mon-Sat. **Map** p108 C4 ⑥④

An assortment of antique furnishings from as early as the 16th century is sold here. The shop also has a workshop that restores gilded ceilings.

VizioVirtù

San Polo 2898A, calle del Campaniel (041 275 0149, www.viziovirtu.com). Vaporetto San Tomà. **Open** 10am-7.30pm daily. **Map** p108 C5 ⑥⑤

At the San Tomà vaporetto stop, VizioVirtù serves up gluttonous pleasures. Witness chocolate being made while nibbling on a spicy praline or sipping an iced chocolate.

Arts & leisure

Palazzo Bru Zane

San Polo 2368, campiello Forner (041 521 1005, www.bru-zane.com). Vaporetto San Stae or San Tomà. **Map** p108 C3 ⑥⑥

Stuccoed and frescoed Palazzo Bru Zane is home to the Centre for French Romantic Music, a research and performance institute that hosts concerts, operas and seminars, and special musical events for children. There are free tours of the palazzo every Thursday, at 2.30pm (Italian), 3pm (French) and 3.30pm (English). Check the website for programme details.

Punta della Dogana p143

Dorsoduro

Cradling the southern flank of
Venice proper, Dorsoduro –
literally 'hard back' – stretches from
its smart, artsy eastern district of
elegant *palazzi* and quiet *campielli* to
the little-visited docks and university
area in the *sestiere*'s far western
reaches. The concentration of art –
from the very contemporary at the
Punta della Dogana through the
modern at the Peggy Guggenheim
Collection to the grand masters at the
Gallerie dell'Accademia – is amazing.
But there are fine churches here too,
including the magnificent Santa
Maria della Salute. In between the
geographical and social extremes
comes the democratic and buzzing
campo Santa Margherita, around
which much of the city's nightlife
action takes place.

West

This was one of the first areas in the
lagoon to be settled. Locals have never

been in the top income bracket (in the
past, they were mostly fishermen or
salt-pan workers) and the area is still
noticeably less sleek than the centre,
although fishing was superseded
as a source of employment by the
port long ago, and subsequently
by the Santa Marta cotton mill –
now stunningly converted into
the **Istituto Universitario di
Architettura di Venezia (IUAV)**.
Ambitious schemes to redevelop
the area fell through and the two
universities of Venice turned to a
more modest development plan,
converting some of the warehouses
into classrooms and lecture halls;
these constitute the Polo didattica di
San Basilio, which was inaugurated
in March 2008.

Moving eastwards, the
atmosphere remains unpretentious
around the churches of **Angelo
Raffaele** and **San Sebastiano**.
Northwards from here, on the rio di
Santa Margherita, are some grander

palazzi, including **Palazzo Ariani** and **Palazzo Zenobio**.

On the southern shore, the final and widest stretch of the **Zattere** passes several notable *palazzi*, including the 17th-century façade of the **Scuola dei Luganegheri** (sausage-makers' school).

Sights & museums

Angelo Raffaele

Dorsoduro, campo Angelo Raffaele (041 522 8548). Vaporetto San Basilio. **Open** 9am-5.30pm daily. **Map** p130 A3 ❶
Tradition has it that this church was founded by St Magnus in the eighth century, but the present free-standing building – one of only two churches in the city that you can walk around – dates from the 17th century. The jewels of the church are on the organ loft, where five compartments, painted by Giovanni Antonio Guardi (or perhaps his brother Francesco), recount the story of *Tobias and the Angel* (1750-53). They are works of dazzling luminosity, quite unlike anything else done in Venice at the time.

Palazzo Zenobio

Dorsoduro 2598, fondamenta del Soccorso (041 241 2397). Vaporetto San Basilio. **Open** events only. **Map** p130 B2 ❷
Built towards the end of the 17th century to a design by Antonio Gaspari, Palazzo Zenobio's broad façade and two wings extending backwards are an unusual design for Venice. It is used as a guesthouse (very basic rooms; 06 8530 1756) and as a venue for exhibitions: grab any opportunity to get inside. The interior is sumptuously decorated with 18th-century frescoes and stucco-work. The showpiece is the Sala degli Specchi, the ballroom frescoed by the French artist Louis Dorigny.

San Nicolò dei Mendicoli

Dorsoduro, campo San Nicolò (041 275 0382). Vaporetto San Basilio or Santa Marta. **Open** 10am-noon, 4-7pm daily. **Map** p130 A3 ❸

One of the few Venetian churches to have maintained its 13th-century Veneto-Byzantine structure, despite numerous refurbishments over the years. The 15th-century loggia at the front is one of only two extant examples of a once-common architectural feature; it originally served as a shelter for the homeless. The interior contains a marvellous mishmash of architectural and decorative styles that creates an effect of cluttered charm. The paintings are mainly 17th century.

San Sebastiano

Dorsoduro, fondamenta di San Sebastiano (041 275 0642, www.chorusvenezia.org). Vaporetto San Basilio. **Open** 10am-5pm Mon-Sat. **Admission** €3 (or Chorus; p12). No credit cards. **Map** p130 A3 ❹
This contains perhaps the most brilliantly colourful church interior in Venice, and it's all the work of one man: Paolo Veronese (who is buried here). His first commission was for the sacristy. From then on, there was no stopping him: between 1556 and 1565 he completed three large ceiling paintings for the nave of the church, frescoes along the upper parts of the walls, organ shutters, huge narrative canvases for the chancel, and the painting on the high altar.

The ceiling paintings depict scenes from the life of Esther and are full of sumptuous pageantry. The enormous canvases on the side walls of the chancel depict, on the right, *The Martyrdom of St Sebastian* and, on the left, *St Sebastian Encouraging St Mark and St Marcellan*. Other paintings in the church include *St Nicholas*, a late painting by Titian, in the first altar on the right.

The sacristy (10am-5pm Sat, 1-5pm Sun) contains ceiling paintings of the *Coronation of the Virgin* and the four panels of *The Evangelists*, which are among Veronese's earliest works in Venice (1555). Around the walls are works by Bonifacio de' Pitati and others. Restoration work on the frescoes and structure of the church is ongoing.

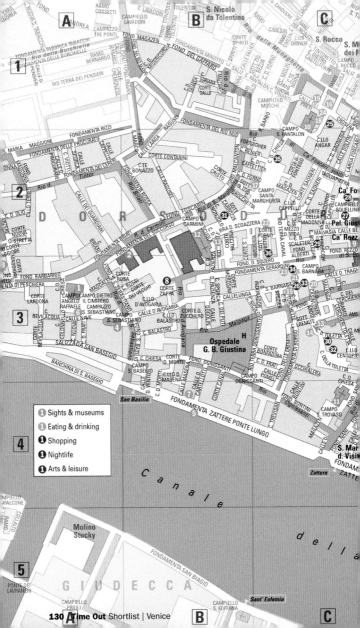

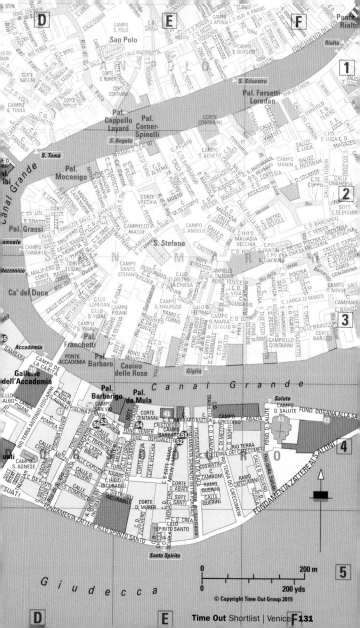

El Chioschetto

Dorsoduro 1406A, fondamenta delle Zattere (348 396 8466 mobile). Vaporetto Zattere. **Open** *Mar-Nov* 8.30am-2am daily. *Jan, Feb, Dec* weather permitting. No credit cards. **Map** p130 B4 **⑤**

A much-loved spot not only for scrumptious panini and nibbles, but also for the tranquillity of sitting outside along the Giudecca Canal with a glass of wine and a sweeping view. There is no inside seating. From April to September, there's blues and jazz out on the *fondamenta* on Wednesday and Sunday evenings (6-9pm).

Pane, Vino e San Daniele

Dorsoduro 1722, campo dell'Angelo Raffaele (041 523 7456). Vaporetto San Basilio. **Meals served** noon-2.30pm, 7-10.15pm daily. **€€. Map** p130 A3 **⑥**

This nouvelle-*osteria* belongs to a chain specialising in the wine and ham of the Friuli region. But the place has a character of its own, determined partly by its high proportion of university patrons, and partly by the fact that the Friulian imprint is varied by dishes reflecting the chef's Sardinian roots, including *coniglio al mirto* (rabbit baked with myrtle). If you just want a drink in the pretty square, it functions as a bar all day (9am-11pm daily). There's another super-friendly and equally good branch nearby at Calle Lungo San Barnaba 3012.

Riviera

Dorsoduro 1473, fondamenta Zattere Ponte Longo (041 522 7621). Vaporetto San Basilio or Zattere. **Meals served** 12.30-3pm, 7-10.30pm Tue-Sun. **€€€€. Map** p130 B4 **⑦**

Riviera is rarely less than an experience. The setting is spectacular: in warm weather, tables on the *fondamenta* afford views across the splendid Giudecca canal, to San Giorgio Maggiore and the Redentore. The service is warm, the ever-present owner – former musician GP Cremonini – makes your enjoyment his business. What's on the plate – mainly but not solely seafood based – is creative, excellent… and pricey: this is a place for special occasions.

Arts & leisure

Teatro a l'Avogaria

Dorsoduro 1607, corte Zappa (041 099 1967, www.teatro-avogaria.it). Vaporetto Ca' Rezzonico or San Basilio. No credit cards. **Map** p130 B3 **⑧**

This experimental theatre (entry to which is by voluntary donation) was founded in 1969 by renowned director Giovanni Poli. Since his death in 1979, Poli's disciples have pressed on with his experimental work, staging plays by lesser-known writers from the 15th to 19th centuries. Places must be booked at the number above between 2.30 and 4.30pm. The theatre opens its doors 15 minutes before performances.

North & centre

A long, irregular-shaped campo with churches at both ends, **campo Santa Margherita** buzzes day and night. There are several ancient *palazzi* around the square. Isolated in the middle is the **Scuola dei Varoteri**, the School of the Tanners. At the north end is the former church of Santa Margherita, long used as a cinema and now beautifully restored as a conference hall for the university. At the other end of the square are the **scuola** and **church of the Carmini**.

North out of Santa Margherita is **campo San Pantalon**. Leaving campo Santa Margherita by the southern end, you reach the charming rio di San Barnaba. At the eastern end of the *fondamenta* is the entrance to **Ca' Rezzonico**, now the museum of 18th-century Venice.

The middle of the three bridges across the canal is ponte dei Pugni, with white marble footprints

San Pantalon p134

indicating that this was one of the bridges where punch-ups were held between the rival factions of the *nicolotti*, from the western quarters of the city, and the *castellani*, from the east. These violent brawls were tolerated by the authorities, who saw them as a chance for the working classes to let off steam in a way that was not disruptive to the state. They were banned, however, in 1705, after a particularly bloody fray.

Across the bridge is campo San Barnaba. The church of San Barnaba (often used for contemporary art shows) has a picturesque 14th-century campanile; the campo is a fine place for sitting outside a bar and watching the world go by.

On the campo of the same name is the church of **San Trovaso**; backing on to the campo is a picturesque *squero*, one of the few remaining yards where gondolas are made.

Sights & museums

Ca' Rezzonico (Museo del Settecento Veneziano)

Dorsoduro 3136, fondamenta Rezzonico (041 241 0100, www.visitmuve.it). Vaporetto Ca' Rezzonico. **Open** 10am-5pm Mon, Wed-Sun. **Admission** €8; €5.50 reductions. See also p12 **Museum Passes. Map** p130 C2 ❾

The Museum of 18th-century Venice is a gleaming (if somewhat chilly) showcase for the art of the Republic's twilight years. For most visitors, the paintings on display here will appear less impressive than the palazzo itself, an imposing Grand Canal affair designed by Baldassare Longhena.

The Sala del Trono has a ceiling by Giambattista Tiepolo; Giovanni Battista Crosato's over-the-top ceiling frescoes in the ballroom have aged less well, together with the Murano chandeliers and intricately carved furniture by Andrea Brustolon, they provide an accurate record of the lifestyles of the rich and famous at the time.

There are historical canvases by Giovanni Battista Piazzetta and Antonio Diziani, plus other gems such as detached frescoes of *pulcinellas* by Giandomenico Tiepolo. A staircase at the far end of the entrance hall leads to the 'Mezzanino Browning', where the poet Robert Browning died in 1889. This contains the Mestrovich Collection of Veneto paintings.

San Pantalon

Dorsoduro, campo San Pantalon (041 523 5893). Vaporetto San Tomà. **Open** 10am-noon, 1-3pm Mon-Sat. **Map** p130 C1 ❿

St Pantaleon's story is depicted inside the church in an extraordinary ceiling painting – a huge illusionist work, painted on 40 canvases, by Gian Antonio Fumiani. It took him 24 years to complete the task (1680-1704), and at the end of it all he fell from the scaffolding to his death. Veronese depicts the saint in less melodramatic fashion in the second chapel on the right, in what is possibly his last work, *St Pantaleon Healing a Child*.

To the left of the chancel is the Chapel of the Holy Nail. The nail in question, supposedly from the Crucifixion, is preserved in a small but richly decorated Gothic altar. On the right wall is a fine *Coronation of the Virgin* by Antonio Vivarini and Giovanni d'Alemagna.

San Trovaso

Dorsoduro, campo San Trovaso (041 522 2133). Vaporetto Zattere. **Open** 8-11am, 2.30-5.30pm Mon-Sat. **Map** p130 C4 ⓫

The two almost identical façades here are both modelled on the sub-Palladian church of Le Zitelle (*p148*) on the Giudecca. The story goes that San Trovaso was built on the very border of the two areas of the city belonging to the rival factions of the *nicolotti* and *castellani*; in the event of a wedding between members of the two factions, each party was able to make its own sweeping entrance and exit.

There are five works by the Tintoretto family in the church; in the left transept is a smaller-than-usual version of one of Tintoretto's favourite subjects, *The Last Supper*; the tavern setting is strikingly realistic.

Santa Maria dei Carmini

Dorsoduro, campo dei Carmini (041 522 6553). Vaporetto Ca' Rezzonico or San Basilio. **Open** 7am-noon, 2.30-7pm Mon-Sat; 8.30am-noon, 2.30-7pm Sun. **Map** p130 B2 ⑫

The church officially called Santa Maria del Carmelo has a tall campanile topped by a statue of the Virgin. It is richly decorated inside, with 17th-century gilt wooden statues over the arcades of the nave and, above, a series of Baroque paintings illustrating the history of the Carmelite order. The best paintings in the church are a *Nativity* by Cima da Conegliano, on the second altar on the right, and *St Nicholas of Bari* by Lorenzo Lotto, opposite; the latter has a dreamy landscape containing tiny figures of St George and the dragon.

Scuola dei Carmini

Dorsoduro 2617, campo dei Carmini (041 528 9420, www.scuolagrande carmini.it). Vaporetto Ca' Rezzonico or San Basilio. **Open** 11am-5pm daily. **Admission** €5; €2-€4 reductions. No credit cards. **Map** p130 B2 ⑬

Begun in 1670 to plans by Baldassare Longhena, the building housing this *scuola* run by the Carmelite order was spared the Napoleonic lootings that dispersed the fittings of most other *scuole*. So we have a good idea of what an early 18th-century Venetian confraternity HQ must have looked like, from the elaborate Sante Piatti altarpiece to the staircase with its excrescence of gilt cherubs.

In the main hall of the first floor is one of the most impressive of Giambattista Tiepolo's Venetian ceilings. These airy panels were painted in the years between 1740 and 1743.

Ai Artisti

Dorsoduro 1169A, fondamenta della Toletta (041 523 8944, www.enoteca artisti.com). Vaporetto Accademia or Ca' Rezzonico. **Meals served** noon-4pm, 7-10pm Mon-Sat. Closed 3wks Dec-Jan. €€. **Map** p130 C3 ⑭

This tiny trattoria expands on to the pretty canal-side in warmer months. In the kitchen, Francesca prepares everything from scratch, from a menu that changes day by day. On Monday, meat dominates; other days, you might find prawn-stuffed squid, or a fillet of john dory pan-fried with artichokes. If prices seem high-ish, bear in mind that main courses have vegetables included (unusual in Italy). Booking essential.

La Bitta

Dorsoduro 2753A, calle lunga San Barnaba (041 523 0531). Vaporetto Ca' Rezzonico. **Meals served** 6.30-11pm Mon-Sat. €€. **Map** p130 C3 ⑮

La Bitta, a warm and rustic *osteria* with a small courtyard, has almost no fish on the menu. Dishes such as *straccetti di pollo ai finferli* (chicken strips with chanterelle mushrooms) or *oca in umido* (stewed goose) make a welcome change. There's also a good selection of cheeses, served with honey or chutney, and intelligent by-the-glass wine options.

Café Noir

Dorsoduro 3805, crosera San Pantalon (041 528 0956). Vaporetto San Tomà. **Open** 8am-2am Mon-Sat; 7pm-2am Sun. No credit cards. **Map** p130 C1 ⑯

Warm and intimate Café Noir is a winter favourite among the university and twentysomething crowd, who while away their days over panini and cups of hot chocolate. As it livens up later, it fills up inside and out with drinkers.

Café Rosso

Dorsoduro 2963, campo Santa Margherita (041 528 7998, www. cafferosso.it). Vaporetto Ca' Rezzonico.

El Sbarlefo

Open 7am-1am Mon-Sat. **No credit cards. Map** p130 C2 ⑰
Laid-back and eclectic, the campo's oldest bar says 'Caffè' over the door, but it's universally known as 'Caffè Rosso' – perhaps for the decor, or for the political leanings of its boho-chic clientele. It attracts a mixed crowd of all ages who spill out from its single room to sip a *spritz* in the campo or to choose from the impressive wine list.

El Sbarlefo

Dorsoduro 3757, calle San Pantalon (041 524 6650). Vaporetto San Tomà. **Open** 10am-midnight daily. **Map** p130 C1 ⑱
Chic and sophisticated with great loungey background music, this new arrival in an ever-livelier corner of northern Dorsoduro updates the typical Venetian *bàcaro* with real class. By-the-glass wines range from the simple-but-good to some really excellent labels; the bar snacks offer a gourmet twist on Venetian traditions.

Estro Vino e Cucina

Dorsoduro 3778, calle della Scuola (041 476 4914). Vaporetto San Tomà. **Open** 11.30am-midnight Mon, Wed-Sun. **Map** p130 C1 ⑲
This recent addition to the flourishing bar scene around San Pantalon might look like just another stylish watering hole, with some fine facial hair behind the bar and a laid-back ambience for matching habitués. But in fact it takes its wines very seriously, with an excellent selection from small producers, and an enlightened by-the-glass policy: they'll open any bottle in the shop if you purchase at least two servings from it. Beside this there are great snacks and a small selection of more filling dishes, using quality organic ingredients.

Grom

Dorsoduro 2761, campo San Barnaba (041 099 1751). Vaporetto Ca' Rezzonico. **Open** 11am-10pm Mon-Thur, Sun; 11am-12.30am Fri, Sat. **Map** p130 C3 ⑳
Founded in Turin and now spreading as far afield as New York, the Grom gelato empire has also begun to colonise Venice. Ice-cream comes with high-quality ingredients such as *sfusato* lemon from Amalfi, *tonda gentile* hazelnut from Lombardy, and pistachios from Bronte in Sicily. Prices are higher than most other *gelaterie* in town. There are also branches at Cannaregio 3844, Strada Nuova and San Polo 3006, campo dei Frari.

Oniga

Dorsoduro 2852, campo San Barnaba (041 522 4410, www.oniga.it). Vaporetto Ca' Rezzonico. **Meals served** noon-2.30pm, 7-10.30pm Mon, Wed-Sun. Closed 3wks Jan. **€€. Map** p130 C3 ㉑
With tables outside on campo San Barnaba, Oniga has a friendly, local feel. The menu is adventurous Venetian and changes frequently, but the pasta is consistently excellent. Among the *secondi*, pork chop with potatoes and figs is good. Marino is a wine expert, and will guide you through the select list.

Orange

Dorsoduro 3054A, campo Santa Margherita (041 523 4740, www.orangebar.it). Vaporetto Ca' Rezzonico. **Open** 9am-2am daily. No credit cards. **Map** p130 C2 ㉒
Orange calls itself a 'restaurant and champagne lounge' but it's far from being as exclusive as this may sound: on any night of the year, you'll find a horde of young locals and students, *spritz* in hand, spilling out from the sleek orange interior and across the campo. The young staff are efficient and friendly, the cocktails are creative and cheap, and the garden inside is wildly popular. There's decent food too, at lunch and dinner.

Osteria ai Pugni

Dorsoduro 2836, fondamenta Gherardini (346 960 7785 mobile). Vaporetto Ca' Rezzonico. **Open** 6.30am-12.30am daily. No credit cards. **Map** p130 C3 ㉓

There's always a warm welcome at this friendly bar at the foot of the Pugni bridge, where locals and students pile in from breakfast time until late at night for drinks and snacks. There's a sister establishment on neighbouring campo San Barnaba; called Ai Artisti (Dorsoduro 2771), it is similarly friendly but not to be confused with the nearby restaurant of the same name.

Tonolo

Dorsoduro 3764, calle San Pantalon (041 523 7209). Vaporetto San Tomà. **Open** 7.45am-8pm Tue-Sat; 7.45am-1pm Sun. Closed Aug. No credit cards. **Map** p130 C1 ㉔

This Venice institution has been operating here since 1953. The coffee is exceptional. On Sundays, the place fills up with locals buying sweet offerings to take to lunch – don't be shy about asserting your rights or you may never get served. The delectable pastries come in miniature sizes.

Shopping

3856 di Elvira Rubelli

Dorsoduro 3749, calle San Pantalon (041 720 595). Vaporetto San Tomà. **Open** 10am-7.30pm Mon-Sat; 11am-6pm Sun. **Map** p130 C1 ㉕

This boutique is popular with fashion-conscious students. Jewellery, scarves and bags sit next to clothes and shoes.

Annelie

Dorsoduro 2748, calle lunga San Barnaba (041 520 3277). Vaporetto Ca' Rezzonico. **Open** 9.30am-1pm, 4-7.30pm Mon-Sat. **Map** p130 C3 ㉖

A delightful shop with a beautiful selection of linens, shirts and baby clothes, either fully embroidered or with lace detailing, plus antique lace.

Arras

Dorsoduro 3235, campiello Squellini (041 522 6460, http://arrastessuti. wordpress.com). Vaporetto Ca' Rezzonico. **Open** 9am-1pm Mon, Fri; 9am-1.30pm, 2-6.30pm Mon-Thur; 10am-7pm Sat. **Map** p130 C2 ㉗

In this venture involving disabled people, a variety of handwoven fabrics are created in a vast range of gorgeous colours and textures. These unique textiles are then worked into bags, clothing and scarves. Arras also has ceramics and homewares.

Cafoscarina 2

Dorsoduro 3259, campiello degli Squellini (041 240 4801, www.cafoscarina.it). Vaporetto Ca' Rezzonico or San Tomà. **Open** 9am-1pm, 2.30-7pm Mon-Fri; 10am-1pm Sat. **Map** p130 C2 ㉘

The official bookstore of the Università Ca' Foscari, selling mostly scholarly texts on a wide variety of topics. On the other side of the campiello (Dorsoduro 3224) is Cafoscarina 3, which stocks a good selection of books in English.

Ca' Macana

Dorsoduro 3172, calle delle Botteghe (041 277 6142, www.camacana.com). Vaporetto Ca' Rezzonico. **Open** 10am-7.30pm daily. **Map** p130 C2 ㉙

This workshop packed with traditional papier-mâché masks from the commedia dell'arte theatre tradition makes all its own masks, unlike so many of the carbon-copy shops that plague the city.

Canestrelli

Dorsoduro 1173, calle della Toletta (041 277 0617, www.venicemirrors.com). Vaporetto Accademia. **Open** 11am-1.30pm, 3.30-7.30pm Mon-Sat. **Map** p130 C3 ㉚

Designer-producer Stefano Coluccio specialises in beautifully framed convex mirrors.

Fustat

Dorsoduro 2904, campo Santa Margherita (041 523 8504). Vaporetto Ca' Rezzonico. **Open** 9.30am-12.30pm Mon-Sat. **Map** p130 B2 ㉛

All the pottery in this little workshop/outlet is handmade by the owner, Cinzia Cingolani.

Libreria Toletta & Toletta Studio

Dorsoduro 1214, calle Toletta (041 523 2034, www.latoletta.com). Vaporetto Accademia or Ca' Rezzonico. **Open** 9.30am-7.30pm Mon-Sat; 3-7pm Sun. **Map** p130 C3 ㉜

Toletta offers 20%-40% off the usual retail prices. Italian classics, art, cookery, children's books and history (mostly in Italian) all feature, along with a vast assortment of dictionaries and reference books. Next door is the Toletta Studio, which specialises in architecture. Toletta Cube is their newest shop, just across the calle, and it carries art and photography books as well as posters, cards and gadgets.

Madera

Dorsoduro 2762, campo San Barnaba (041 522 4181, www.maderavenezia.it). Vaporetto Ca' Rezzonico. **Open** 10am-1pm, 3.30-7.30pm Tue-Sat. **Map** p130 C3 ㉝

Fusing minimalist design with traditional techniques, the young architect and craftswoman behind Madera creates unique objects in wood. She also sells lamps, ceramics, jewellery and textiles by other crafts-people, many of them Venice-based. Some of the homewares are now on sale down the road in calle Lunga San Barnaba (Dorsoduro 2729).

Signor Blum

Dorsoduro 2840, campo San Barnaba (041 522 6367, www.signorblum.com). Vaporetto Ca' Rezzonico. **Open** 10am-7pm daily. **Map** p130 C3 ㉞

Mr Blum's colourful handmade wooden puzzles of Venetian *palazzi*, gondolas and animals make great gifts for children and adults.

Vinaria Nave de Oro

Dorsoduro 3664, campo Santa Margherita (041 522 2693). Vaporetto Ca' Rezzonico. **Open** 9am-1pm, 5-8pm Mon, Tue, Thur-Sat; 9am-1pm Wed. No credit cards. **Map** p130 C2 ㉟

Bring your own bottles here and the staff will fill them with anything from pinot grigio to merlot. For something different, try *torbolino*, a sweet and cloudy first-pressing white wine.

Nightlife

Venice Jazz Club

Dorsoduro 3102, fondamenta dei Pugni (041 523 2056, www.venicejazzclub.com). Vaporetto Ca' Rezzonico. **Open** 7pm-2am Mon-Wed, Fri, Sat. **Map** p130 C2 ㊱

The intimate setting makes this club, just behind campo Santa Margherita, a perfect place for a night out for fans of high-quality jazz. Concerts start at 9pm, and some food is served.

East

The eastern reaches of Dorsoduro, from the rio di San Trovaso, past the **Accademia** and the **Salute** to the punta della Dogana, is an area of elegant, artsy prosperity. Ezra Pound spent his last years in a small house near the Zattere; Peggy Guggenheim hosted her collection of modern art in her truncated palazzo on the Grand Canal (now the **Peggy Guggenheim Collection**); artists use the vast spaces of the old warehouses on the Zattere as studios. On Sunday mornings, British expats home in on the Anglican church of St George on campo San Vio.

It is a district of quiet canals and cosy *campielli*. But all that money has driven out the locals: nowhere in Venice are you further from a simple *alimentari* (grocery store).

The colossal magnificence of Longhena's church of Santa Maria della Salute brings the residential area to an end. Beyond is the old Dogana di Mare (Customs House). Debate about redeploying this empty space raged for years, but with the **Punta Della Dogana** gallery open and building work over, it is once again possible to stroll around the *punta*, with its spectacular view across the water towards St Mark's.

South from punta della Dogana, the mile-long stretch of Le Zattere, Venice's finest promenade after the riva degli Schiavoni, leads westwards past the churches of **I Gesuati** and **Santa Maria della Visitazione** to the San Nicolò zone. This long promenade bordering the Giudecca Canal is named after the *zattere* (rafts) that used to moor here.

The eastern end is usually quiet, with the occasional flurry of activity around the rowing clubs now occupying the 14th-century salt warehouses, one of which hosts the **Fondazione Vedova** gallery.

Westward from these are the new premises of the Accademia di Belle Arti (the school of fine arts that was recently evicted from the Accademia), the church of Spirito Santo and the long 16th-century façade of the grimly named Ospedale degli Incurabili.

The liveliest part of the Zattere is around the church of I Gesuati. Venetians flock here at weekends and on warm evenings to savour ice-cream or sip drinks at canalside tables.

Sights & museums

Fondazione Vedova

Dorsoduro 50, fondamenta Zattere ai Saloni (041 522 6626, www.fondazione vedova.org). Vaporetto Salute or Zattere. **Open** 11.30am-6.30pm Tue-Sun. **Admission** varies. **Map** p131 F4 ③⑦
Works by Venetian artist Emilio Vedova (1919-2006) are housed in a stunning new gallery, designed by Renzo Piano, in the Magazzini del Sale (salt warehouses). Immense canvases by this leading member of the European avant-garde are suspended from moving brackets.

Galleria Cini

Dorsoduro 864, piscina del Forner (041 271 0111, www.cini.it). Vaporetto Accademia. **Open** *Feb-June, Sept-Nov* 10am-6pm Tue-Sun. *Closed Jan, July, Aug, Dec.* **Admission** €6.50; €5.50 reductions. No credit cards. **Map** p131 D4 ③⑧
This lovely collection of Ferrarese and Tuscan art was put together by industrialist Vittorio Cini, who created the Fondazione Cini on the island of San Giorgio Maggiore (p151). It's small but there are a few gems, such as the unfinished Pontormo double *Portrait of Two Friends* (on the first floor), and Dosso Dossi's *Allegorical Scene* (on the second).

Gallerie dell'Accademia

Dorsoduro 1050, campo Carità (041 522 2247, www.gallerieaccademia.org). Vaporetto Accademia. **Open** 8.15am-2pm Mon; 8.15am-7.15pm Tue-Sun. **Admission** €9; €6 reductions; free under-18s and EU students (incl Palazzo Grimani, p12). *Audio guide* €6. **Map** p131 D3 ③⑨
Early in 2014, the Accademia galleries threw open the doors of a long-awaited extension, which added to the existing exhibition halls parts of the Scuola della Carità (the oldest of the Venetian *scuole*, founded in the 13th century), the monastery of the Lateran Canons (a 12th-century structure remodelled by Andrea Palladio, with a superb oval staircase by the architect now on view) and the church of the Carità. At the time of writing, the new area was bare; a complete overhaul was scheduled as the artworks were rehung. The following description refers to the original body of the gallery; the arrangement of works inside may be altered considerably in time.

The Accademia is the essential one-stop shop for Venetian painting, and one of the world's greatest art treasure houses. It was Napoleon who made the collection possible: first, by suppressing hundreds of churches, convents and religious guilds, confiscating their artworks for the greater good of the state; and second, by moving the city's Accademia di Belle Arti art school here, with the mandate both to train students and to act as a gallery and

I Gesuati p142

storeroom for all the evicted artworks. The art school moved to a new site in 2004, leaving the freed-up space for the gallery extension.

In its old layout, the collection is arranged chronologically, with the exception of the 15th- and 16th-century works in rooms 19-24 at the end. It opens with 14th- and 15th-century devotional works by Paolo Veneziano and others. Rooms 2 and 3 have devotional paintings and altarpieces by Carpaccio, Cima da Conegliano and Giovanni Bellini (a fine *Enthroned Madonna with Six Saints*).

Rooms 4 and 5 are the Renaissance heart of the collection: here are Mantegna's *St George* and Giorgione's mysterious *Tempest*. In Room 6, the three greats of 16th-century Venetian painting – Titian, Tintoretto and Veronese – are first encountered. But the battle of the giants gets under way in earnest in Room 10, where Tintoretto's ghostly chiaroscuro *Transport of the Body of St Mark* vies for attention with Titian's moving *Pietà* – his last painting – and Veronese's huge *Christ in the House of Levi*.

Room 11 covers two centuries, with canvases by Tintoretto (the exquisite *Madonna dei Camerlenghi*), Bernardo Strozzi and Tiepolo. The series of rooms beyond brings the plot up to the 18th century, with all the old favourites: Canaletto, Guardi, Longhi and soft-focus, bewigged portraits by female superstar Rosalba Carriera.

Rooms 19 and 20 take us back to the 15th century; the latter has the rich *Miracle of the Relic of the Cross* cycle, a collaborative effort by Gentile Bellini, Carpaccio and others, which is packed with telling social details. An even more satisfying cycle has Room 21 to itself. Carpaccio's *Life of St Ursula* (1490-95) tells the story of the legendary Breton princess who embarked on a pilgrimage to Rome with her betrothed.

Room 23 is the former church of Santa Maria della Carità: here are devotional works by Vivarini, the Bellinis

and others. Room 24 – the Albergo room (or secretariat) of the former *scuola* – contains the only work in the whole gallery that is in its original site: Titian's magnificent *Presentation of the Virgin*.

I Gesuati

Dorsoduro, fondamenta Zattere ai Gesuati (041 275 0642, www.chorus venezia.org). Vaporetto Zattere. **Open** 10am-5pm Mon-Sat. **Admission** €3 (or Chorus; p12). No credit cards. **Map** p131 D4 ⑩

This church is officially Santa Maria del Rosario, but it is always known as the Gesuati, after the minor religious order that owned the previous church here. I Gesuati is a great piece of teamwork by a trio of remarkable rococo artists: architect Giorgio Massari, painter Giambattista Tiepolo and sculptor Giovanni Morlaiter.

The façade deliberately reflects the Palladian church of the Redentore opposite, but the splendidly posturing statues give it a typically 18th-century touch of histrionic flamboyance. Inside is a magnificent ceiling by Tiepolo, with three frescoes on Dominican themes. These works reintroduced frescoes to Venetian art after two centuries of canvas ceiling paintings. There is another brightly coloured Tiepolo on the first altar on the right, *The Virgin and Child with Saints Rosa, Catherine and Agnes*.

Peggy Guggenheim Collection

Dorsoduro 701, fondamenta Venier dei Leoni (041 520 6288, www.guggenheim-venice.it). Vaporetto Accademia or Salute. **Open** 10am-6pm Mon, Wed-Sun. **Admission** €14; €8-€12 reductions. **Map** p131 E4 ㉑

This remarkable establishment, tucked behind a high wall off a quiet street (but with a Grand Canal frontage), is the third most visited museum in the city. It was founded by one of Venice's most colourful expat residents, Peggy Guggenheim. She turned up in 1949 looking for a home for her already sizeable art collection. Peggy found a perfect, eccentric base in Palazzo Venier dei Leoni, a truncated 18th-century Grand Canal palazzo.

There are big European names in her collection, including Picasso, Duchamp, Brancusi, Giacometti and Max Ernst, plus a few Americans such as Calder and Jackson Pollock. Highlights include the beautifully enigmatic *Empire of Light* by Magritte and Giacometti's disturbing *Woman with Her Throat Cut*. The flamboyant *Attirement of the Bride*, by Peggy's husband, Max Ernst, often turns up as a Carnevale costume. But perhaps the most startling exhibit of all is the rider of Marino Marini's *Angel of the City* on the Grand Canal terrace, who thrusts his manhood towards passing *vaporetti*.

Another wing has been given over to Futurist works on long-term loan from the collection of Gianni Mattioli. The gallery has a pleasant garden and café.

Punta della Dogana

Dorsoduro 2, campo della Salute (041 523 1680, www.palazzograssi.it). Vaporetto Salute. **Open** 10am-7pm Mon, Wed-Sun. **Admission** €15 (€20 Punta & Palazzo Grassi; p12); €10 (€14 both) reductions. **Map** p131 F4 ㊷

Inaugurated in June 2009 after a remarkable makeover by Japanese star architect Tadao Ando (see box p144), the Punta della Dogana gallery confirms Venice's key place on Europe's contemporary art circuit. French tycoon François Pinault beat the Peggy Guggenheim Collection with his bid for the lease on this 17th-century bonded warehouse – much to the annoyance of many who felt that Pinault's outpost at Palazzo Grassi (p63) was more than enough. On show here are exhibitions based around Pinault's own immense contemporary art collection.

Santa Maria della Salute

Dorsoduro, campo della Salute (041 241 1081, www.seminariovenezia.it). Vaporetto Salute. **Open** 9am-noon,

3-5.30pm daily. **Admission** *Church* free. *Sacristy* €2. No credit cards. **Map** p131 F4 ㊸

This magnificent Baroque church is almost as recognisable an image of Venice as St Mark's or the Rialto bridge. It was built between 1631 and 1681 in thanksgiving for the end of Venice's last bout of plague, which had wiped out at least a third of the population in 1630. The church is dedicated to the Madonna, as protector of the city.

The terms of the competition won by 26-year-old architect Baldassare Longhena presented a serious challenge. The church was to be colossal but inexpensive; the whole structure was to be visually clear on entrance, with an unimpeded view of the high altar (the ambulatory and side altars coming into sight only as one approached the chancel); the light was to be evenly distributed; and the whole building should *creare una bella figura* – show itself off to good effect. Longhena succeeded brilliantly in satisfying all of these requisites.

The architect said he chose the circular shape with the reverent aim of offering a crown to the Madonna. This Marian symbolism continues throughout the church.

The three side altars on the right have paintings by Luca Giordano, a prolific Neapolitan painter. On the opposite side is a clumsily restored *Pentecost*, by Titian, transferred here from the island monastery of Santo Spirito (demolished in 1656). The high altar has a splendidly dynamic sculptural group by Giusto Le Corte, the artist responsible (with assistants) for most of the statues inside and outside the church. This group represents *Venice Kneeling before the Virgin and Child*, while the plague, in the shape of a hideous old hag, scurries off to the right, prodded by a tough-looking *putto*. Amid this marble hubbub is a serene Byzantine icon of the *Madonna and Child*, brought from Crete in 1669.

Tadao Ando

The Japanese architect who's made his mark on the city.

Teatrino Grassi

Self-taught and without the shadow of an academic qualification, Japanese architect Tadao Ando has put his stamp on Venice thanks to his close collaboration with French magnate and collector of contemporary art Francois Pinault.

When Pinault bought the Grand Canal-side **Palazzo Grassi** (p63) from Fiat in 2005, he called on Ando to rationalise the exhibition spaces inside the immense 18th-century pile. The result was clean but cold.

Two years later, Pinault was handed the lease on the **Punta della Dogana** (p143), a 17th-century bonded warehouse at a strategic and hugely scenic spot facing across St Mark's basin to the Doge's Palace. Once again, Ando was given charge of the makeover of the immense, unstructured spaces inside the triangular customs building. He set to work with his usual gusto, sweeping aside the bureaucratic complications that can make renovations in Italy a decades-long calvary. The result is a stunning series of halls with a subtle play of wood and brick, concrete (Ando's signature material) and dazzling light off the water that laps all around.

Ando's latest Venetian outing was a bagatelle in comparison: the **Teatrino Grassi** (p64) is a sheer space of curves and diagonals in shiny white.

Sacristy

The best paintings – including Tintoretto's *Marriage at Cana* (1551) – are in the sacristy (open 10am). On the altar is a very early Titian of *Saints Mark, Sebastian, Roch, Cosmas and Damian*, saints who were all invoked for protection against the plague; the painting was done during the outbreak of 1509-14. Three later works by Titian (c1540-49) hang on the ceiling, violent Old Testament scenes also brought here from the church of Santo Spirito. More Old Testament turbulence can be seen in Salviati's *Saul Hurling a Spear at David* and Palma il Giovane's *Samson and Jonah*, in which the whale is represented mainly by a vast lolling rubbery tongue.

Santa Maria della Visitazione

Dorsoduro, fondamenta Zattere ai Gesuati (041 522 4077). Vaporetto Zattere. **Open** 8am-noon, 3-6pm daily. **Map** p130 C4 ㉔

Confusingly, this has the same name as the Vivaldi church on the riva degli Schiavoni – though the latter is usually known as La Pietà. Santa Maria della Visitazione is now the chapel of the Istituto Don Orione, which has taken over the vast complex of the monastery of the Gesuati next door.

Designed by Tullio Lombardo or Mauro Codussi and built in 1423, the church has an attractive early Renaissance façade. It was suppressed (by Napoleon) at the beginning of the 19th century and stripped of all its works of art with the exception of the original coffered ceiling, an unexpected delight containing 58 compartments with portraits of saints and prophets by an Umbrian painter of Luca Signorelli's school, one of the few examples of central Italian art in Venice. To the right of the façade is a lion's mouth for secret denunciations: the ones posted here went to the *Magistrati della sanità*, who dealt with matters of public health.

Ai Gondolieri

Dorsoduro 366, fondamenta Ospedaletto (041 528 6396, www.aigondolieri.com). Vaporetto Accademia or Salute. **Meals served** noon-3pm, 7-11.15pm Mon, Wed-Sun. €€€€. **Map** p131 E4 ㊺

If you're looking to splash out, Ai Gondolieri offers a creative menu that belies its ultra-traditional decor and service. It's also, unusually for Venice, fish-free. Rooted in the culinary traditions of north-east Italy, dishes include a warm salad of venison with blueberries, and pork fillet in pear sauce with wild fennel. Enquire about the price before tasting truffle delights in autumn. You can take the sting out of the bill at lunch time with less expensive half-portions and taster menus.

Cantinone (già Schiavi)

Dorsoduro 992, fondamenta Nani (041 523 0034). Vaporetto Accademia or Zattere. **Open** 8am-8pm Mon-Sat. **Map** p130 C4 ㊻

Two generations of the Gastaldi family work in the Cantinone (also, confusingly, known as Il Bottegon) filling glasses, carting cases of wine, and preparing huge panini with mortadella or more delicate *crostini* with, for example, creamed pistachio. Come before the crowds pour in at 1pm. When the bar itself is full, you'll be in good company on the bridge outside – a fine setting for *spritz* and prosecco consumption.

Da Gino

Dorsoduro 853A, calle Nuova Sant'Agnese (041 528 5276). Vaporetto Accademia. **Open** 6am-7.30pm Mon-Sat. **No credit cards. Map** p131 D4 ㊼

You will always be greeted with a smile by the Scarpa family; they take customer service seriously in a city where the number of tourists makes for some cranky hosts. Gino's serves some of the best *tramezzini* and made-to-order panini around. At the time of writing, the rumour that the bar was about to

Gelateria Lo Squero

Dorsoduro 989-990, fondamenta Nani (347 269 7921 mobile). Vaporetto Accademia or Zattere. **Open** 11am-9pm daily. No credit cards. **Map** p130 C4 ④⑧

Simone Sambo makes some of the finest ice-cream in Venice, with the freshest ingredients available. His mousse series (blueberry, strawberry, chocolate and hazelnut, among others) is exceptionally light and creamy.

Osteria al Squero

Dorsoduro 944, fondamenta Nani (335 600 7513 mobile). Vaporetto Accademia or Zattere. **Open** 9am-9.30pm Tue-Sun. No credit cards. **Map** p130 C4 ④⑨

This simple, friendly *bàcaro* looks like it has been here since time immemorial, but that's an illusion. The former teachers who run the place, however, have captured the spirit of the traditional Venetian drinking den, adding only some gourmet *cicheti* at very reasonable prices: many customers turn up for a single glass of wine, and end up making a full meal out of a plate of these delicious tidbits. There are no tables, just benches and perching places.

Shopping

Cornici Trevisanello

Dorsoduro 662, fondamenta Bragadin (041 520 7779). Vaporetto Accademia. **Open** 9am-1pm, 3-7pm Mon-Fri; 9am-1pm Sat. **Map** p131 D4 ⑤⓪

This workshop is home to a father, son and daughter team that makes beautiful gilded frames, many with pearl, mirror and glass inlay. Custom orders and shipping are not a problem.

Le Forcole di Saverio Pastor

Dorsoduro 341, fondamenta Soranzo de la Fornace (041 522 5699, www.forcole. com). Vaporetto Salute. **Open** 8am-6pm Mon-Fri. **Map** p131 E4 ⑤①

The place to come for a new *forcola* or pair of oars for your gondola. Saverio Pastor is one of only three recognised *marangon* (oar-makers) in Venice. There are bookmarks, postcards and books (in English) on Venetian boatworks too.

Genninger Studio

Dorsoduro 364, campiello Barbaro (041 522 5565, www.genningerstudio.com). Vaporetto Accademia or Salute. **Open** 9.30am-6.30pm Mon-Sat; 11am-6pm Sun. **Map** p131 E4 ⑤②

Designer Leslie Ann Genninger's flame-worked and blown beads, custom jewellery, knick-knacks, lighting and mirrors offer a contemporary take on Venetian luxury and decadence.

Marina & Susanna Sent

Dorsoduro 669 & 681, campo san Vio (041 520 8136, www.marinaesusanna sent.com). Vaporetto Accademia. **Open** 10am-6pm daily. **Map** p131 D4 ⑤③

Some of Venice's finest contemporary glass jewellery is created by the Sent sisters. There's also a good selection of pieces from design house Arcade.

Il Pavone

Dorsoduro 721, fondamenta Venier dei Leoni (041 523 4517). Vaporetto Accademia. **Open** 9.30am-1.30pm, 2.30-6.30pm daily. **Map** p131 E4 ⑤④

Handmade paper with floral motifs in a variety of colours, plus boxes, picture frames and other objects.

Nightlife

Piccolo Mondo

Dorsoduro 1056A, calle Contarini-Corfù (041 520 0371, www.piccolomondo.biz). Vaporetto Accademia. **Open** 10.30pm-4am daily. **Map** p131 D3 ⑤⑤

Called 'El Souk' in better days, this 'small world' remains one of the few places to dance in Venice proper. If you find yourself on the dancefloor, you'll be mixing with ageing medallion men, lost tourists and foreign students so desperate to dance, they'll go anywhere.

Isola di San Giorgio p151

La Giudecca & San Giorgio

Once a place of flourishing monasteries and lush gardens, the island of La Giudecca, just across the water to the south of Venice proper, is less impressive today. Its nature changed in the 19th century when city authorities began converting abandoned religious houses into factories and prisons. The factories have almost all closed down, but the prisons remain in use. Giudecca now has a reputation as one of the poorer areas of the city, but it manages to attract more than its fair share of celebrities, and locals in the know come here for its community spirit and alternative arty scene.

With its splendid Palladian church facing the Doge's Palace across the lagoon, the island of San Giorgio is an immediately recognisable Venetian icon.

La Giudecca

The Giudecca was once known as 'Spinalonga', from an imagined resemblance to a fish skeleton (*spina* means fish bone). Some claim that the present name derives from an early community of Jews; others cite the fact that the island was a place of exile for troublesome nobles, who had been *giudicati*, 'judged'. The exile was sometimes self-chosen, however, as people used the islands as a place of rural retreat: Michelangelo, when exiled from Florence in 1529, chose to mope here.

The Giudecca's industrial heritage is in the process of being shaken up: some of the factories remain abandoned, contributing to the run-down appearance of the

Secret gardens

Seek out the Giudecca's green spaces.

Once famous for its gardens, the Giudecca island keeps its greenery well hidden these days. But the magnificent courtyards – one with a maze – inside the Fondazione Cini (p151) may be visited, as may the garden inside the Fortuny Tessuti Artistici (p150), which is open by appointment and beautiful to see despite being in the middle of a painstaking restoration as this guide went to press. Also worth a peek if you're craving greenery is the gem that lies behind the Bauer group's Palladio and Villa F hotels (for both, p178); four separate gardens have been restored and brought back to life, adding contemporary verve to historically documented elegance.

south side of the island, but a few have been converted into new residential complexes. The greatest transformation has been that of the Molino Stucky, the vast turreted and crenellated Teutonic mass at the western end of the Giudecca. The largest building in the lagoon, it was built as a flour mill in 1896 and continued to function until 1955. After decades of abandonment, it now hosts the Hilton Hotel with its conference centre, rooftop Skyline Bar and swimming pool, and private flats.

The *palazzi* along the northern *fondamenta* enjoy a splendid view of Venice and attract well-heeled outsiders (Elton John and Giorgio Armani, for example) in search of picturesque holiday homes. Apart from the Hilton, there are a number of other major hotels, including the swanky Cipriani (p179), at the eastern end. The island's disused warehouses are popular as studios for artists.

The main sights of the Giudecca are all on this northern *fondamenta*. Santa Eufemia, with its charming mix of styles ranging from the 11th to the 18th century, and the Palladian church of Le Zitelle ('the spinsters': the convent ran a hospice for poor girls who were trained as lace-makers) are both nearly always closed. Several fine *palazzi* are here, as well as **Il Redentore**.

Near Le Zitelle is the neo-Gothic Casa De Maria, with its three large inverted-shield windows. The Bolognese painter Mario De Maria built it for himself from 1910 to 1913, and it's the only private palazzo to have the same patterned brickwork as the Doge's Palace. It's now home to Tre Oci (www.treoci.org), a space hosting photography exhibitions.

On the fondamenta Rio della Croce (no.149, close to the Redentore) stands the Palazzo Munster, a former infirmary for English sailors.

Sights & museums

Il Redentore

Giudecca, campo del Redentore (041 275 0462, www.chorusvenezia.org). Vaporetto Redentore. **Open** 10am-5pm Mon-Sat. **Admission** €3 (or Chorus; p12). No credit cards. **Map** p150 B2 ❶

Venice's first great plague church was commissioned to celebrate deliverance from the bout of 1575-77. A conspicuous site was chosen, one that could be approached in ceremonial fashion. Palladio designed an eye-catching building with a solemn, harmonious interior. The Capuchin monks, the austere order to whom the building was entrusted, were not pleased by its grandeur; Palladio attempted to mollify them by designing their choir stalls in a plain style. The best paintings are in the sacristy, which is rarely open; they include a *Virgin and Child* by Alvise Vivarini and a *Baptism* by Veronese.

Eating & drinking

Alla Palanca

Giudecca 448, fondamenta del Ponte Piccolo (041 528 7719). Vaporetto Palanca. **Meals served** noon-2.30pm Mon-Sat. €€. No credit cards. **Map** p150 A2 ❷

One of the cheapest meals-with-a-view in Venice is on offer at this hugely friendly bar-trattoria on the Giudecca quay. It's a lunch-only place: the rest of the day (7.30am-8.30pm) it operates as a bar. The menu includes some surprisingly gourmet options: tagliatelle with prawns and *funghi porcini*, or tuna steaks in balsamic and sesame.

Harry's Dolci

Giudecca 773, fondamenta San Biagio (041 522 4844, www.cipriani.com). Vaporetto Sant'Eufemia. **Open** 10.30am-11pm Mon, Wed-Sun. Closed Nov-Mar. **Meals served** noon-3pm, 7-10.30pm Mon, Wed-Sun. €€€€. **Map** p149 C1 ❸

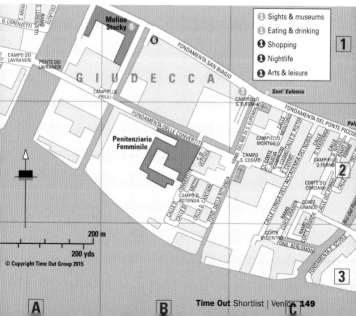

Arrigo Cipriani's second Venetian stronghold (after Harry's Bar; p70), this open-air restaurant is a fair-weather-only venue. The cuisine is supposedly more summery than chez Harry, but in practice many dishes are identical. Outside of mealtimes, you can order just a coffee and one of the delectable pastries made on the premises. Come prepared for mosquitoes.

Mistrà

Giudecca 53C, calle Michelangelo (041 522 0743). Vaporetto Zitelle. **Meals served** noon-3pm, 6.30-10.30pm Tue-Sun. **€€. Map** p151 D2 ❹

At lunchtime, Mistrà is not a bad spot, with its open-to-view kitchen and friendly mix of workers from local galleries and boatyards. There's pizza as well as fish-based Venetian classics at reasonable prices. The place aims to go upmarket in the evenings but the result doesn't merit the higher price tag.

Skyline Bar

Molino Stucky Hilton Hotel, Giudecca 810, campo San Biagio (041 272 3310). Vaporetto Palanca. **Open** 5.30pm-1am Tue-Sun. **Map** p149 B1 ❺

It's a hike across to the Hilton Hotel in the former Molino Stucky flour mill (p148) – and the bar is an expensive extravagance – but sit out on the roof-top terrace and survey Venice beneath you, beyond the grand sweep of the Giudecca Canal, and you'll probably feel that it's all worth it. Meals and light snacks are served too, for those with deep pockets.

Shopping

Fortuny Tessuti Artistici

Giudecca 805, fondamenta San Biagio (041 528 7697, www.fortuny.com). Vaporetto Palanca. **Open** Apr-Sept 10am-1pm, 2-6pm Mon-Sat. Oct-Mar 10am-1pm, 2-6pm Mon-Fri. **Map** p149 B1 ❻

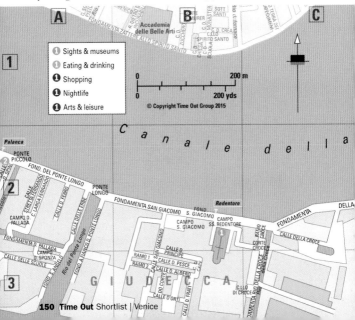

- ❶ Sights & museums
- ❶ Eating & drinking
- ❶ Shopping
- ❶ Nightlife
- ❶ Arts & leisure

© Copyright Time Out Group 2015

This wonderful factory showroom space glows with the exquisite colours and patterns of original Fortuny prints. At €427 a metre, you may not be tempted to buy, but it's worth the trip just to see it. The marvellous garden inside the factory can be visited by appointment. Check the Fortuny blog for occasional clearance sales and cut-price discontinued lines.

Isola di San Giorgio

Sights & museums

The island of San Giorgio, facing St Mark's across the lagoon, realised its true potential under set designer extraordinaire Andrea Palladio, whose church of **San Giorgio Maggiore** is one of Venice's most recognisable landmarks. Known originally as the Isola dei Cipressi (Cypress Island), it soon became an important Benedictine monastery

and centre of learning – a tradition that is carried on today by the **Fondazione Giorgio Cini**, which operates a research centre and craft school on the island.

Fondazione Giorgio Cini, Benedictine Monastery & Le Stanze del Vetro

(041 524 0119, www.cini.it). Vaporetto *San Giorgio.* **Open** *Monastery* (guided tours every hour) 10am-4pm Sat, Sun. Mon-Fri by appt. *Le Stanze del Vetro* 10am-7pm Mon, Tue, Thur-Sun during exhibitions. **Admission** *Monastery* €10; €8 reductions. *Le Stanze del Vetro* free. No credit cards. **Map** p151 E1/F1 ⑦

There has been a Benedictine monastery here since 982, when Doge Tribuno Memmo donated the island to the order. The monastery continued to benefit from ducal donations, acquiring large tracts of land both in and around Venice and abroad. After the church acquired the remains of

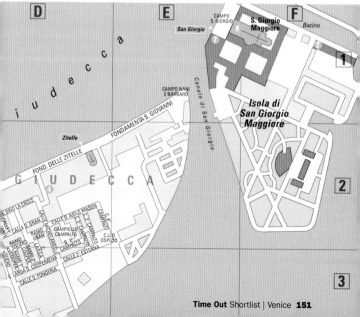

St Stephen (1109), it was visited yearly by the doge on 26 December, the feast day of the saint. The city authorities often used the island as a luxury hotel for particularly prestigious visitors, such as Cosimo de' Medici in 1433.

In 1800, the island hosted the conclave of cardinals that elected Pope Pius VII, after they had been expelled from Rome by Napoleon. In 1806, the French got their own back, suppressing the monastery and sending its chief artistic treasure – Veronese's *Marriage Feast at Cana* – off to the Louvre, where it still hangs. For the rest of the century, the monastery did ignominious service as a barracks and ammunition store. In 1951, industrialist Vittorio Cini bought the island to set up a foundation in memory of his son, Giorgio, killed in a plane crash in 1949.

The Fondazione Giorgio Cini uses the monastery buildings for its activities, including artistic and musical research (it holds a collection of Vivaldi manuscripts, plus illuminated manuscripts), and as a naval college. A portion of the complex was given back to the Benedictines; there are currently a handful of monks in the monastery. The foundation is now open to the public at weekends for guided tours (in Italian, English, French and German). There are two beautiful cloisters – one by Giovanni Buora (1516-40), the other by Palladio (1579) – an elegant library and staircase by Longhena (1641-53), and a magnificent refectory by Palladio (1561). The tour also includes the splendid garden, including a JL Borges-inspired maze by the late British designer Randoll Coate, behind the monastery.

Inside the monastery complex, Le Stanze del Vetro (www.lestanzedelvetro.it) is an exhibition space that hosts excellent shows on Venetian glass.

San Giorgio Maggiore

(041 522 7827). Vaporetto San Giorgio. **Open** 8.30am-8pm daily. **Admission** *Church* free. *Campanile* €6; €4 reductions. No credit cards. **Map** p151 E1 ⑧

This unique spot cried out for a masterpiece. Palladio provided it. This was his first complete solo church; it demonstrates how confident he was in his techniques and objectives. With no hint of influence from the city's Byzantine tradition, Palladio here develops the system of superimposed temple fronts with which he had experimented in the façade of San Francesco della Vigna (p73). The interior maintains the same relations between the orders as the outside, with composite half-columns supporting the gallery, and lower Corinthian pilasters supporting the arches. The effect is of luminosity and harmony, decoration being confined to the altars.

There are several good works of art. Over the first altar is an *Adoration of the Shepherds* by Jacopo Bassano. The altar to the right of the high altar has a *Madonna and Child with Nine Saints* by Sebastiano Ricci.

On the side walls of the chancel hang two vast compositions by Tintoretto, a *Last Supper* and the *Gathering of Manna*, painted in the last years of his life. The perspective of each work makes it clear that they were intended to be viewed from the altar rails. Tintoretto's last painting, a moving *Entombment*, hangs in the Cappella dei Morti (open for 11am Mass on Sundays in winter only). It's possible that Tintoretto included himself among the mourners; he has been identified as the bearded man gazing intently at Christ.

In the left transept is a painting by Jacopo and Domenico Tintoretto of the *Martyrdom of St Stephen*, placed above the altar containing the saint's remains (brought from Constantinople in 1109).

From the left transept, follow the signs to the campanile. Just in front of the ticket office stands the huge statue of an angel that crowned the bell tower until it was struck by lightning in 1993. To the left of the statue, a corridor gives access to the lift that takes you up to the bell tower. The view from the top of the tower is extraordinary: the best possible panorama across Venice and the lagoon.

Molino Stucky p148

Lido

Lido & Lagoon

Venice lies more or less in the middle of a saltwater lagoon, separated from the open sea by two slender sand barriers – the Lido and Pellestrina. In high season, much-visited islands such as Murano and Burano can seem only marginally less crowded than St Mark's or the Rialto. Other islands, such as Sant'Erasmo, are always bucolically tranquil and almost entirely tourist-free. But even at the busiest times, the views from the vaporetto of the lagoon's empty reaches are enough to soothe the most frayed of nerves.

The Lido

The Lido is the northernmost of the two strips of land that separate the lagoon from the open sea. It is no longer the 'bare strand/Of hillocks heaped from ever-shifting sand' that Shelley described in *Julian and Maddalo*, nor is it the playground for

wealthy aesthetes that fans of *Death in Venice* might come in search of. These days, Venice-by-the-sea is a placidly residential suburb, full of supermarkets and cars. Now, the only moment when the place stirs to anything like its former vivacity is at the beginning of September for the film festival (p28).

The Lido has few tourist sights as such. Only the church of San Nicolò on the riviera San Nicolò – founded in 1044 – can claim any great antiquity. It was here that the doge would come on Ascension Day after marrying Venice to the sea in the ceremony known as *lo sposalizio del mare* (p27 Festa e Regata della Sensa).

Fans of art nouveau and deco have plenty to look at on the Lido. On the Gran Viale there are two gems: the tiled façade of the Hungaria Hotel (no.28), formerly the Ausonia Palace, with its Beardsley-esque nymphs; and Villa Monplaisir at no.14, an art deco design from 1906. There are serve excellent mixed seafood antipasti, fishy pasta dishes and grilled fish to contented diners out on the portico of the former produce market.

La Favorita

Via Francesco Duodo 33 (041 526 1626). Vaporetto Lido. **Meals served** 7.30-10.30pm Tue; 12.30-2.30pm, 7.30-10.30pm Wed-Sun. Closed Jan. **€€€**.

With a lovely vine-shaded pergola for summer dining, this is an old-fashioned and reassuring sort of place that does textbook Venetian seafood classics such as *spaghetti ai caparossoli* or *scampi in saor* (sweet-and-sour sauce), plus a few more-audacious dishes such as pumpkin gnocchi with scorpion fish and radicchio. Service is professional, and the wine list has a fine selection of bottles from the north-east.

The Northern Lagoon

San Michele

Halfway between Venice and Murano, this is the island where tourists begin their lagoon visit. For many Venetians, it's the last stop: San Michele is the city's cemetery (open Apr-Sept 7.30am-6pm daily, Oct-Mar 7.30am-4.30pm daily). Early in the morning, *vaporetti* are packed with locals coming over to lay flowers. This is not a morbid spot, though: it is an elegant city of the dead, with more than one famous resident.

In a booth to the left of the entrance by the vaporetto stop, staff hand out maps that are indispensable for searching out the graves of the famous, including Igor Stravinsky, Ezra Pound and Joseph Brodsky. There's a corner dedicated to the city's gondoliers, their tombs decorated with carvings and statues of gondolas.

Before visiting the cemetery, take a look at the recently restored church of San Michele in Isola (open 7.30am-12.15pm, 3-4pm daily). Designed by

San Nicolò

other smaller-scale examples in and around via Lepanto. For full-blown turn-of-the-century exotica, though, it's hard to beat the Hotel Excelsior (p178) on lungomare Marconi, a neo-Moorish party-piece.

Getting there & around

The main Lido–Santa Maria Elisabetta vaporetto stop (often just called 'Lido') is served by frequent boats from Venice and the mainland. The San Nicolò stop, to the north, is served by the no.17 car ferry from Tronchetto. Bus routes are confusing, but cover the island pretty well. Cycling is a good way of getting around the pancake-flat Lido.

Eating & drinking

Al Mercà

Via Enrico Dandolo 17A (041 243 1663). Vaporetto Lido. **Meals served** June-Oct 10.30am-3pm, 6.30pm-midnight Tue-Sun. Closed Nov-May. **€€**.

The Lido's coolest dining hangout, with a lively *aperitivo* scene in the evening before eating begins. Charming hosts

Mauro Codussi in the 1460s, this white building of Istrian stone was Venice's first Renaissance church.

An orderly red-brick wall runs around the whole of the island, with a line of tall cypress trees rising high behind it – the inspiration for Böcklin's famously lugubrious painting *Island of the Dead*.

Murano

After San Michele, the vaporetto continues to Murano, one of the larger and more populous islands. In the 16th and 17th centuries, when it was a world centre of glass production and a decadent resort for pleasure-seeking Venetians, Murano had a population of more than 30,000. These days, only around 5,000 people live here, with many workers commuting from the mainland.

Murano owes its fame to the decision taken in 1291 to transfer all of Venice's glass furnaces to the island because of a fear of fire in the main city. Their products were soon sold all over Europe. At first sight, Murano looks close to being ruined by glass tourism. Dozens of 'guides' swoop on visitors as they pile off the ferry, to whisk them off on tours of furnaces. Even if you head off on your own, you'll find yourself on fondamenta dei Vetrai, full of shops selling glass knick-knacks, most of which are made far from Murano. But there are some serious glass-makers on the island and even the tackiest showroom usually has one or two gems.

There's more to Murano, however, than glass. At the end of fondamenta dei Vetrai is the nondescript façade of the 14th-century parish church of **San Pietro Martire**, which holds important works of art including Bellini's impressive altarpiece triptych. The Palazzo Giustinian holds the **Museo dell'Arte Vetrario**, the best place to learn about the history of glass. Just beyond this is Murano's greatest architectural treasure: the 12th-century basilica of **Santi Maria e Donato**.

Sights & museums

Museo dell'Arte Vetrario
Fondamenta Giustinian 8 (041 739 586). Vaporetto Museo. **Open** 10am-5pm daily. **Admission** €5.50; €3 reductions.
Housed in beautiful Palazzo Giustinian, built in the late 17th century for the bishop of Torcello, the museum has a huge collection of Murano glass. As well as the famed chandeliers, which were first produced in the 18th century, there are ruby-red beakers, opaque lamps and delicate Venetian *perle* – glass beads that were used in trade and commerce all over the world from the time of Marco Polo.

San Pietro Martire
Fondamenta dei Vetrai (041 739 704). Vaporetto Colonna or Faro. **Open** 9am-6pm Mon-Fri; 1-6pm Sat; 8am-5pm Sun.
Behind its unspectacular façade, the church of San Pietro Martire conceals an important work by Giovanni Bellini: *The Virgin and Child Enthroned with St Mark, St Augustine and Doge Agostino Barbarigo*. There is also a Tintoretto *Baptism*, two works by Veronese and his assistants (mainly the latter) and an ornate altarpiece – *Deposition* – by Salviati.

Santi Maria e Donato
Campo San Donato (041 739 056). Vaporetto Museo. **Open** 8am-7pm daily.
Although altered by over-enthusiastic 19th-century restorers, the exterior of this church is a classic of the Veneto-Byzantine style, with an ornate blind portico on the rear of the apse. Inside is a richly coloured mosaic floor, laid down in 1140 (at the same time as the floor of the Basilica di San Marco), with floral and animal motifs. Above,

Clockwise from top left: **Busa alla Torre p158**; **Santi Mariae Donato**; **Murano glass**; view towards **San Pietro Martire**

a Byzantine apse mosaic of the Virgin looms out of the darkness surrounded by a field of gold.

Eating & drinking

Acquastanca
Fondamenta Manin 48 (041 319 5125, www.acquastanca.it). Vaporetto Faro.
Open *Bar* 9am-4pm, 6-11pm Mon, Fri; 9am-4pm, 6-8.30pm Tue-Thur, Sat. **Meals served** noon-3.30pm, 7-10.30pm Mon, Fri; noon-3.30pm Tue-Thur, Sat. **€€**.
This new arrival on the Murano eating scene is helmed by two local ladies and frequented, to date, more by fellow islanders than by visitors. Housed in a former bakery, it's an all-day kind of place, where you can drop by for a cappuccino, a bar snack or a full-blown meal. The menu features fishy Venetian classics.

B-Restaurant alla Vecchia Pescheria
Campiello Pescheria 4 (041 527 957). Vaporetto Faro. **Meals served** noon-3.30pm Mon, Tue; noon-3.30pm, 6-10pm Thur-Sun. Closed 3 wks Dec. **€€**.
A sideline for the glass-making Berengo dynasty, this trattoria in Murano's old fish market is chic and stylish inside, with tables beneath big green umbrellas outside on a pretty square. The welcome is friendly, and some very good, creative seafood cooking is served up at reasonable prices (for Venice). The hours given above refer to meal times: but B-Restaurant opens early in the morning for breakfast, and is good for an aperitivo too.

Busa alla Torre
Campo Santo Stefano 3 (041 739 662). Vaporetto Faro. **Meals served** noon-3.30pm daily. **€€€**.
In summer, tables spill out into a pretty square opposite the church of San Pietro Martire. The service is deft and professional. The cuisine is no-frills seafood cooking, with good primi that

might include tagliatelle with *canoce* (mantis shrimps) or ravioli filled with *branzino* (bream) in a spider-crab sauce. Note the lunch-only opening.

La Perla ai Bisatei
Campo San Bernardo 1 (041 739 528). Vaporetto Museo or Venier.
Meals served noon-3pm daily. **€€**. No credit cards.
La Perla is a rare gem in Venice: spit-and-sawdust, local, family-run, unreconstructed, with great mainly fishy dishes at sub-Venetian prices and an atmosphere that makes anyone who wanders this far into Murano feel like they've stumbled across a roomful of old friends. The traditional Venetian fare is well prepared, served in generous helpings and very fresh.

Shopping

Berengo Fine Arts
Fondamenta dei Vetrai 109A (041 739 453, www.berengo.com). Vaporetto Colonna or Faro. **Open** 9am-5.30pm daily.
Adriano Berengo commissions international artists to design brilliantly coloured sculptures – in glass, of course.

Davide Penso
Riva Longa 48 (041 527 4634, www.davidepenso.com). Vaporetto Museo.
Open 9.30am-6.30pm daily.
Davide Penso makes and shows exquisite glass jewellery. His own creations are all one-off or limited edition pieces with designs drawn from nature: zebra-striped, mother-of-pearl or crocodile-skinned. The shop sometimes closes 1.30-2.30pm.

Galliano Ferro
Fondamenta Colleoni 6 (041 739 477, www.gallianoferro.it). Vaporetto Faro.
Open by appt. No credit cards.
Inspired by 18th-century classics of design, Ferro's rich, vibrant and intricate works in glass are some of Murano's most sought-after pieces.

There are early 20th-century and Islamic art-inspired designs too.

Luigi Camozzo

Fondamenta Venier 3 (041 736 875, www.luigicamozzo.com). Vaporetto Venier. **Open** 10am-6pm Mon-Fri; by appt Sat, Sun.

It would be over-simplifying things to describe Luigi Camozzo as a glass-engraver. He carves, sculpts and inscribes wonderfully soft, natural bas-reliefs into glass. Drop by and you may even catch him in action.

Manin 56

Fondamenta Manin 56 (041 527 5392). Vaporetto Faro. **Open** 10am-6pm daily. Closed Jan.

This place sells modern (though slightly staid) lines in glassware and vases from prestigious houses such as Salviati and Vivarini.

Marina e Susanna Sent

Fondamenta Serenella 20 (041 527 4665, www.marinaesusannasent.com). Vaporetto Colonna. **Open** 10am-5pm Mon-Fri.

In the Sent sisters' recently expanded Murano workshop, you'll find clean, modern jewellery in glass, as well as innovative jewellery in other materials. See also p146.

Murano Collezioni

Fondamenta Manin 1C (041 736 272, www.muranocollezioni.com). Vaporetto Colonna. **Open** 10.30am-5.30pm Mon-Sat. Closed 2wks Jan.

This shop sells pieces by some of the lagoon's most respected glass producers, including Carlo Moretti, Barovier e Toso, and Venini.

Rossana e Rossana

Riva Longa 11 (041 527 4076, www.ro-e-ro.com). Vaporetto Museo. **Open** 10am-6pm daily.

The place to come for traditional Venetian glass, all produced by master glass-maker Davide Fuin.

Seguso Viro

Fondamenta Venier 29 (041 527 4255, www.segusoviro.com). Vaporetto Museo or Venier. **Open** 11am-4pm Mon-Sat.

Giampaolo Seguso's modern blown-glass pieces are enhanced by experiments around Murano traditions.

Venini

Fondamenta Vetrai 47 (041 273 7204, www.venini.com). Vaporetto Colonna. **Open** 9.30am-5.30pm Mon-Sat.

Venini was the biggest name in Murano glass for much of the 20th century, and remains in the forefront.

Burano & Mazzorbo

Mazzorbo, the long island next to Burano, is a haven of peace, rarely visited by tourists. It is worth getting off here just for the sake of the quiet walk along the canal and then across the long wooden bridge that connects Mazzorbo to Burano. The view from the bridge across the lagoon to Venice is stunning. Mazzorbo is a lazy place of small farms with a pleasant walk to the 14th-century Gothic church of Santa Caterina (opening times vary).

Burano is picturesque in the extreme. Together with its lace, its multicoloured houses make it a magnet for tourists armed with cameras. The street leading from the main quay throbs with souvenir shops selling lace, lace and more lace – much of it machine-made in the Far East. Lace was first produced in Burano in the 15th century, originally by nuns, and then by fishermen's wives and daughters. Today, most work is done on commission.

It was in Burano that Carnevale (p30) was revived in the 1970s; the modest celebrations here are still far more authentically joyful than the antics of masked tourists cramming piazza San Marco.

The busy main square of Burano is named after the island's most

Top to bottom: **Burano p159;
Mazzorbo p159; Santa Fosca,
Torcello p162**

famous son, Baldassare Galuppi, a 17th-century composer who collaborated with Carlo Goldoni on a number of operas and who was the subject of a poem by Robert Browning. The square is a good place for sipping a glass of prosecco. Across from the lace museum is the church of San Martino (open 8am-noon, 3-7pm daily), containing an early Tiepolo *Crucifixion* and, in the chapel to the right of the chancel, three small paintings by the 15th-century painter Giovanni Mansueti. There's a lively morning fish market (Tue-Sat) on the fondamenta della Pescheria.

Sights & museums

Museo del Merletto

Burano, piazza B Galuppi 187 (041 730 034, http://museomerletto.visitmuve.it). Vaporetto Burano. **Open** 10am-5pm Tue-Sun. **Admission** €5; €3.50 reductions. No credit cards.
Following a major revamp, the Lace School's rooms with painted wooden beams are looking resplendent. The displays cover elaborate examples of lace-work from the 17th century onwards. Some of Burano's remaining lace-makers can regularly be found at work here, displaying their handicraft to visitors.

Eating & drinking

Alla Maddalena

Mazzorbo, via Mazzorbo 7B (041 730 151). Vaporetto Mazzorbo. **Meals served** noon-3pm Mon-Wed, Fri-Sun. **€€.**
Opposite the jetty on the island of Mazzorbo is this lunch-only trattoria, which serves good lagoon cuisine. During the hunting season, wild duck is sourced directly from local hunters; the rest of the year, seafood dominates the menu. You'll need to book for Sunday lunch in summer, when tables by the water and in the quiet garden

behind fill up. Service is professional, though not always cheerful.

Venissa

Mazzorbo, fondamenta Santa Caterina 3 (041 527 2281, www.venissa.it). Vaporetto Mazzorbo. **Meals served** noon-2.30pm, 7-9.30pm daily. **€€€€.**
Inside a high-walled vineyard, with a hotel attached (p179), Venissa serves exquisite fare inspired by super-fresh local produce, conjured up by Michelin-starred chef Antonia Klugmann. Many of the raw ingredients come from the on-site vegetable garden, but fish also features heavily. There are taster menus at €75 and €95. The main restaurant is open only six months a year, but a less formal (and considerably cheaper) eating alternative and winebar runs year-round. The initiative is the brainchild of prosecco producers Bisol, who have brought back to life the well-nigh-forgotten Dorona grape here. Book to arrive an hour before lunch and enjoy a tour of the walled estate, plus a tasting (€25).

San Francesco del Deserto

From behind the church of San Martino on Burano, there is a view across the lagoon to the idyllic monastery island of San Francesco del Deserto. The island, with its 4,000 cypress trees, is inhabited by a small community of Franciscan monks. Getting there can be a challenge. If you take the water taxi from Burano, expect to pay at least €60 for the return ride. Individuals or smaller groups should call the Laguna Fla boat hire service (339 778 1132, mobile), which charges €10 per person return (no credit cards).
The otherworldly monk who shepherds visitors around will tell the story (only in Italian) of how the island was St Francis's first stop in Europe on his journey back from the Holy Land in 1220. The medieval

monastery (Convento di San Francesco del Deserto, 041 528 6863, www.sanfrancescodeldeserto.it; open 9-11am, 3-5pm Tue-Sun) – all warm stone and cloistered calm – is about as far as you can get from the worldly bustle of the Rialto.

Torcello

This sprawling, marshy island is where the history of Venice began. Torcello today is a picturesquely unkempt place with a resident population of about 15 (plus infinitely more mosquitoes). It's difficult to believe that in the 14th century more than 20,000 people lived here. It was the first settlement in the lagoon, founded in the fifth century by the citizens of the Roman town of Altino on the mainland. But Torcello's dominance of the lagoon did not last: Venice itself was found to be more salubrious (malaria was rife on Torcello) and more easily defendable. But past decline is present charm, and rural Torcello is a great antidote to the pedestrian traffic jams around San Marco.

From the ferry jetty, the cathedral campanile can already be made out; to get there, simply follow the path along the main canal through the island. Halfway along the canal is the ponte del Diavolo (one of only two bridges in the lagoon without a parapet).

Torcello's main square has some desultory souvenir stalls, the small but interesting **Museo di Torcello** with archaeological finds from around the lagoon, a battered stone seat known arbitrarily as Attila's throne, and two extraordinary churches. The 11th-century church of Santa Fosca (open 10am-5pm daily, free) looks somewhat like a miniature version of Istanbul's St Sophia, more Byzantine than European with its Greek-cross plan and external colonnade; its bare

interior allows the perfect geometry of the space to come to the fore. Next door is the imposing cathedral of **Santa Maria Assunta**.

Sights & museums

Museo di Torcello

Palazzo del Consiglio (041 730 761). *Vaporetto Torcello.* **Open** 10am-5pm Tue-Sun. **Admission** €3. No credit cards. The Museum of Torcello has a small but worthwhile collection of sculptures and archaeological finds from the cathedral and elsewhere in Torcello.

Santa Maria Assunta

041 270 2464. Vaporetto Torcello. **Open** 10.30am-5pm daily. **Admission** €5. No credit cards. Dating from 639, the basilica of Santa Maria Assunta is the oldest building on the lagoon. The interior has an elaborate 11th-century mosaic floor, but the main draws are the vivid mosaics on the ceiling vault and walls, which range in date from the ninth century to the end of the 12th. The apse has a simple but stunning mosaic of a *Madonna and Child* on a plain gold background, while the other end of the cathedral is dominated by a huge mosaic of the *Last Judgement*. It's worth picking up an audio-guide (€2) for a very good explanation of the church's history and artistic treasures.

Eating & drinking

Locanda Cipriani

Torcello, piazza Santa Fosca 29 (041 730 150, http://locandacipriani.com). *Vaporetto Torcello.* **Meals served** noon-3pm Mon, Wed-Sun. Closed Jan. €€€€. There is a lot to like about the high-class Locanda Cipriani, which was one of Hemingway's haunts. The setting, just off Torcello's pretty square, is idyllic; tables are spread over a large vine-shaded terrace during the summer. The food is good in an old-fashioned way. Specialities such as *risotto alla* *torcellana* (with seasonal vegetables) are done to perfection. Dinner is served (7-9pm) on Friday and Saturday, by prior arrangement only. If you want to stay here, see p179.

La Certosa

Situated between Sant'Elena and Le Vignole, La Certosa was the seat of a monastery, that from 1422 was run by the Certosini monks of Florence. Napoleon suppressed the monastery and the army moved in, staying until 1968, when the island fell into decay. In 2004, the remaining warehouses and huts became the home of a sailing club (www.ventodivenezia.it), which runs a sailing school and a hotel. The rest of the island is open to the public, and makes for a pleasant walk, though views are limited by perimeter walls.

Sant'Erasmo

The largest island in the northern lagoon, Sant'Erasmo is a well-kept secret, with a tiny population that contents itself with growing most of the vegetables eaten in *La Serenissima* (on Rialto market stalls, the sign 'San Rasmo' is a mark of quality). Venetians refer to the islanders of Sant'Erasmo as *i matti* ('the crazies') because of their shallow gene pool – everybody seems to be called Vignotto or Zanella. There are cars on this island, but as they are only used to drive the few miles from house to boat and back, few are in top-notch condition, a state of affairs favoured by the fact that the island does not have a single policeman. It also lacks a doctor, pharmacy and high school, but there is a supermarket and a tiny primary school.

There are also some restaurants: Ca' Vignotto (via Forti 71, 041 528 5329, www.vignotto.com, average €30-€50, closed dinner Tue, Wed,

Sun and all Mon), where bookings are essential; and a fishermen's bartrattoria – Ai Tedeschi (041 521 0738, open 9am-11pm daily) – hidden away on a small sandy beach by the Forte Massimiliano. This latter is a moat-surrounded 19th-century Austrian fort that has been restored and is open to the public on summer afternoons (3-7pm Wed-Sun) and some weekend mornings too.

The main attraction of the island lies in the beautiful country landscapes and lovely walks past traditional Veneto farmhouses, through vineyards and fields of artichokes and asparagus. For those wanting to get around more swiftly, bicycles can be hired from the Lato Azzurro guesthouse (041 523 0642). It's a ten-minute walk southwards from the vaporetto stop Capannone.

By the main vaporetto stop (Chiesa) is the 20th-century church, technically named Santi Erme ed Erasmo, but widely known as simply 'Chiesa'. Over the entrance door is a gruesome painting, attributed to Domenico Tintoretto, of the martyrdom of St Erasmus, who had his intestines wound out of his body on a windlass. The resemblance of a windlass to a capstan resulted in St Erasmus becoming the patron saint of sailors.

Lazzaretto Nuovo & Vignole

Opposite Sant'Erasmo's Capannone vaporetto stop is the tiny island of Lazzaretto Nuovo. In the 15th century, the island was fortified as a customs depot and military prison; during the 1576 plague outbreak it became a quarantine centre. The island is now home to a research centre for the archaeologists of the Archeo Club di Venezia, who are excavating its ancient remains, including a church that may date back to the sixth century.

On the smaller island of Vignole (also served by the 13 vaporetto, on request), there is a medieval chapel dedicated to St Erosia.

The Southern Lagoon

The southern part of the lagoon – between Venice, the Lido and the mainland – has 14 small islands, a few of which are still inhabited, though most are out of bounds to tourists. La Grazia was for years a quarantine hospital but the structure has now been closed. The huge San Clemente, originally a lunatic asylum and later a home for abandoned cats, is now a plush hotel (p179).

San Servolo

From the 18th century until 1978, San Servolo was Venice's mental hospital; it is now home to Venice International University. In 2006, the Museo del Manicomio di San Servolo (San Servolo Asylum Museum; 041 524 0119) was inaugurated. The museum is open for guided visits only (€3; minimum five people); booking is essential. It reveals the different ways in which mental illnesses have been treated over the years; there are not only examples of the more or less brutal methods of restraint (chains, straitjackets, handcuffs) but also early examples of such treatments as hydro-massage and electrotherapy. After the tour, it is possible to visit the island's extensive and charming gardens.

San Lazzaro degli Armeni

A further five minutes on the no.20 will take you to the island of San Lazzaro degli Armeni. There are tours (€6 ; 41 526 0104) of the island every afternoon for visitors from the mid-afternoon boat (times vary seasonally) from San Zaccaria.

A black-cloaked Armenian priest meets the boat and takes visitors on a detailed tour of the Monastero Mechitarista. The tiny island is a global point of reference for Armenia's Catholic minority, visited and supported by Armenians from Italy and abroad. Near the entrance stand the printing presses that helped to distribute Armenian literature all over the world for 200 years. They are now silent, with the monastery's retro line in dictionaries and liturgical texts farmed out to a modern press.

Originally a leper colony, in 1717 the island was presented by the doge to an Armenian abbot called Mekhitar, who was on the run from the Turkish invasion of the Peloponnese. There had been an Armenian community in Venice since the 11th century, centring on the tiny Santa Croce degli Armeni church, just around the corner from piazza San Marco, but the construction of this church and monastery made Venice a world centre of Armenian culture.

The tour takes in both the cloisters and the church, rebuilt after a fire in 1883. The museum and the modern library contain 40,000 priceless books and manuscripts, and a bizarre collection of gifts donated over the years by visiting Armenians that range from Burmese prayer books to an Egyptian mummy.

The island's most famous student was Lord Byron, who used to take a break from his more earthly pleasures in Venice and row over three times a week to learn Armenian. He helped the monks to publish an Armenian-English grammar, although by his own confession he never got beyond the basics of the language. You can buy a completed version of this, plus period maps and an illustrated children's Armenian grammar, in the shop just inside the monastery gate.

Essentials

Aman Grand Canal Venice p173

Hotels

Venice is a city of immense accommodation price swings, so placing hotels under category headings is as difficult as it is misleading. We've divided the hotels by area, while in the listings we've rated them according to the standard prices (not including seasonal offers or discounts) for one night in a double room with en suite shower/bath. For deluxe hotels (€€€€) you can expect to pay from €500 upwards; €€€ means it will cost from €300 up to €500 per night; €€ means a moderate hotel at €150-€300, and € is a budget hotel with a bill below €150.

However, it really does pay to check hotel websites carefully, especially at peak times, and to book directly with the selected establishment. A room that costs €500 in high season might plummet to €150 in late November; and even mid-range options at around €200 will be on offer at €75 a night or less in the dog days.

In the know

In general, room prices include breakfast, though this is of wildly varying freshness and generosity; check when booking.

Reaching your hotel in this labyrinthine city can be a challenge. Ask for very clear directions, including the nearest vaporetto (ferry) stop or church, or GPS coordinates. If you have mobility problems and/or don't fancy dragging your suitcase over too many bridges with steps, ask whether your hotel of choice has a *porta d'acqua* (canal-side entrance) where a water taxi can pull right up to reception.

Facilities for the disabled are scarce in Venetian hotels, mainly due to the nature of the buildings. Many establishments spread over several floors but do not have lifts; always check first. See p184 for information on disabled travel in Venice.

ESSENTIALS

Most hotels will charge more for rooms with canal or lagoon views. As some canals are muddy backwaters, and others are major highways with a constant procession of bellowing gondoliers, it pays to ask exactly what this water view consists of.

San Marco

AD Place

San Marco 2557A, fondamenta della Fenice (041 241 3234, www.adplace venice.con). *Vaporetto Giglio.* €€€.
Tucked away on a quiet canal behind La Fenice opera house, AD Place has a friendly atmosphere and great service. Bedrooms and public spaces revel in a wild combination of candy-stripe colours and baroque touches. Rooms vary in size; one on the ground-floor is wheelchair-adapted. The private water entrance means you can get straight here by water taxi. The roof terrace is a great place to watch the sun set.

Bauer Hotels

San Marco 1459, campo San Moisè (041 520 7022, www.bauerhotels.com). *Vaporetto San Marco Vallaresso.* €€€€.
This is a hotel of many parts. The main block – Bauer's L'Hotel – occupies a 1940s extension of the original 18th-century hotel building; though the place is brutal outside, the vast hall inside with its marble, gold and black looks like a grand old ocean liner. Luxurious, antique Il Palazzo is housed in an older building and has Grand Canal frontage. Adjacent to L'Hotel, Casanova has a series of comfortable, sunny serviced apartments.

Ca' del Nobile

San Marco 987, rio terà delle Colonne (041 528 3473, www.cadelnobile.com). *Vaporetto Rialto.* €€.
The last five years have seen a rash of six-room *locande* with near-identical websites opening in Venice, but this compact charmer has an edge on the competition. It's two minutes' walk

ESSENTIALS

from piazza San Marco, service is spot-on, and the classic-contemporary decor is a cut above the usual cookie-cutter Casanova look.

Corte di Gabriela

San Marco 3836, calle degli Avvocati (041 523 5077, www.cortedigabriela. com). Vaporetto Sant'Angelo. €€€.
This recent addition marries classic Venetian frescoes and stucco with some *molto-mod* design details to produce a very stylish four-star boutique hotel with obliging, well informed staff. Spacious bedrooms come with iPads and kettles; the bathrooms are large and chic. The breakfast is a rich feast of home-baked goodies.

Flora

San Marco 2283A, calle Bergamaschi (041 520 5844, www.hotelflora.it). Vaporetto San Marco Vallaresso. €€.
Book well in advance if you want to stay at the perennially popular Flora. It offers a tranquil stay in rooms that are classic Venetian, varying significantly from quite opulent to relatively spartan; some are tiny. There's a cosy bar and a delightful garden. The Flora prides itself on its child-friendly features.

Gritti Palace

San Marco 2467, campo Santa Maria del Giglio (041 794 611, www.thegritti palace.com). Vaporetto Giglio. €€€€.
With much fanfare, the 15th-century Gritti Palace reopened in 2013 after a massive makeover that upped the already considerable luxury quotient. Each room is uniquely decorated; one is lined with antique floor-to-ceiling mirrors. If you want a canal or campo view, specify when booking: some rooms overlook a dingy courtyard. Breakfast, or just an *aperitivo* on the canal terrace, is an experience in itself.

Hotel Monaco & Grand Canal

San Marco 1332, calle Vallaresso (041 520 0211, www.hotelmonaco.it). Vaporetto San Marco Vallaresso. €€€.
This Grand Canal fixture is a curious hybrid. The lobby and bar area is a fussy mix of classic and modern; the rooms in the main building are untouched by the design revolution, while those on the Grand Canal are ultra-traditional Venetian. More *charmant* is the Palazzo Selvadego residence: no lagoon views, but modern Mediterranean-style rooms.

Locanda Novecento

San Marco 2683-4, calle del Dose (041 241 3765, www.novecento.biz). Vaporetto Giglio. €€.
This home-from-home is a real pleasure after a hard day's sightseeing. With its friendly, helpful staff, little garden, and reading and sitting rooms, Novecento is a special place to stay. Wooden floors, ethnic textiles, oriental rugs, Indonesian furniture and individually decorated rooms make a refreshing change.

Locanda Orseolo

San Marco 1083, corte Zorzi (041 520 4827, www.locandaorseolo.com). Vaporetto Rialto. €€.
This welcoming *locanda* has beamed ceilings, painted wood panelling, leaded windows and rich colours; there's even a tiny water entrance. The immaculate bedrooms are furnished in a fairly restrained Venetian style. Choose between a canal view (which can be noisy) or quieter rooms overlooking the square. Breakfast is generous; staff are very helpful.

Luna Hotel Baglioni

San Marco 1243, calle larga dell'Ascensione (041 528 9840, www.baglionihotels.com). Vaporetto San Marco Vallaresso. €€€€.
In a 15th-century palazzo, this hotel has little remaining period decor. Shiny marble, swathes of rich fabric and lots of Murano glass provide the backdrop for luxurious bedrooms and communal areas. Views from the rooms are of the Giardinetti Reali, the lagoon and San Giorgio Maggiore.

ESSENTIALS

Palazzo Sant'Angelo sul Canal Grande

San Marco 3878B, fondamenta del Teatro a Sant'Angelo (041 241 1452, www.palazzosantangelo.com). Vaporetto Sant'Angelo. €€€.

While it enjoys a superb location on the Grand Canal and luxurious facilities, Palazzo Sant'Angelo is rather lacking in soul. The red and gold bedrooms are traditional in style; all have whirlpool baths, fine bed linen, fluffy robes and slippers. Rooms overlooking the Grand Canal cost extra; instead, watch the gondolas drift by from the sitting room and bar area.

San Samuele

San Marco 3358, salizada San Samuele (041 522 8045, www.hotelsansamuele. it). Vaporetto San Samuele or Sant'Angelo. €€.

Flowers cascade from the window boxes of this friendly little hotel in an excellent location. The spotlessly clean rooms have a simple, sunny aspect and the welcome from manager Judith is always warm. There's free Wi-Fi throughout. Breakfast is not included, though there's a coffee machine in reception for guests, and a fridge to keep your supplies in.

Saturnia & International

San Marco 2398, via XXII Marzo (041 520 8377, www.hotelsaturnia.it). Vaporetto San Marco Vallaresso. €€€.

An old-fashioned, friendly air pervades this bustling hotel. The 14th-century building's interior has been done up in an eclectic faux-Renaissance style. The bedrooms vary considerably: most are in traditional Venetian style, but a handful have been given a more contemporary makeover in the retro style of sister hotel Ca' Pisani (p176). The roof terrace has a view of Santa Maria della Salute.

Castello

B&B San Marco

Castello 3385L, fondamenta San Giorgio degli Schiavoni (041 522 7589, 335 756 6555, www.realvenice.it/ smarco). Vaporetto San Zaccaria. **Closed** Jan & 2wks Aug. €.

One of the few Venetian B&Bs that come close to the British concept of the genre. Two of the three cosy, antique-filled bedrooms share a bathroom; the other is en-suite. There's also an apartment that sleeps four. Marco and his wife Alice serve breakfast in their own kitchen and guests are treated as part of the family.

Ca' del Nobile p167

ESSENTIALS

Bed & Breakfast

The personal touch.

B&Bs in Venice vary from spartan squats to rooms in glorious antiques-filled *palazzi*, with an equally wide range of prices reflecting location and facilities.

In addition to the cosy **B&B San Marco** (p169) and the charming **Campiello Zen** (p173), a few other places are worth considering. A pretty plant-filled courtyard with a well is the main draw of **Corte 1321** (San Polo 1321, campiello Ca' Bernardi, 041 522 4923, www.corte1321.com), a three-room ethno-chic B&B. The welcome from hosts Maria and Rodolfo makes **Residenza de l'Osmarin** (Castello 4960, calle Rota, 347 450 1440, www.residenzadelosmarin.com) a hit, and you'll need to book well in advance to bag one of the pretty, airy rooms – especially the huge top-floor suite. Similarly, it's Lorenzo's personal touch that gives **B&B Ai Tagliapietra** (pictured above; Castello 4943, salizada Zorzi, 347 323 3166, www.aitagliapietra.com) its edge; but the three comfortable rooms also come with all the help you need, at a reasonable price.

The handy **www.bed-and-breakfast.it** website has many more Venice options.

Bed & Venice – Casa per Ferie

Castello 3701, calle della Pietà (041 244 3639, www.bedandvenice.it). Vaporetto San Zaccaria. €-€€.

This bright hostel is spacious, sunny and spotlessly clean, with around 40 beds; a couple of singles and six doubles, with the rest in dormitory rooms sleeping up to six. None have private baths. Families with children are very welcome, and can make use of cots and other baby equipment. The rooms occupy the top two floors of the building, so there are some great views, especially from the terrace at the top.

Casa Querini

Castello 4388, campo San Giovanni Novo (041 241 1294, www.locandaquerini. com). Vaporetto San Zaccaria. **Closed** Jan. €€.

This friendly hotel has a pretty little terrace area on a quiet square; breakfast is served here when the weather is fine. From a tiny reception area, stairs lead up to bedrooms pleasantly decorated in sober Venetian style; all are spacious, but try for one with a view of the square rather than the side alley.

Casa Verardo

Castello 4765, calle della Sacrestia (041 528 6138, www.casaverardo.it). Vaporetto San Zaccaria. €€.

Tucked away at the end of a narrow *calle*, and across its own little bridge only minutes from piazza San Marco, the first impression of Casa Verardo is of cool and calm. Bedrooms are decorated in elegant, tasteful fabrics. There's a pretty courtyard at the back, and a terrace off the elegant salon where tables are laid for breakfast. The level of comfort and facilities is above what you might expect at these prices.

Charming House i Qs

Castello 4425, campiello Querini Stampalia (041 241 0062, www.the charminghouse.com). Vaporetto San Zaccaria. €€€.

The latest addition to the Charming House boutique hotel group is as radical a design statement as you'll find in play-safe Venice. If it weren't for the *porta d'acqua* gondola entrance and the overhead beams, i Qs' four accommodation options (including a two-bedroom, self-catering apartment) could almost be in Milan or New York. Service is impeccable.

Locanda La Corte
Castello 6317, calle Bressana (041 241 1300, www.locandalacorte.it). Vaporetto Fondamente Nove. €€.
Housed in a small 16th-century palazzo, La Corte is removed from noisy tourist trails. Bedrooms are decorated in restful greens or striking russets and there is a little courtyard where breakfast is served in summer.

Locanda Vivaldi
Castello 4150-2, riva degli Schiavoni (041 277 0477, www.locandavivaldi.it). Vaporetto San Zaccaria. €€€.
This luxurious hotel offers tasteful rooms with modern comforts. Located partly in the house where composer Antonio Vivaldi lived, and next to the church where he taught music (La Pietà; p84), the Vivaldi offers views of the island of San Giorgio from the magnificent roof terrace – where breakfast is served in summer – and from the front bedrooms.

Londra Palace
Castello 4171, riva degli Schiavoni (041 520 0533, www.hotelondra.it). Vaporetto San Zaccaria. €€€€.
It's no wonder that Tchaikovsky found this hotel – with no fewer than 100 of its bedroom windows facing San Giorgio Maggiore across the lagoon – a congenial spot in which to write his fourth symphony in 1877. Today, the Londra Palace is elegant but restrained. You can sunbathe on the roof terrace or enjoy a romantic dinner at the restaurant where, in good weather, tables are laid out on the *riva*.

Metropole
Castello 4149, riva degli Schiavoni (041 520 5044, www.hotelmetropole.com). Vaporetto San Zaccaria. €€€€.
Of all the grand hotels nearby, the Metropole is arguably the most characterful. Owner-manager Pierluigi Beggiato is a passionate collector, and his antiques and curios are dotted in the elegant and varied bedrooms. In winter, tea and cakes are served in the velvet-draped *salone*; in summer, guests relax in the pretty garden. The hotel's Met restaurant, with a slew of impressive young chefs, has one Michelin star and prices to match. Breakfast is not always included in the room rates.

Savoia & Jolanda
Castello 4187, riva degli Schiavoni (041 520 6644, 041 522 4130, www.hotel savoiajolanda.com). Vaporetto San Zaccaria. €€€.
A hotel of two different but lovely halves, the Savoia offers rooms with balconies and views across the Bacino di San Marco to San Giorgio Maggiore in one direction, or facing back over Castello towards the glorious façade of San Zaccaria. The decor is pleasantly luxurious without going over the top, and breakfast is a sumptuous spread.

Cannaregio

Al Ponte Antico
Cannaregio 5768, calle dell'Aseo (041 241 1944, www.alponteantico.com). Vaporetto Rialto. €€€.
With its festooned curtains and lashings of brocade, the family-run Al Ponte Antico takes the traditional Venetian hotel decor idiom and turns it into something faintly decadent. In a 16th-century palazzo on the Grand Canal, with views over the Rialto bridge, Al Ponte Antico's exquisite little balcony overlooks the water, as do some doubles and suites. Owner-manager Matteo Peruch will make you feel totally at home; the breakfasts here are famous and fêted.

Palazzo Abadessa

Ca' Dogaressa

*Cannaregio 1018, calle del Sotoportego
Scuro (041 275 9441, www.cadogaressa.
com). Vaporetto Guglie or Tre Archi.* €€.
This welcoming, family-run hotel offers
a modern take on 'traditional' Venetian
accommodation decor: the Murano
glass light fittings and brocade-covered
walls are there, but so are neat marble
bathrooms, comfortable beds and air-
con. Breakfast is served at tables along
the canalside on fine days. There's also a
roof terrace with fantastic views.

Ca' Sagredo

*Cannaregio 4198, campo Santa Sofia
(041 241 3111, www.casagredohotel.
com). Vaporetto Ca' d'Oro.* €€€€.
This Grand Canal palazzo dating from
the 15th century is as much a museum
as a hotel, with a magnificent double
staircase, a huge rococo ballroom and
frescoes by Giambattista Tiepolo
among its many treasures. There are
six stunning historical suites, and
rooms in which decor is standard luxe-
Venetian, albeit of the bright, light-
filled sort. Service is mostly charming,
especially at the impressive breakfast.

Domus Orsoni

*Cannaregio 1045, sottoportego dei Vedei
(041 275 9538, www.domusorsoni.it).
Vaporetto Crea or Guglie.* €€.

The Orsoni dynasty has been produc-
ing glass in its foundry attached to this
charming B&B for generations, and
their magnificent wares decorate floors
and walls here in richly coloured mosaics. Many guests stay here while attend-
ing mosaic-making courses at the
foundry. The five rooms (including one
single) are large, airy and uncluttered,
with great bathrooms; some look out
over the property's beautiful garden.
Breakfast is served on a pleasant terrace in fine weather. Request a tour of
the fascinating foundry – the only one
allowed to remain in Venice after 1291.

Giorgione

*Cannaregio 4587, calle larga dei Proverbi
(041 522 5810, www.hotelgiorgione.
com). Vaporetto Ca' d'Oro.* €€.
Just off the busy campo Santi Apostoli,
the Giorgione exudes warmth. A
15th-century palazzo joins the newer
extension around a flower-filled
courtyard with a lily pond (a rather
less picturesque salt-water whirlpool
tub was also planned for this space).
Some split-level rooms have terraces
overlooking the rooftops.

Locanda ai Santi Apostoli

*Cannaregio 4391A, strada Nuova (041
521 2612, www.locandasantiapostoli.
com). Vaporetto Ca' d'Oro.* €€.

A pair of handsome dark green doors lead to the courtyard of this palazzo, where a lift sweeps you up to the third floor. The hotel feels like a genteel private apartment. The two best rooms overlook the Grand Canal; book well ahead and be prepared to pay extra. A comfortable sitting room, filled with antiques and books, overlooks the water.

Locanda del Ghetto

Cannaregio 2892-3, campo del Ghetto Nuovo (041 275 9292, www.locanda delghetto.net). Vaporetto Guglie or San Marcuola. €€.

The building that houses this guesthouse dates from the 15th century, and several rooms still retain the original decorated wooden ceilings. Upstairs, light and airy bedrooms have cream walls, honey-coloured parquet floors and pale gold bedcovers; two of them have small terraces on the campo side. A sparse kosher breakfast is served in the ground-floor dining room, which overlooks a canal.

Palazzo Abadessa

Cannaregio 4011, calle Priuli (041 241 3784, www.abadessa.com). Vaporetto Ca'd'Oro. €€€.

A beautiful, shady walled garden is laid out in front of this 16th-century palazzo, where the prevailing atmosphere is that of an aristocratic private home (which it is). A magnificent stone double staircase leads to the impressive bedrooms, all of which are beautifully appointed with richly coloured brocade-covered walls. Some are vast, but three low-ceilinged doubles on the mezzanine floor are rather cramped. Bathrooms tend to be small too.

San Polo & Santa Croce

Ai Due Fanali

Santa Croce 946, campo San Simeon Grande (041 718 490, www.aiduefanali. com). Vaporetto Riva di Biasio. €€.

Housed in the old annexe of the church of San Simeon Grande, this neat little hotel faces the Grand Canal across a pretty campo. On a terrace at the front, tables are set out under big umbrellas; there's also a rooftop breakfast room and *altana* (roof terrace). The reception area has antiques, oriental rugs and fresh flowers, and the 16 smallish bedrooms have a refreshing lack of brocade, and good modern bathrooms.

Al Ponte Mocenigo

Santa Croce 2063, fondamenta Rimpetto Mocenigo (041 524 4797, www.alponte mocenigo.com). Vaporetto San Stae. €€

A delightful hotel across its own little bridge on a quiet canal near campo San Stae, this has to be one of Venice's best-value accommodation options. It has tastefully decorated mod-Venetian rooms and well-appointed bathrooms, not to mention a bar, a Turkish bath, a pretty courtyard garden and genuinely charming owners – Walter and Sandro. The eight-room annexe nearby has similarly decorated accommodation.

Aman Grand Canal Venice

San Polo 1364, calle Tiepolo Baiamonte (041 270 7333, www.amanresorts.com). Vaporetto San Silvestro. €€€€.

Aman's Venetian outpost – opened in 2013 – is exactly what you'd expect of this hotel group: immaculate service and deluxe surroundings. The hotel is housed in palazzo Papadopoli (not to be confused with Sofitel's Papadopoli hotel; p174), whose count-owner still lives on the top floor. The bedrooms and suites are exercises in pared-back luxury: one has frescoes by GB Tiepolo; another has a magnificent fireplace designed by Sansovino.

Campiello Zen

Santa Croce 1285, rio terà di Biasio (041 710 431, www.campiellozen.com). Vaporetto Riva di Biasio. €€.

This three-room charmer is in a quiet, untouristy spot but handy for the Riva di Biasio vaporetto stop, for some very good restaurants and for the railway station. Welcoming host Andrea will plot itineraries, organise restaurant bookings and generally make sure that your Venice experience is a special one. The rooms are tastefully decorated: one is on the ground floor and the others are up two flights of stairs (no lift). Breakfast is a sumptuous spread.

Ca' Nigra Lagoon Resort

Santa Croce 927, campo San Simeon Grande (041 275 0047, www.hotel canigra.com). €€€.

Ca' Nigra is a classy little hotel with a fantastic position on the Grand Canal, in a 17th-century villa painted deep red and set in a beautiful waterside garden. Public spaces and the spacious junior suites are done out with interesting antique oriental pieces, while the piano nobile has partially retained the period decor. Ultra-contemporary bathrooms are particularly impressive. Pick of the bedrooms is the Loggia Suite with its private terrace; light sleepers should avoid ground-floor rooms close to the breakfast room.

Casa Peron

Santa Croce 84, salizada San Pantalon (041 710 021, www.casaperon.com). Vaporetto San Tomà. **Closed** Jan. €.

Casa Peron is an excellent budget choice. The friendly Scarpa family and their parrot Pierino preside over the very simple, very clean hotel. It's located in the bustling university area, with the shops, restaurants and bars of campo Santa Margherita nearby. Two rooms at the top of the house have private terraces; all have showers, though four are without toilets.

Locanda Marinella

Santa Croce 345, rio terà dei Pensieri (041 275 9457, www.locandamarinella. com). Vaporetto Piazzale Roma. €€.

On a tree-lined street near piazzale Roma, the Locanda Marinella offers stylish, comfortable rooms done out in pale yellow and blue. A tiny garden at the back is shaded by white umbrellas. This is a good choice for those with late arrivals or early departures, and is favoured by people over-nighting in the city before or after cruises. Two smart little apartments sleep four to five people.

Locanda Sturion

San Polo 679, calle dello Sturion (041 523 6243, www.locandasturion.com). Vaporetto Rialto Mercato or San Silvestro. €€.

Established in the late 13th century by the doge as an inn for visiting merchants, this hotel is still thriving – not surprising, given its Grand Canal location. Only two of the rooms overlook the canal (rooms one and two; the others give on to a quiet *calle*), but even if you can't afford the view, you can enjoy it from the breakfast room. It's a long haul up steep stairs, and there's no lift. Staff can be terse.

MGallery Papadopoli

Santa Croce 245, Giardini Papadopoli (041 710 4004, www.mgallery.com). Vaporetto Piazzale Roma. €€€.

Well placed for piazzale Roma and the railway station, this Accor-Sofitel hotel somehow avoids the total anonymity that chains often deliver. Rooms at the front of the modern building overlook a canal and bustling campo Tolentini; those on the top floors have stunning views. There is an elegant cocktail bar, and a restaurant in a plant-lined winter garden where breakfast is also served.

Oltre il Giardino

San Polo 2542, fondamenta Contarini (041 275 0015, www.oltreilgiardino-venezia.com). Vaporetto San Tomà. €€.

Tucked away at the end of a *fondamenta* and accessed through a garden, this attractive villa was once owned by Alma Mahler, widow of the composer Gustav. Today, host Lorenzo Muner welcomes guests to this stylish yet homely hotel, where neutral shades and wood floors provide the backdrop for a mix of antique furniture and contemporary *objis*. Bedrooms vary considerably in size, but all are equipped with TVs, robes, slippers and luxurious bath goodies. Next door, two large suites are great for groups or families.

Salieri

Santa Croce 160, fondamenta Minotto (041 710 035, www.hotelsalieri.com). €.
This simple one-star located between the railway station and piazzale Roma offers ten smartish bedrooms on three floors. Unusually for a hotel of this category, all have bathrooms, air-con, TV and free Wi-Fi. Some rooms look over a canal; others have garden or rooftop views.

San Cassiano – Ca' Favretto

Santa Croce 2232, calle de la Rosa (041 524 1768, www.sancassiano.it). Vaporetto San Stae. €€€.
In a 14th-century Gothic building on the Grand Canal, the San Cassiano has its own private jetty, but if you're arriving on foot, get good directions as the hotel is difficult to find. Rooms are, on the whole, quite elegant, though some are showing their age. The airy breakfast room has huge windows overlooking the Grand Canal and there is a tiny but charming veranda right on the water – a great spot for an early evening *spritz*. Staff are friendly, but there's a charge for Wi-Fi and the three flights of steps (no lift) can be daunting for some.

La Villeggiatura

San Polo 1569, calle dei Botteri (338 853 1264, 041 524 4673, www.la villeggiatura.it). Vaporetto Rialto Mercato or San Silvestro. €€.
A scruffy entranceway and a steep climb (there's no lift) lead to Francesca Adilardi's charming third-floor apartment, which has six tastefully decorated bedrooms, each with its own character and all spacious and bright. Thai silks are draped over the generous-sized beds and at the windows of the subtly themed rooms, two of which have lovely old parquet floors. Windows in the two loft rooms are ceiling lights: bright, but offering views of nothing but the sky. Breakfast is served around a big table in the sunny dining area.

Dorsoduro

Accademia – Villa Maravege

Dorsoduro 1058, fondamenta Bollani (041 521 0188, www.pensioneaccademia. it). Vaporetto Accademia. €€€.
This wonderful secluded 17th-century villa used to be the Russian embassy; it's perennially popular with visitors seeking comfortable *pensione*-style accommodation within easy reach of Dorsoduro's galleries but also handy for more central sights. Located at the junction of the Toletta and Trovaso canals with the Canal Grande, it has a waterside patio where a generous breakfast buffet is served, as well as a grassy rear garden. The rooms are stylish, if fairly traditional, with antiques and marble or wood floors.

Agli Alboretti

Dorsoduro 884, rio terà Foscarini (041 523 0058, www.aglialboretti.com). Vaporetto Accademia. **Closed** 3wks Jan. **€€.**
The model ship in the window of the tiny, wood-panelled reception area of this friendly hotel lends a nautical air to the place. The simply decorated rooms are comfortable and well equipped, though some are truly tiny. Each has an electric kettle for tea and coffee. There is a pretty, pergola-covered terrace at the back of the hotel where meals are served in summer. The staff are exceptionally helpful. A fully equipped three-bed apartment is also available.

American – Dinesen

Dorsoduro 628, fondamenta Bragadin (041 520 4733, www.hotelamerican. com). Vaporetto Accademia. €€€.

Ca' Maria Adele

A well-run and popular hotel with friendly service. Set on the delightful rio di San Vio, its generally spacious rooms are decorated in antique Venetian style; some have balconies with bright geraniums and look over the canal. Try to secure one of the corner rooms, where multiple French windows make for wonderful light. There's a tiny terrace where breakfast is served under a pergola. In low season, rooms here are remarkably inexpensive.

Ca' Foscari

Dorsoduro 3887B, calle della Frescada (041 710 401, www.locandacafoscari. com). Vaporetto San Tomà. **€**.
The Scarpa family has been offering a friendly welcome to guests at this *locanda* since the 1960s. The rooms – some of which could do with a makeover – are on the second and third floors of the building (no lift); they are spotlessly clean. The quietest of them have views over neighbouring gardens while others face the street; not all have private bathrooms.

Ca' Maria Adele

Dorsoduro 111, rio terà dei Catecumeni (041 520 3078, www.camariaadele.it). Vaporetto Salute. **€€€**.
Situated in the shadow of the basilica of Santa Maria della Salute, Ca' Maria Adele marries sumptuous 18th-century Venetian decadence to modern design, with some Moorish elements and a host of quirky details. Brothers Alessio and Nicola Campa preside attentively over 12 luxurious bedrooms, five of which are themed; the red and gold Doge's Room is voluptuous, the Sala Noire ultra-sexy. There's an intimate sitting room on the ground floor, plus a Moroccan-style roof terrace. Breakfast can be consumed in bed or in any of the hotel's public spaces. Next door in Palazzetto 113 are two elegant-chic new rooms, with downstairs lounge, gorgeous roof terrace and – if you take the whole place – a kitchen for self-catering. Note that there is no lift in this four-floor hotel.

Ca' Pisani

Dorsoduro 979A, rio terà Foscarini (041 277 1478, www.capisanihotel.it). Vaporetto Accademia. **€€€**.
Ca' Pisani's luxurious, designer-chic rooms decorated art deco style make a refreshing change from the usual fare of brocade, gilt and Murano glass; this was the first hotel to throw off the yawn-making pan-Venetian style, and though it's no longer the only one, it's still one of the most effective. Bedrooms are all generously sized and there's a restaurant with tables outside

in the summer, a sauna and a roof terrace. The hotel is located right behind the Accademia gallery.

Ca' Zose

Dorsoduro 193B, calle del Bastion (041 522 6635, www.hotelcazose.com). Vaporetto Salute. €€.

The enthusiastic Campanati sisters run this immaculate little guesthouse. There's a tiny, neat breakfast room off the cool white reception area; upstairs, the dozen bedrooms are done out in a fairly restrained traditional Venetian style with painted furniture.

La Calcina

Dorsoduro 780, fondamenta delle Zattere (041 520 6466, www.lacalcina. com). Vaporetto Accademia or Zattere. €€.

La Calcina is a perennial favourite and has an air of civilised calm. The open vistas of the Giudecca canal provide the backdrop for meals taken on the terrace, a view shared by the bedrooms at the front of the building. Rooms have parquet floors, 19th-century furniture and a refreshingly uncluttered feel; one single is without private bath. There is an *altana* (suspended roof terrace), and a number of suites and self-catering apartments are available in adjacent buildings. La Calcina is one of the best value hotels in its category.

DD 724

Dorsoduro 724, ramo da Mula (041 277 0262, www.dd724.com). Vaporetto Accademia. €€€.

Off a gated cul-de-sac (there is a sign, but it's easy to miss), DD 724 is a design hotel in miniature. The bedrooms are stylishly understated in pale shades and dark wood, with contemporary artworks from the owner's collection dotted around; one has a little terrace. Bathrooms in pale travertine are tiny but super-modern with walk-in showers. Public spaces (and some bedrooms) are cramped, though, and the atmosphere isn't exactly warm. A

recent annexe, DD 694, is located two minutes' walk away and has three similarly smart rooms.

Locanda San Barnaba

Dorsoduro 2785-6, calle del Traghetto (041 241 1233, www.locanda-san barnaba.com). Vaporetto Ca' Rezzonico. €€.

Situated at the end of a quiet alleyway, the friendly San Barnaba has 13 comfortable, individually decorated rooms featuring a mix of antique furniture and elegant fabrics, and extremely helpful staff. There's a pretty little courtyard and a roof terrace, and no bridges to cross to get to the nearest vaporetto. Besides the regular boat services, the airport boats also stop here. Note that there's no lift.

Palazzetto da Schio

Dorsoduro 316B, fondamenta Soranzo (041 523 7937, www.palazzettodaschio. it). Vaporetto Salute or Zattere. €€.

The gracious antique-packed family home of Contessa Anna da Schio has been divided into four superb apartments, sleeping between two and six people. The *contessa* is very hands-on, helping guests get the best out of her city. All the apartments have been restored, and fitted with modern fully equipped kitchens and well appointed bathrooms. Two look over the small canal out front, the others over the little garden and the rooftops of Dorsoduro. The Peggy Guggenheim Collection is a short stroll away.

Palazzo Stern

Dorsoduro 2792, calle del Traghetto (041 277 0869, www.palazzostern.com). Vaporetto Ca' Rezzonico. €€€.

Built in the early 20th century in eclectic pastiche style, Palazzo Stern is now home to this elegant hotel. A magnificent wooden staircase leads up to rooms decorated in classic Venetian style in pale shades. Pricier rooms have views over the Grand Canal but the standard doubles at the back overlook a lovely garden. On the rooftop terrace is a jacuzzi. A wonderful breakfast terrace overlooks the canal.

Silk Road

Dorsoduro 1420E, calle Cortelogo (388 119 6816, www.silkroadhostel.com). Vaporetto San Basilio. €.

Sparse, basic but well placed and extremely clean, Silk Road offers six beds in a women's dorm, six in a mixed dorm and one double room. There are lockers for all in the dorms, and the kitchen – where owner Alex will spontaneously cook meals for guests from time to time – is equipped with a big fridge and other facilities. The vibe is convivial, and lone women travellers will feel totally safe.

La Giudecca

Belmond Hotel Cipriani

Giudecca 10, fondamenta San Giovanni (041 520 7744, www.hotelcipriani.com). Hotel launch from San Marco Vallaresso vaporetto stop, or Vaporetto Zitelle. €€€€.

Set amid verdant gardens, the Cipriani has great facilities as well as a private harbour for your yacht and a better-than-average chance of rubbing shoulders with an A-list film star (especially during the film festival, when many make this their base). Rooms are as luxurious and well-appointed as you'd expect in this category. If this seems too humdrum, take an apartment in the neighbouring 15th-century Palazzo Vendramin, with butler service and private garden. Facilities include tennis courts, a pool, a sauna, a spa and a gym. There's a motorboat to San Marco, but many guests never even leave the premises.

Generator

Giudecca 86, fondamenta delle Zitelle (041 523 8211, http://generatorhostels. com). Vaporetto Zitelle. €.

Venice's once-dowdy youth hostel has undergone the Generator treatment, emerging with some hip decor, infinitely more inviting public spaces, a lively nightlife scene and a restaurant that is rather less like a sad canteen. There are double, triple and quad rooms suitable for families, and dorms sleeping up to 16 people, some of which are women-only.

Palladio Hotel & Spa/ Villa F

Giudecca 33, fondamenta Zitelle (041 270 3806, www.bauerhotels.com). Vaporetto Zitelle. €€€€.

This luxury hotel group has expanded across the lagoon on to the Giudecca, where the Palladio Hotel & Spa and the super-elegant self-catering accommodation in Villa F look over the Giudecca canal towards San Marco out front and over Bauer's own lush gardens – one of the city's largest – at the back. Rooms at Palladio are all that you would expect at this level: large, with beautiful fabrics, a modern-classic feel, lashings of marble in the large bathrooms and superb views. At Villa F, apartments full of heirloom antiques have huge windows, fully fitted kitchens and sizeable reception rooms.

Lido & Lagoon

Hotel Excelsior

Lido, Lungomare Marconi 41 (041 526 0201, www.excelsiorvenezia.com). Vaporetto Lido. €€€€.

This Moorish extravaganza overlooking the serried ranks of candy-striped bathing huts on the Lido's long strip of sand has been catering to the luxe hotel trade since early in the 20th century. Come during the film festival and luvvies galore will be mixing with A-list celebrities and caffeine-fuelled journalists on the Excelsior's spreading terraces. New for 2014 is the San Marco Suite – at 2,260 sq ft, the largest on the lagoon – with massive windows giving a 360° view.

Il Lato Azzurro

Sant'Erasmo, Via Forti 13 (041 523 0642, www.latoazzurro.it). Vaporetto Capannone. €.

This friendly guesthouse is the ideal place to stay if you want a really quiet retreat. Colourful triple and quad rooms come with a balcony. There is a restaurant, and you can hire bikes to explore the island.

Locanda Cipriani

Torcello, piazza Santa Fosca (041 730 150, www.locandacipriani.com). Vaporetto Torcello. €€€.

Some people might argue that there's no point in going to Venice and staying on the island of Torcello, but this famous green-shuttered inn is special enough to justify the remoteness of the setting, at least for a couple of nights. Some of the five rooms (in understated, elegant country style) look over the hotel's gorgeous garden; you might end up in the one where Ernest Hemingway wrote *Across the River and into the Trees*. You can opt to limit yourself to the *locanda*'s wonderful breakfast, or go for half-board, allowing you to sample one of Venice's dining classics (p162).

San Clemente Palace

Isola di San Clemente (041 475 0001, www.stregisvenice.com). Hotel launch from jetty at piazza San Marco. €€€€.

Over time, the island of San Clemente has hosted a hospice for pilgrims, a powder store, an ecclesiastical prison for unruly priests and, more recently, a mental hospital. Today, the buildings house a St Regis group luxury hotel set in extensive, landscaped grounds. Reopened in spring 2015 after extensive renovation, the hotel has 146 rooms, suites with butler service, three restaurants and two bars, conference facilities, an elegant pool, tennis courts and all the attendant pampering. A hotel launch shuttles back and forth to central Venice regularly.

Venissa

Mazzorbo, fondamenta Santa Caterina 3 (041 527 2281, www.venissa.it). Vaporetto Mazzorbo. €€.

Many visitors make the trip to Burano. Few alight at the stop just before – Mazzorbo. It is on this picturesquely rural island (linked to Burano by a footbridge) that the prosecco producer Bisol has taken over an ancient walled vineyard, cajoled a long-forgotten grape variety (Dorona) back to life and created a Michelin-starred restaurant (p161) with hotel attached. Venissa's attractive minimal-chic boutique rooms can be taken with a host of plush amenities at a higher price, or with not much more than a bed at budget rates. In both cases, breakfast is extra, and à la carte.

Generator

Getting Around

Arriving & leaving

By air

Venice Marco Polo Airport

Switchboard 041 260 6111, flight & airport information 041 260 9260, www.veniceairport.it.

You can get a bus or taxi to Venice's piazzale Roma, but you may find that the **Alilaguna boat service** (041 240 1701, www.alilaguna.it) drops you nearer your hotel. The dock is seven minutes' walk from the arrivals hall; porter service costs €5 per bag. Alilaguna services call at San Marco, Rialto, Fondamente Nove, Guglie, Zattere, Ca' Rezzonico, Sant'Angelo, San Stae, Zitelle, San Zaccaria, Arsenale, Lido, Bacini, Ospedale, Murano Colonna and Orto vaporetto stops, as well as the Mulino Stucky Hilton on the island of Giudecca, and at the Stazione Marittima cruise ship terminal: check which is handiest for your final destination.

Main services are hourly, others less frequent. Tickets (€15 to Venice, the Lido or the Stazione Marittima) can be purchased at Alilaguna's counter in the arrivals hall or on board. Allow 70mins for the journey to/from San Marco.

Two companies run **bus services** between the airport and piazzale Roma. The non-stop bus service operated by **ATVO** (0421 594 671, www.atvo.it) takes 20mins. Buy tickets (€6; €11 return) from the ATVO counter at the airport, or at their piazzale Roma office. You may also be able to pay the driver directly if you have exact change.

Bus 5, run by **ACTV** (041 272 2111, timetable information 041 2424, www.actv.it) leaves every 15mins, but the journey time is slower (25-30mins). Buy tickets (€6) at the machine next to the bus stop at the airport, or at any ACTV/Hellovenezia ticket office.

A regular **taxi** from the airport to piazzale Roma costs €40 and takes about 20mins. You can pay in advance by credit card in the arrivals hall at the Cooperativa Artigiana Radio Taxi desk (041 5964, information 041 936 222).

The most luxurious way to reach the city centre is by **water taxi**. Consorzio Motoscafi Venezia (041 522 2303) charges from €100 for the half-hour crossing.

Sant'Angelo Airport (Treviso)

0422 315 111, www.trevisoairport.it.

ATVO (0422 315 381, www.atvo.it) **bus services** run from piazzale Roma and back to coincide with flights – if the flight arrives late, the bus will wait. The journey takes 70mins, and costs €11 one way, €18 return (valid for ten days). Buses from piazzale Roma leave ridiculously early, so ensure your timely arrival.

Alternatively, take a **train** from Venice to Treviso (35mins) and then a bus or taxi (Taxi Padova, 049 651 333) to the airport. ACTT (0422 3271) bus 6 does the 20-minute trip from in front of Treviso train station to the airport at frequent intervals throughout the day, and costs €1.30.

Valerio Catullo Airport (Verona)

045 809 5666, www.aeroportoverona.it.

A bus (0458 057 911) runs every 20mins to Verona train station, from 5.35am to 11.35pm. The 20-minute journey costs €6 (pay on board). There are regular train links between Verona and Venice (70-90mins).

By train

Santa Lucia is Venice's main station. Most long-distance trains stop here, though some only go as far as Mestre on the mainland; if so, change to a local train (every ten minutes or less during the day) for the short hop across the lagoon.

By bus

Buses to Venice all arrive at piazzale Roma, which is connected by vaporetto (below) to the rest of the city centre.

By car

Prohibitive parking fees make cars one of the least practical modes of arrival. Many Venetian hotels offer their guests discounts at car parks, and VeneziaUnica (p187) has special offers too.

Public transport

Public transport – including *vaporetti* (water buses) and local buses – in Venice itself and in some mainland areas is run by **ACTV** (www.actv.it). **ATVO** (0421 594 671, www.atvo.it) runs more extensive bus services to numerous destinations on the mainland.

Information

Hellovenezia (p187) is ACTV's ticketing, information and merchandising wing. Its extremely helpful call centre (041 2424) provides information on vaporetto and bus schedules. Its outlets at many vaporetto stops sell tickets and VeneziaUnica passes (p187), which allow users to buy multiple services and access them all through one ticket. If you're lucky, you can also pick up one of the free transport timetable booklets, but these are published at the start of the season and tend to run out swiftly; timetables are posted at all vaporetto stops. The free VeneziaUnica app has real-time transport information.

Fares & tickets

Vaporetto tickets and passes can be purchased at *tabacchi* (p186) and at Hellovenezia counters at many vaporetto stops. Stops without ticket counters have automatic ticket machines. On board *vaporetti*, you can only buy single tickets.

Ticket costs are: single trip €7 (valid 60mins on multiple boats); 12hrs €18; 24hrs €20; 36hrs €25; 48hrs €30; 72hrs €40; 1 week €60. A shuttle journey (for example, one stop across the Grand Canal, the hop across to the Giudecca, or from Sant'Elena to the Lido) is €4.

Tickets must be validated prior to boarding the vaporetto, by swiping them in front of the machines at the entrance to the jetty. For multiple-journey tickets, you need only stamp your ticket once, at the start of the first journey.

Vaporetti

Venice's *vaporetti* (water buses) run to a very tight schedule, with sailing times for each line marked clearly at stops. Regular services run from about 5am to around midnight, after which a frequent night service (N) operates. Strikes sometimes occur, but are always announced in advance; look out for notices posted inside vaporetto stops bearing the title *sciopero* (strike). Services are also curtailed and rerouted for Venice's many rowing regattas; these disruptions are also announced with posters in vaporetto stops.

Taking a boat in the wrong direction is all too easy. Remember: if you're standing with your back to the station and want to head down

ESSENTIALS

the Grand Canal, take Line 1 (slow) or Line 2 (faster) heading left.

Not all passenger ferries are, strictly speaking, *vaporetti*. A vaporetto is larger, slower and more rounded in shape, and has room for 230 passsengers; older boats have outside seats at the front that are much sought after. These vessels follow routes along the Grand Canal. The *motoscafo* is sleeker, smaller (160 passengers) and has outside seats only at the back. It runs on routes encircling the island. *Motonave* are large double-decker steamers, taking 600-1,200 passengers, and cross the lagoon to the Lido.

Traghetti

The best way to cross the Grand Canal when you're far from a bridge is to hop on a *traghetto*. These unadorned *gondole* are rowed back and forth at fixed points along the canal. At €2 (70c for resident travel card holders), this is the cheapest gondola ride in the city – Venetians make the short hop standing up.

Traghetti ply between the following points:

Santa Sofia–Pescheria 7.30am-8pm Mon-Sat; 8.45am-7pm Sun.
Riva del Carbon–Riva del Vin 8am-12.30pm Mon-Sat.
Ca' Garzoni–San Tomà 7.30am-8pm Mon-Sat; 8.30am-7.30pm Sun.
San Samuele–Ca' Rezzonico 7.45am-12.30pm Mon-Sat.
Santa Maria del Giglio–Santa Maria della Salute 9am-6pm daily.
Punta della Dogana–Vallaresso 9am-2pm daily.

Buses

ACTV buses operate to both Mestre and Marghera on the mainland, as well as serving the Lido, Pellestrina and Chioggia. Services for the mainland depart from piazzale

Roma. From midnight until 5am, buses N1 (leaving every 30mins) and N2 (leaving every hour) depart from Mestre for piazzale Roma, and vice versa. There are also regular night buses from the Lido (departing at least hourly) to Malamocco, Alberoni and Pellestrina.

Bus tickets, costing €1.30 (also available in blocks of ten tickets for €12), are valid for 75mins, during which you may use several buses, though you can't make a return journey on the same ticket. They can be purchased from ACTV/Hellovenezia ticket booths (p187) or from *tabacchi* (p186) anywhere in the city. They should be bought before boarding the bus and then be stamped on board.

Trains

Trenitalia's national rail information and booking number is 892 021 (24 hours daily). Press 1 after the recorded message, then say '*altro*' to speak to an operator (who may not speak English). The website (www.trenitalia.com) gives exhaustive information on timetables.

The information office in the main hall of **Santa Lucia station** is open 7am to 9pm daily. Buy tickets from the ticket windows (open 6am-9pm daily, all major credit cards accepted), vending machines in the station, travel agents around the city bearing the Trenitalia logo or online at www.trenitalia.com.

If you have a regular railways-issued ticket, you must stamp it in the machines on the platform before boarding or face a fine. If you forget to stamp your ticket, locate the inspector as soon as possible to waive the fine.

The private train operator **Italo** (www.italotreno.it) also runs high-speed services from Venice's Santa Lucia to Rome, Florence, Bologna, Naples, Padua and Salerno.

Water taxis

Water taxis are hugely expensive: expect to pay €100 from the airport directly to any single destination in Venice, and more for multiple stops. The minimum possible cost for a 15-minute trip from hotel to restaurant is €60, with most journeys averaging €110 once numbers of passengers and baggage have been taken into account. In all cases, tariffs are for five people or fewer, with each extra passenger charged €10 (up to a maximum of ten people). Between the hours of 10pm and 7am, there is a surcharge of €10.

Taxi pick-up points can be found at piazzale Roma, outside the train station, next to the Rialto vaporetto stop, and next to San Marco Vallaresso vaporetto stop, but it's more reliable to call and order yourself. Pre-booking through the Motoscafi Venezia website can give discounts on some routes. Avoid asking your hotel to book a taxi for you, as they frequently add a 10% mark-up. Beware of unlicensed taxis, which charge even more than authorised ones. The latter have a black number on a yellow background.

Consorzio Motoscafi Venezia
041 522 2303, www.motoscafivenezia.it.
Open 24hrs daily.

Gondolas

Official gondola stops can be found at (or near) the following locations:

Fondamenta Bacino Orseolo.
Riva degli Schiavoni in front of the Hotel Danieli.
San Marco Vallaresso vaporetto stop.
Santa Lucia railway station.
Piazzale Roma bus terminus.
Santa Maria del Giglio vaporetto stop.
Piazzetta San Marco jetty.

Campo Santa Sofia near Ca' d'Oro vaporetto stop.
San Tomà vaporetto stop.
Campo San Moisè by the Hotel Bauer.
Riva del Carbon at the southern end of the Rialto bridge, near the vaporetto stop.

Fares are set by the Istituzione per la Conservazione della Gondola e Tutela del Gondoliere (Gondola Board; 041 528 5075, www.gondola venezia.it). In the event that a gondolier tries to overcharge you – and it does happen: be prepared to stick to your guns – complain to the Gondola Board. Prices below are for the hire of the gondola, for six passengers or fewer. Having your own personal crooner will push the fare up.

8am-7pm €80 for 30mins.
7pm-8am €100 for 35mins.

Driving

Driving is an impossibility in Venice: even if your vehicle was capable of going up and down stairs and squeezing through the narrowest of alleyways, it wouldn't be legal for you to do so. Instead, you'll need to park on the outskirts and walk or use alternative means of transport. You can drive on the Lido, but there aren't many places to go. It's certainly worth hiring a car (do upgrade to comprehensive insurance cover) if you are planning to visit the Veneto countryside and its fine villas.

Car hire

Avis *041 523 7377, www.avisautonoleggio.it.*
Europcar *041 523 8616, www.europcar.it.*
Hertz *041 528 4091, www.hertz.it.*
Maggiore National *041 935 300, www.maggiore.it.*

ESSENTIALS

Resources A-Z

For information on travelling to Italy from within the European Union, including details of visa regulations and healthcare provision, see the EU's travel website: http://europa.eu/travel.

Accident & emergency

Ambulance *118.*
Coastguard *1530 or 041 240 5711.*
Fire *115 or 041 257 4700.*
Infant emergency *114.*
Police – Carabinieri *112.*
Police – Polizia di Stato *113.*

The hospitals below all have 24-hour casualty facilities.
Ospedale dell'Angelo *Via Tosatto, Mestre (041 965 7111).*
Ospedale Civile *Castello 6777, campo Santi Giovanni e Paolo (041 529 4111, casualty 041 529 4516).*
Ospedale di Padova *Via Giustiniani 2, Padua (049 821 1111).*
Ospedale di Verona *Piazzale Stefani 1, Verona (045 812 1111).*

Credit card loss

American Express *06 7290 0347*
Diners Club *800 393 939*
MasterCard *800 870 866*
Visa *800 819 014*

Customs

If you arrive from an EU country, you are not required to declare goods imported into or exported from Italy as long as they are for personal use.

For people arriving from non-EU countries, limits apply. For more information, consult www. agenziadoganemonopoli.gov.it.

Dental emergency

For urgent dental issues, go to the Ambulatorio Odontostomatologico at the **Ospedale Civile** (left).

Disabled

With its narrow streets, 400-plus stepped bridges and lack of barriers between canals and pavements, this city is no easy task for anyone with impaired mobility or vision to negotiate. But with determination and planning, Venice is far from impossible, and recent efforts to make the city more negotiable for disabled travellers have helped.

Start your research on the city council website, www.comune. venezia.it. Type 'Venezia accessibile' into the search box; once you reach the page, you'll find the English option button. Here, you'll find itineraries and a useful map of barrier-free zones; at time of writing, the map still showed long-removed stairlifts previously installed on some bridges.

VeniceConnected (041 2424, www.veniceconnected.com) also provides information and shows itineraries without barriers, as well as hosting a helpful FAQ section on its 'Accessible Venice' pages.

Alilaguna (www.alilaguna.it) services between the airport and Venice proper can carry wheelchairs, as can most *vaporetti*. Staff will help you on and off the boats, and ensure that assigned areas are available. Tickets for wheelchair users cost €1.30 for 75 minutes; an *accompagnatore* travels free.

Public transport is one area where Venice scores higher than many other destinations, as standard *vaporetti* and *motonavi* have a reasonably

ESSENTIALS

large, flat deck area and there are no steps or steep inclines on the route between quayside and boat, enabling easy travel along the Grand Canal, on lines 1 and 2. Lines that circle the city use *motoscafi*; some of their older models have not yet been adapted to accommodate wheelchairs, although the onboard ACTV personnel are unerringly helpful. The vaporetto lines that currently guarantee disabled access (though peak times should be avoided if possible) are 1, 2, LN and N. Some of the buses that run between Mestre and Venice also have wheelchair access.

Electricity

Italy's electricity system runs on 220/230V. To use British or US appliances, you will need two-pin adaptor plugs and, for the latter, a voltage converter.

Embassies & consulates

For most information, and in emergencies, you will probably have to contact offices in Rome or Milan. There is a US Consular Agency in Venice, open by appointment only (041 541 5944).

Consulates in Milan
Australia 02 7767 4200.
Ireland 02 5518 7569.
New Zealand 02 7217 0001.
South Africa 02 885 8581.
United Kingdom 06 4220 2431.
United States 02 290 351.

Embassies in Rome
Australia 06 852 721.
Canada 06 85444 2911.
Ireland 06 585 2381.
New Zealand 06 853 7501.
South Africa 06 8525 4262.
United Kingdom 06 4220 0001.
United States 06 46741.

ID

You are legally obliged to carry photo ID with you at all times.

Pharmacies

Pharmacies (*farmacie*), are run by qualified chemists who will dispense informal advice on, and assistance for, minor ailments, as well as filling prescriptions. Most chemists are open 9am-12.30pm, 3.45-7.30pm Mon-Fri and 9am-12.45pm Sat. A small number remain open on Saturday afternoon, Sunday and at night on a duty rota system, details of which are posted outside every pharmacy.

Police

For emergencies, see p184.
Both the (nominally military) Carabinieri and the Polizia di Stato deal with crimes and emergencies of any kind. If you have your bag or wallet stolen, or are otherwise made a victim of crime, go as soon as possible to either force to report a *scippo* ('bagsnatching'). A *denuncia* (written statement) of the incident will be made for you. It is unlikely that your things will be found, but you will need the *denuncia* for making an insurance claim.
The **Polizia di Stato**'s main station is at Questura Santa Croce 500, piazzale Roma (041 271 5586, www.questura.poliziadistato.it); the **Carabinieri**'s is at Castello 4693A, campo San Zaccaria (041 27411).

Post

Italy's postal service (www.poste.it) is generally reliable. Letterboxes are red and have two slots: *Per la città* (for Venice, Mestre and Marghera), and *Tutte le altre destinazioni* (all other destinations). Stamps can be bought at *tabacchi* (p186) and post

ESSENTIALS

offices. Each district has its own sub-post office, open 8.20am-1.45pm Mon-Fri, 8.20am-12.45pm Sat. The main post office below has longer opening hours.

Posta Piazzale Roma *Santa Croce 511, fondamenta Santa Chiara (041 244 6811). Vaporetto Piazzale Roma.* **Open** 8.20am-7.05pm Mon-Fri; 8.20am-12.35pm Sat.

Smoking

Smoking is banned anywhere with public access – including bars, restaurants, stations, offices and on all public transport – except in clearly designated smoking rooms.

Tabacchi

Tabacchi or *tabaccherie* (identified by a white T on a black or blue background) are the only places in Italy where you can legally buy tobacco products. They also sell stamps, telephone cards, individual or season tickets for public transport and lottery tickets. Most of Venice's *tabacchi* pull their shutters down by 7.30pm.

Telephones

Italian landline numbers must be dialled with their prefixes, even if you're phoning within the local area. Numbers in Venice and its province begin 041; numbers in Padua province begin 049; in Vicenza they begin 0444; in Verona 045.

When calling an Italian landline from abroad, the whole prefix, including the 0, must be dialled. So dial 00 39 041… for Venice from the UK. To make an international call from Venice, dial 00, then the country code, then the area code (usually without the initial 0) and the number. Common country codes include Australia 61, Canada 1, Ireland 353, New Zealand 64, South Africa 27, UK 44, USA 1.

Time

Italy is one hour ahead of London, six ahead of New York, eight behind Sydney and 12 behind Wellington.

Tipping

Venetians know that foreigners tip generously back home, and expect them to be liberal. Some upmarket restaurants (and a growing number of cheaper ones) will add a service charge to your bill; ask: '*Il servizio è incluso?*' If not, leave whatever you think the service merited (Italians leave 5%-10%). Bear in mind that all restaurants charge a cover charge (*coperto*) – a quasi-tip in itself.

Toilets

Public toilets (*servizi igienici pubblici*) are numerous and relatively clean in Venice, but you have to pay (€1) to use them, unless you have invested in the appropriate VeneziaUnica package (p187). Follow blue and green signs marked WC. By law, all cafés and bars should allow anyone to use their facilities; however, many Venetian bar owners don't.

Tourist information

Cards & passes

See also p12 **Chorus**. For transport-only passes, see p181.

The museums around piazza San Marco (but not the paying parts of the basilica) can only be visited on one of these museum passes:

Musei di Piazza San Marco Valid for three months, with one visit to each of the sights covered; costs €16 (€10 reductions, free under-5s). Covers Doge's Palace, Museo Correr, Museo Nazionale Archeologico and Biblioteca Marciana.

Museum Pass Valid six months with one visit to each museum covered; costs €24 (€18 reductions, free under-5s). Covers the sights listed above plus Ca' Rezzonico, Casa di Carlo Goldoni, Ca' Pesaro, Museo dell'Arte Vetrario, Museo del Merletti, Museo di Storia Naturale and Palazzo Mocenigo.

Passes can be bought at the sights themselves, by phone (041 4273 0892) or online (www. visitmuve.it). Alternatively, they can be booked through the city council's **VeneziaUnica** website, www.veneziaunica.it, where they can be purchased as part of a sightseeing and transport deal that may bring costs down.

Visitors can get a top-upable VeneziaUnica swipe card, permitting them to add events and services at prices that – for some things – come in at slightly lower levels than purchasing directly and/or individually.

The card can be ordered and paid for online through the website (not easy to navigate but worth the struggle) or purchased in the city.

In both cases, it can be picked up at offices of **Hellovenezia** (www.hellovenezia.it) – the sales outlet of the ACTV transit company, generally open 8am-8pm daily – at points of entry to the city (railway station, piazzale Roma, Marco Polo airport, Tronchetto cruise ship terminal) and at those vaporetto stops where Hellovenezia has its larger sales counters (Rialto, San Marco Vallaresso, San Zaccaria).

In addition to the two museum passes, the extensive menu of goodies on offer with VeneziaUnica includes city-wide Wi-Fi, use of public toilets, transport to and from the airport, the Chorus church pass (p12), tours of the La Fenice opera house, car parks and audio-guides.

Information

The APT tourist board's website, www.turismovenezia.it, has useful information for visitors.

Hellovenezia's extremely helpful call centre (041 2424) provides information on sights, events, and vaporetto and bus timetables, in English. Hellovenezia offices dispense tourist information, and issue and add services to the VeneziaUnica card (left); outlets at the railway station, Tronchetto and piazzale Roma also sell tickets for events.

Azienda di Promozione Turistica (APT)
San Marco 71F, piazza San Marco (041 529 8711, www.turismovenezia.it). Vaporetto San Marco Vallaresso.
Open 9am-7pm daily.
Other locations Venice Pavilion, San Marco 2, Giardinetti Reali (041 529 8711); Santa Lucia railway station (041 529 8711); Marco Polo Airport arrivals hall (041 529 8711); Piazzale Roma Garage ASM, Santa Croce, piazzale Roma (041 529 8711).

Visas

For EU citizens, a passport or a national identity card valid for travel abroad is sufficient. Non-EU citizens must have full passports. Citizens of the US, Canada, Australia and New Zealand do not need visas for stays of up to 90 days.

What's on

Venezia News (www.venezia news.it) is an information-packed magazine which comes out on the first of each month. It encompasses music, film, theatre, art and sports listings, and also contains interviews and features, written in both Italian and English.

ESSENTIALS

Vocabulary

Pronunciation

a – as in ask
e – like a in age or e in sell
i – like ea in east
o – as in hotel or in hot
u – as in boot
c before a, o or u – like c in cat; otherwise like ch in check (sh as in ship in Venetian)
g before a, o or u – like g in get; otherwise like j in jig
h – makes the consonant preceding it hard (ch – cat, gh – get)
gl followed by i – like lli in million
gn – like ny in canyon
s – two sounds, as in soap or rose
sc before e or i – like sh in shame
sch – like sc in scout

Useful phrases

(**English** – Italian/*Venetian*)

hello, goodbye ciao (used informally in other parts of Italy; in all social situations in Venice); **good morning, hello** buongiorno; **good afternoon, good evening** buonasera; **please** per favore, per piacere; **thank you** grazie; **you're welcome** prego; **excuse me** mi scusi (polite), scusami (informal)/*scusime, me scusa*; **I'm sorry** mi dispiace/*me dispiaxe*; **I don't understand** non capisco, non ho capito/*no gò capio*; **do you speak English?** parla inglese?; **open** aperto/*verto*; **closed** chiuso; **when does it open?** quando apre?; **it's closed** è chiuso/*xè serà*; **what's the time?** che ore sono? **I'd like to book**… vorrei prenotare…; **…a table for four at eight** …una tavola per quattro alle otto; **…a single/twin/double bedroom** …una camera singola/doppia/matrimoniale; **the bill** il conto; **shop** negozio/*botega*; **how much does it cost/is it?** quanto costa?, quant'è?/*quanto xè?*

Transport

car macchina; **bus** autobus; **taxi** tassì, taxi; **train** treno; **plane** aereo; **stop** (bus/vaporetto) fermata; **station** stazione; **platform** binario; **ticket/s** biglietto, biglietti; **one way** solo andata; **return** andata e ritorno.

Directions

entrance entrata; **exit** uscita; **where is…?** dov'è…?/*dove xè…?*; **(turn) left** (gira) a sinistra; **(it's on the) right** (è sulla/a) destra; **straight on** sempre dritto; **could you tell me the way to…?** mi può indicare la strada per…?

Days & times

Monday lunedì; **Tuesday** martedì; **Wednesday** mercoledì; **Thursday** giovedì; **Friday** venerdì; **Saturday** sabato; **Sunday** domenica; **yesterday** ieri; **today** oggi/*ancùo*; **tomorrow** domani; **morning** mattina; **afternoon** pomeriggio; **evening** sera; **this evening** stasera; **night** notte; **tonight** stanotte.

Numbers

0 zero; **1** uno; **2** due; **3** tre; **4** quattro; **5** cinque; **6** sei; **7** sette; **8** otto; **9** nove; **10** dieci; **11** undici; **12** dodici; **13** tredici; **14** quattordici; **15** quindici; **16** sedici; **17** diciassette; **18** diciotto; **19** diciannove; **20** venti; **21** ventuno; **22** ventidue; **30** trenta; **40** quaranta; **50** cinquanta; **60** sessanta; **70** settanta; **80** ottanta; **90** novanta; **100** cento; **1,000** mille; **2,000** duemila.

Menu

Antipasti (starters)

The dozens of different *cicheti* – tapas-style snacks – that are served from the counters of Venice's traditional *bàcari* (trattorias) are essentially *antipasti*. The choice may include:

baccalà mantecato stockfish beaten into a cream with oil and milk, often served on grilled polenta; **bovoleti** tiny snails cooked in olive oil, parsley and garlic; **carciofi** artichokes, even better if they are **castrauri** – baby artichokes; **canoce** (or **cicale di mare**) mantis shrimps; **folpi/folpeti** baby octopus; **garusoli** sea snails; **moleche** soft-shelled crabs, usually deep-fried; **museto** boiled pork-brawn sausage, generally served on a slice of bread with mustard; **nervetti** boiled veal cartilage; **polpetta** deep-fried spicy meatball; **polenta** yellow or white cornmeal mush, served either runny or in firm sliceable slabs; **sarde in saor** sardines marinated in onion, vinegar, pine nuts and raisins; **schie** tiny grey shrimps, usually served on a bed of soft white polenta; **seppie in nero** cuttlefish in its own ink; **spienza** veal spleen, usually served on a skewer; **trippa e rissa** tripe cooked in broth.

Primi (first courses)

Bigoli in salsa fat spaghetti in an anchovy and onion sauce; **gnocchi con granseola** potato gnocchi in spider-crab sauce; **pasta e ceci** pasta and chickpea soup; **pasta e fagioli** pasta and borlotti bean soup; **spaghetti alla busara** in anchovy sauce; **spaghetti al nero di seppia** in squid-ink sauce; **spaghetti con caparossoli/vongole veraci** with clams; **risotto di zucca** pumpkin risotto.

Secondi (main courses)

Meat eaters are not that well catered for in Venice, but local specialities include **fegato alla veneziana** veal liver cooked in onions, and **castradina** lamb and cabbage broth.

Fish lovers, however, will find themselves spoiled for choice. In addition to the *antipasti* mentioned above, you may find:

anguilla eel; **aragosta/astice** spiny lobster/lobster; **branzino** sea bass; **cape longhe** razor clams; **cape sante** scallops; **cernia** grouper; **coda di rospo** anglerfish; **cozze** mussels; **granchio** crab; **granseola** spider crab; **orata** gilt-headed bream; **rombo** turbot; **pesce san pietro** john dory; **pesce spada** swordfish; **sogliola** sole; **tonno** tuna; **vongole/caparossoli** clams.

Dolci (desserts)

Venice's restaurants are not the best place to feed a sweet habit – with a few exceptions, there are far more tempting pastries to be found on the shelves of the city's *pasticcerie*.

The classic conclusion to a meal here is a plate of **buranei** – sweet egg biscuits – served with a dessert wine such as Fragolino. Then it's quickly on to the more important matter of which grappa to order.

Index

ESSENTIALS